Leaders of the City

Leaders of the City

Dublin's first citizens, 1500–1950

Ruth McManus & Lisa-Marie Griffith

EDITORS

FOUR COURTS PRESS

Typeset in 11pt on 14pt AGaramondPro by
Carrigboy Typesetting Services for
FOUR COURTS PRESS LTD
7 Malpas Street, Dublin 8, Ireland
www.fourcourtspress.ie
and in North America for
FOUR COURTS PRESS
c/o ISBS, 920 NE 58th Avenue, Suite 300, Portland, OR 97213.

A catalogue record for this title is available
from the British Library.

ISBN 978–1–84682–347–3 hbk

ACKNOWLEDGMENT

Published with the support of the
Research Committee, St Patrick's College, Drumcondra.

Printed in England
by Antony Rowe Ltd, Chippenham, Wilts.

Contents

Illustrations

CREDITS

19 Board of Trinity College Dublin; 1, 2, 5 Joe Brady; 30 Dublin City Council, photograph by Joanna Travers; 3, 4, 8–14, 16–18, 21–6, 28, 29 Dublin City Library and Archive; 15 Jacqueline Hill; 6, 7 Ruth McManus.

Foreword

As lord mayor of Dublin, and first citizen of the city, I am delighted to welcome this book *Leaders of the city: Dublin's first citizens, 1500–1950*. It is very interesting to read about my illustrious, and not so illustrious, predecessors who have worn the Great Chain of the City of Dublin.

I hold a very ancient title with the office of the mayor of Dublin having been created in 1229 by King Henry III of England and the first lord mayor of Dublin, Sir Daniel Bellingham, elected in 1665. I find it fascinating that I follow in the footsteps of diverse characters such as Blessed Francis Taylor who was mayor in 1595 and who died in prison for refusing to give up his faith; Sir Mark Rainsford, lord mayor in 1700 and the original founder of the Brewery at St James' Gate that went on to become the world famous Guinness Brewery; and the Liberator Daniel O'Connell who was lord mayor in 1841 and achieved Catholic emancipation in Ireland by peaceful means – an inspiration to future world leaders such as Mahatma Gandhi and Martin Luther King. More recently, Alfie Byrne was famously elected lord mayor nine times during the 1930s and – uniquely – served first as an MP in the House of Commons and later as a TD in Dáil Éireann. In 1939, Dublin had its first woman lord mayor in Caitlín Bean Ui Chléirigh, widow of Thomas Clarke, leader of the 1916 Rising, while in 1956 Robert Briscoe was elected as the first Jewish lord mayor.

This publication brings together a series of essays on many of Dublin's first citizens by leading academics, telling their stories in a most vivid manner, while presenting the historical background and context which informed their service to the city. My congratulations to each of the contributors and in particular to the two editors, Dr Lisa-Marie Griffith and Dr Ruth McManus, on this achievement, and also to the publishers Four Courts Press for producing such a readable and elegant book.

The role of lord mayor has changed over the years with former duties such as Chief Magistrate abolished in 1926 and titles such as The Right Honourable abolished in 2001. However, the role of the lord mayor remains to this day as one of service to the citizens of Dublin and the principal duty is still to represent the people of Dublin at home and abroad. The Mansion House, which has been Dublin's mayoral residence since 1715, has always been known for its hospitality and warm welcome to visitors. This publication brings to life many of those First Citizens who resided here in the past and ensures that their contribution as Leaders of the City will be remembered now and into the future.

NAOISE Ó MUIRÍ
Ardhmhéara Bhaile Átha Cliath
Lord Mayor of Dublin

The Mansion House
Spring 2013

Notes on contributors

DR RUTH McMANUS lectures in the Geography Department at St Patrick's College, Drumcondra, and with the Open University. She is the author of *Dublin, 1910–1940: shaping the city and suburbs* (2002) and *Crampton built* (2008), as well as articles on different aspects of urban geography, suburban history, population, heritage, tourism and geography education. She is the editor of *Irish Geography, the Journal of the Geographical Society of Ireland*, produced by Taylor & Francis.

DR LISA-MARIE GRIFFITH is coordinator of the Culture and Heritage Studies programme at the National Print Museum where she teaches Irish and local history. Her research interest is in eighteenth-century history and the fields of social and economic history. She graduated with her IRCHSS-funded PhD in 2009, which examined social mobility and the merchants of Dublin (1760–1800), and she has published articles on this topic in several volumes.

She is also a coordinator of the History of the City of Dublin Research Group, which organized a symposium on lord mayors of Dublin in 2009 (from which this volume arises) and another one on Dublin commerce in 2012.

CONTRIBUTORS

DR LYDIA CARROLL was awarded her PhD in 2008, entitled 'More than a man's part: Sir Charles Cameron, public analyst and medical officer of health for Dublin, 1862–1921'. Her biography, *In the fever king's preserves: Sir Charles Cameron and the Dublin slums*, was published in November 2011.

DR MARY E. CLARK is the Dublin city archivist. She is currently working on the digitization of Freedom Rolls of Dublin, 1468–1918; the digitization of Electoral Rolls, 1937–63; the development of Dublin City Archaeological Archive; and a biographical dictionary of Dublin's lord mayors. She has published with Raymond Refaussé, *Directory of historic Dublin guilds* (Dublin, 1993), and with Gráinne Doran, *Serving the city: Dublin city managers and town clerks* (Dublin; 1st edition, 1996; 2nd edition, 2006).

PROFESSOR RAYMOND GILLESPIE lectures on local history, methodologies and sources of history at the Department of History, NUI Maynooth. He is editor of the Four Courts Press series Maynooth Studies in Local History. He has published extensively on urban history in Ireland. He is author of three books on Belfast: *Early Belfast: the origins and growth of an Ulster town to 1750* (Belfast, 2007), with S.A. Royle, *Belfast c.1600 to c.1900: the making of the modern city* (Dublin, 2007), and with C.E. Brett and W.A. Maguire, *Georgian Belfast, 1750–1850: maps, buildings and trades* (Dublin, 2004). He edited with Peter Clark *Two capitals: London and Dublin, 1500–1840* (Oxford, 2001).

PROFESSOR JACQUELINE HILL lectures at the Department of History, NUI Maynooth. She is author of *From patriots to unionists: Dublin civic politics and Irish Protestant patriotism, 1660–1840* (Oxford, 1997) and has edited *A new history of Ireland* vii: *Ireland, 1921–1984* (Oxford, 2003). Her publications include 'Mayors and lord mayors of Dublin' in T.W. Moody, F.X. Martin & F.J. Byrne (eds), *A new history of Ireland* ix: *maps, genealogies, lists* (Oxford, 1984), and she has published extensively on urban history and Dublin.

DR MÁIRE KENNEDY is divisional librarian, Special Collections and Early Printed Books, with Dublin City Libraries. She is author of *French books in eighteenth-century Ireland* (Oxford, 2001) and edited *A directory of Dublin for 1738: compiled from the most authentic sources* (Dublin, 2000). She has published numerous articles on her research interests: eighteenth-century print culture and the Dublin book trade.

PROFESSOR COLM LENNON lectures at the Department of History, NUI Maynooth. His publications include *The lords of Dublin in the age of Reformation* (Dublin, 1989), *The urban patriciates of early modern Ireland: a case-study of Limerick* (NUI O'Donnell lecture (1999), Dublin, 2000), and *An Irish prisoner of conscience of the Tudor era: Archbishop Richard Creagh of Armagh, 1523–86* (Dublin, 2000). He is interested in social, cultural and religious history of late medieval and early modern Ireland; Irish Reformation and Counter-Reformation studies; and the history of Dublin and other urban communities.

HELEN LITTON has worked in freelance in publishing since 1979 (proofreader, editor, indexer). She is editor of *Revolutionary woman* (Dublin, 1991), the autobiography of her great-aunt Kathleen Clarke. She is author of six illustrated histories for Wolfhound Press (1994–2001), and is currently writing a biography of her great-uncle Commandant Edward Daly (executed 1916), which will be published in 2013.

DAVID McELLIN was born in Co. Leitrim. He was educated at Marian College, Mohill, and at University College, Dublin. His particular research interest is in late nineteenth-century and early twentieth-century Irish political and ecclesiastical history.

JANET REDMOND is a teacher with a background in education, history and geography who holds an MA in design history and material culture. She uses a multi-disciplinary analytical approach to her research, drawing on the key areas of history, sociology, social and urban geography. She has written numerous articles on many aspects of design history and material culture. She is currently working on a history of Dublin's South City Markets (George's St Arcade) and has presented on this subject at home and abroad.

DR PATRICIA STAPLETON is the extramural officer for the School of Histories and Humanities, Trinity College Dublin, where she completed her IRCHSS-funded PhD in 2008, which examined the merchant community in Dublin and their interaction with other social and political groupings in the early seventeenth century.

DR CIARÁN WALLACE completed his IRCHSS-funded PhD in 2010 on local politics and government in Dublin city and suburbs, 1899–1914, at the School of Histories and Humanities, Trinity College Dublin. He has completed a Government of Ireland postdoctoral fellowship and is working on his monograph *Divided city: Dublin and its unionist townships, 1899–1916*. He is currently lecturing on 'Ireland and the Great War' at the School of Histories and Humanities, Trinity College Dublin, and is one of the coordinators of the History of the City of Dublin Research Group.

Acknowledgments

This collection emerged from a one-day symposium hosted by the History of the City of Dublin Research Group and held in the Gilbert Library, which was entitled 'Leaders of the City? Dublin mayors 1500–2000'. We would like to thank all of those who assisted in organizing the event, including members of the History of the City of Dublin Research Group – David Dickson, Patrick Geoghegan, Justyna Pyz and Ciarán Wallace – and the staff of Dublin City Library and Archive, particularly Mary Clark and Máire Kennedy. We would also like to thank all of the contributors on the day, including Lydia Carroll, Mary Clark, David Dickson, Raymond Gillespie, Jacqueline Hill, Máire Kennedy, Colm Lennon, David McEllin and Patricia Stapleton, as well as session chairs, Ciarán Brady, Deirdre Ellis-King and James Kelly. Helen Litton and Janet Redmond very kindly added to our volume after the symposium to ensure that the first lord mayor and the first female lord mayor had a place in this collection.

From the outset, Dublin City Library and Archives and Margaret Hayes, Dublin City Librarian, have been hugely supportive of this volume. We would like to express our great appreciation to Mary Clark, Dublin City Archivist, who has contributed time, expertise and resources for which we are very grateful. In addition to compiling the appendices, she has also assisted considerably in sourcing many of the images which enhance these pages. Joe Brady's help in relation to images has also been invaluable He supplied maps and also kindly sourced the postcard which appears as figure 6 and which serves as a fascinating reminder of the varied demands of the office of lord mayor. Michael Hinch, Editorial Imaging Manager at Independent Newspapers, was kind enough to search for the image of Kathleen Clark stirring the Christmas pudding and then to spend time making the image of publishable quality.

The staff at Four Courts Press, especially Martin Fanning, have been instrumental in bringing this volume to fruition. Particular thanks are due to the Research Committee of St Patrick's College, Drumcondra, who made a generous subvention towards publication costs.

Finally, we would like to thank the Office of the Lord Mayor, especially Joanna Travers, for their assistance. We are especially honoured that the present lord mayor, Naoise Ó Muirí, has supplied the foreword to this volume, which we hope does justice to some of the individuals who have held that office over the centuries.

An introduction to Dublin's first citizens

LISA-MARIE GRIFFITH & RUTH McMANUS

The lord mayor is the first citizen of Dublin city and chairperson of the elected city council. Their role is to provide civic leadership, facilitate dialogue with organizations and with citizens and to be proactive in raising the profile of the city. The office of mayor of Dublin was created by King Henry III in 1229, while in 1665 Sir Daniel Bellingham became the first person to hold the title of lord mayor of Dublin. In exploring the experience of some of the individuals who held the office between 1500 and 1950, this volume attempts to shed light on the role of these civic leaders within a broader social and political context and, in so doing, provides a sense of the evolution of the city and its people.

Between 1500 and 1950 the office of chief magistrate of Dublin changed continuously to meet the demands of a growing population and a changing religious and political backdrop. Over this period significant changes occurred; the office itself was elevated from that of mayor to lord mayor, the method of election to the position was altered, the guild system that operated the corporation was dissolved, the corporation itself was at various times dissolved, re-formed, suspended and renamed, the office was restricted by confessional faith and then opened up again, the composition of the electorate changed, and women were eventually allowed to vote in civic elections and, later, to hold the office of lord mayor. Arguably the one constant in civic politics throughout this period was the existence of an annually elected mayor (and lord mayor from 1665).

As chief magistrate, the mayor was to be the figurehead of the city, the chair of the civic government and the person responsible for the maintenance of law and order within the city boundaries. This meant that his actions and policies would both influence and reflect day-to-day life on the streets, within the jails and markets and at the port. The politics and belief system of the lord mayor during his term of office reflected the concerns of the population, or at least the voting population. For these reasons, an exploration of the role of the first citizen of Dublin reveals more than just the operation of civic government and can say much about the average person who lived in the city.

This volume evolved from a one-day symposium that was held in Dublin
City Library and Archive in November 2009 and that aimed to discuss
whether the lord mayor was the leader of the city. Each speaker was asked to
look at one mayor and their response to a city-wide problem or issue that arose
during their mayoralty. Although the issues varied greatly across this broad
timespan, a number of recurring themes emerged, including issues of planning
and growth, the constitutional relationship between Britain and Ireland,
confessional politics and the sometimes-complex intertwining of national
politics and local business interests. For many of the mayors portrayed in this
volume, the realities of balancing the demands of making a living with
performing their civic duty were challenging. There was a fine line between
availing of the power and commercial opportunities afforded by the office, and
experiencing financial hardship due to the high costs that it sometimes
entailed. This is not simply a story of the city's figureheads, but of real people
whose human frailties led to at times spectacular falls from grace, whether due
to allegations of financial impropriety or misconduct, political miscalculation,
or simply being in the wrong place at the wrong time. Among the individuals
considered here are some who were elected as 'firsts', including the first *lord*
mayor, the first Catholic lord mayor after the penal laws, the first woman
mayor, and others who presided over particularly troubled times in the life of
the city.

The biggest external influence on corporation politics and policies was
national government. Parliament met outside of Dublin in the sixteenth and
seventeenth centuries and it was not until the late seventeenth century that
parliament began to reside frequently and then permanently in Dublin.
Nevertheless, the fact that Dublin Castle housed the office of the chief
governor of Ireland, the lord lieutenant or viceroy, ensured that national
politics played its part in influencing civic government throughout this period.
As Dublin evolved to become the focal point for national politics, this had
consequences for civic government. Three developments occurred to strengthen
the position of the corporation but also to undermine their powers in the face
of national government. First, by the seventeenth century the corporation had
become a more professional body with increased civic power and functions
distributed to its members.[1] Second, parliament (as we shall see below in
relation to municipal reform legislation) became more likely to get involved in
how the corporation was run. After the Glorious Revolution, which saw the

1 Lennon, *Lords of Dublin,* p. 42.

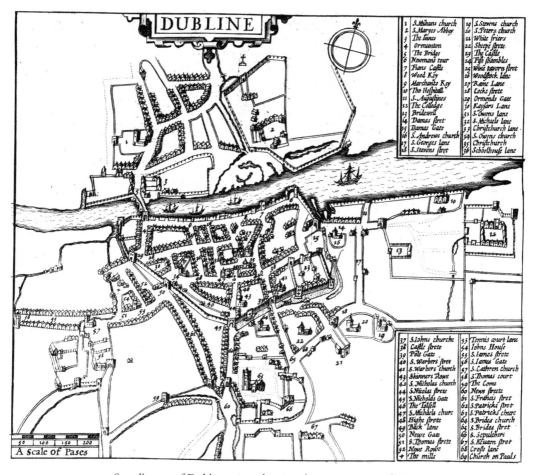

DUBLINE

1	S. Mihans church	19	S. Stevens church
2	S. Maryes Abbey	20	S. Peters church
3	The Innes	21	White friers
4	Ormunton	22	Sheepe strete
5	The Bridge	23	The Castle
6	Newmans tour	24	Fish shambles
7	Friars Castle	25	Wine tavern stret
8	Wood Key	26	Woodstock lane
9	Marchants Key	27	Rome Lane
10	The Hospitall	28	Cocks strete
11	S. Augustines	29	Ormonds Gate
12	The Colledge	30	Kayfars Lane
13	Bridewell	31	S. Owens lane
14	Damas strete	32	S. Michaels lane
15	Damas Gate	33	Chrystchurch lane
16	S. Andrews church	34	S. Owens church
17	S. Georges lane	35	Chryst church
18	S. Stevens strete	36	Schoolhouse Lane

37	S. Johns churche	53	Tennis court lane
38	Castle strete	54	Johns House
39	Pole Gate	55	S. Iames strete
40	S. Warbers stret	56	S. Iames Gate
41	S. Warbers church	57	S. Cathren church
42	Skinners Rowe	58	S. Thomas court
43	S. Nicolas church	59	The Come
44	S. Nicolas strete	60	Newe streets
45	S. Nicholas Gate	61	S. Francis stret
46	The Tolsell	62	S. Patricks stret
47	S. Michaels churc	63	S. Patricks churc
48	Highe strete	64	S. Brides church
49	Back Lane	65	S. Brides stret
50	Newe Gate	66	S. Sepulchers
51	S. Thomas strete	67	S. Kevam stret
52	Nowe Rowe	68	Crosse lane
+	The mills	69	Church on Pauls

A Scale of Pases

1 Speed's map of Dublin, 1610, showing the compact size of the city: reproduced courtesy of Joe Brady.

overthrow of King James II, there was a marked move away from the tradition of the monarchy granting municipal charters to increase the power and function of a corporation. Instead, parliament was increasingly legislating for that body and interfering in how it operated. Finally, while this outside interference could weaken the corporate structure, the corporation also weakened themselves through internal disputes that spilled over onto the national arena.

If the policies and politics of national government were the greatest external influence on corporation politics, certainly the growth of the city and the maintenance of its infrastructure was the greatest internal issue facing the corporation. The population of Dublin was, with the exception of times of war

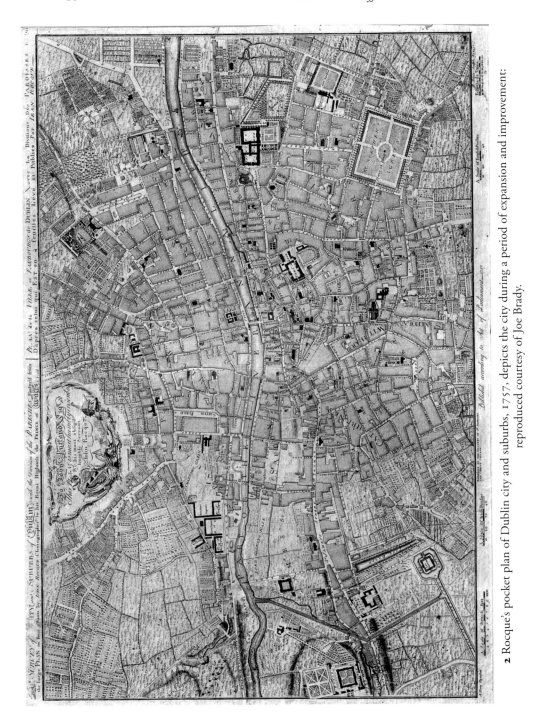

2 Rocque's pocket plan of Dublin city and suburbs, 1757, depicts the city during a period of expansion and improvement: reproduced courtesy of Joe Brady.

or during economic crises, expanding throughout this period. Louis Cullen estimates that when John Speed's map (fig. 1) was drawn in 1610, the population of Dublin was probably somewhere between 15,000 and 20,000. It doubled to *c*.40,000 by 1680, reached about 60,000 by 1700 and 180,000 by the end of the eighteenth century.[2] Cities were desirable places to live and this process of urbanization was occurring across Europe at a similar pace. The growth of the city's population meant more work for the city corporation. As the population increased so too did trade, crime and waste. The city infrastructure, including the Custom House, the city docks and the largely medieval street layout, became inadequate. It was the role of the corporation, sometimes in partnership with parliament or the Dublin Castle administration, to try to improve facilities and deal with the impact of this population increase on the city. As this workload increased throughout this period, the need for more regular corporation and trade offices became evident. In his essay, Raymond Gillespie discusses the erection of the city tholsel that became home to the corporation from the late seventeenth century to the early nineteenth century. Other buildings, such as the Royal Exchange, which coincidentally later became City Hall, were erected in order to encourage trade and business in the city.

When construction of the Parliament House on College Green began in 1729, it confirmed what had become reality since the restoration of Charles II in 1660, that Dublin was the centre of Irish political life. Despite the presence of the parliament and the lord lieutenant in the city, however, the corporation was still affected by the big issues of the day and had to respond to them. More often than not, the serving lord mayor was called upon to argue the interest of the corporation or freemen and guilds of the city. The big issues governing national politics – confessional freedom (see Lennon, Hill, Griffith and Clark), policing (see Griffith), re-zoning of land (see Gillespie), housing (see Carroll and McManus), trade (see Kennedy and Stapleton) and the constitutional connection with Great Britain (see Kennedy, Wallace, McManus, Litton and McEllin) – affected not just citizens but also the government and smooth running of the city. But when speaking up about how these issues affected the city was the mayor simply voicing the opinions of the electorate or affecting change? To what extent was the mayor reactionary rather than proactive? Each of these essays seeks to assess how a serving mayor dealt with an issue over the course of their term, revealing how the national politics of the day, just as

2 H. Clarke, *Irish cities,* pp 98–9.

much as the serving personality, could affect the degree to which a mayor led the city on a particular issue or simply reacted to events.

THE MAYORALTY IN THE EARLY MODERN PERIOD

The legal structures and government of Dublin city evolved gradually from medieval times. By 1500 a pattern of civic government had been established in large cities across Ireland, by means of a series of charters granted by the English government (see figs 3, 4 and 8). Sometimes intended to garner the support and loyalty of city inhabitants for the crown, charters were also directed at city defences, trade and good government within the city walls. In 1485 Richard III conferred corporate status on Dublin and in 1548 Edward VI bestowed a charter upon Dublin that distinguished the boundaries of the city from the county.[3] There was a further confirmation of the city charters by King James I in 1611.[4] By 1641 Charles I had bestowed the title of 'lord mayor' on the chief magistrate of the city, although this title was not taken up until the Restoration (see Janet Redmond).[5]

Colm Lennon has shown that 'the larger the municipality, the more complex were the councillor structures'.[6] In Dublin and Drogheda, for example, the corporation was divided into two boards, the common council (lower council) and alderman board (upper council). In Dublin twenty-four aldermen sat on the board and elected the mayor (as previously noted, Dublin was allowed to grant a mayor from 1229, a lord mayor from 1641). The common council had 144 members. By the eighteenth century a total of 169 men sat on the corporation; the aldermen and common council meetings took place at the same time but in different rooms for privacy. Although city powers evolved in this period, this bicameral structure did not change until 1840.

Involvement in corporations and elections was restricted to freemen and the freedom of the city conferred the most basic of rights. As well as the right to vote (the civic franchise), freemen could enter trade associations, guilds and corporations.[7] The city had twenty-four guilds, based on the medieval guild structure, although the corporation and guilds were becoming more akin to

3 H.B. Clark, *Dublin, Part 1: to 1610, Irish Historic Towns Atlas* (Dublin, 2002), p. 12.   4 Haliday MSS, 12/E/2, 307.   5 *CARD*, iv, p. ix.   6 Colm Lennon, *Sixteenth-century Ireland* (Dublin, 2005), p. 24. 7 Dublin City Library and Archive have put together, using extant sources of lists of freemen, an online listing of early city freemen. The site also details the position of freemen within the city and can be found here: http://www.dublinheritage.ie/freemen/about.php.

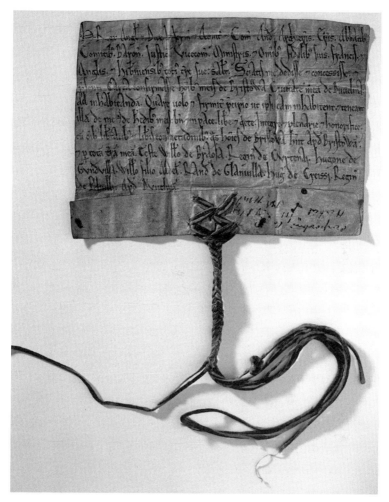

3 Dublin's earliest charter, issued by Henry II in 1171–2:
reproduced courtesy of Dublin City Library and Archive.

professional bodies from 1500 onwards. Freedom was granted in several ways: 'by birth', to sons of a freeman; 'by marriage' to a daughter of a freeman; 'by service' or on completion of a seven-year apprenticeship in one of the Dublin trade guilds; 'by act of parliament', which was introduced to encourage foreign Protestants (particularly Huguenots) to settle in Dublin, 'by fine', a fee paid, or by 'grace especial', which was special circumstance normally reserved for those who had undertaken their apprenticeship in another city or country.

Freemen could be elected to seats in the common council through their guilds. From the common council they could be elected to the position of

4 Charles I's charter granting the title 'Lord Mayor of Dublin' in 1641, although the new title was not exercised until after the Restoration: reproduced courtesy of Dublin City Library and Archive.

high sheriff for a year and then to the alderman board. The common council, or lower chamber of the corporation, consisted of members of each of the twenty-four guilds. Forty-eight men sat as sheriff-peers and ninety-six sat as direct representatives of the guilds.

The high sheriffs were the legal arm of the corporation and their tasks included issuing warrants, empanelling juries, managing and delivering prisoners, making arrests in the market place and presiding over executions.[8] Elections for the office of high sheriff took place on an annual basis and on completing a term as sheriff, the corporation member then sat as a master of the city works and would become a sheriff-peer (which was the title conveyed to someone who had served as a sheriff). The position would have been very time-consuming, involving the city-wide tasks enumerated above, as well as sitting on several committees.

The next higher position open to members of the corporation was the office of alderman, or city magistrate. Aldermen held their positions for life and, while members could resign, the only circumstances that led to the loss of their positions on the board were gross misconduct or conversion to Catholicism. The powers of the alderman board were curtailed under the Corporation Reform Act of 1760, which removed the alderman veto over guild represen-tatives thus allowing guilds to elect whomever they liked. Under this act, the electoral process for offices in the corporation was taken out of the hands of the aldermen and placed in the commons.[9]

The office of lord mayor, although only an annual position, was the highest ranking office. It was held by members of the alderman board. The lord mayor was charged with presiding over the corporation as a whole, appointing members to committees, calling, dismissing and chairing corporation assemblies and post assemblies, swearing in freemen, regulating weights and measures in the markets, regulating prices, permitting plays and theatre productions within the city and administering the punishment of groups or individuals who disrupted the peace of city.

A key task was inspection and regulation of the market place. The lord mayor was an important figure involved in trade and commerce in the city and held the power to punish fraudulent traders. If he was displeased with produce, then he was responsible for penalizing the trader and he was expected

8 Joanne Innes, 'Managing the metropolis, London's social problems and their control, *c.*1660–1830' in P. Clark and R. Gillespie (eds), *Two capitals: London and Dublin, 1500–1840. Proceedings of the British Academy* (London, 2001), p. 84.   **9** 33 Geo. II, c.16 (1760).

'to seize, burn or publicly destroy' the goods.[10] As corporation members were elected by their city guilds they were active tradesmen and had an interest in the trade of the city. As such it was believed that they were best suited to carry out these duties. Máire Kennedy examines the overlap between corporation duties and trade in her essay on Lord Mayor Exshaw.

Socializing was a facet of the office of lord mayor that received much attention in the press and was facilitated by a mayoral stipend introduced in the late sixteenth century. The office was a costly one to run and, from its inception, there were frequent petitions to increase the grant. The mayor stipend amounted to £20 in 1558, was raised to £40 st. in the early 1570s, and to £45 st. by 1575.[11] By the late seventeenth century, this had risen to £500 and was intended to pay for the cost of the lord mayor's socializing while in office. This sum was considered inadequate and was increased in the early eighteenth century to £1,350. In August 1760, following the Corporation Reform Act, a committee which met to 'ascertain for the succeeding lord mayors … the income of that office by the late act of parliament',[12] resolved to increase the sum from £1,350 to £2,000. They believed that the increased amount would be adequate to keep the lord mayor in 'splendour and hospitality necessary to preserve respect and conciliate the good affections of the citizens by promoting a social and friendly intercourse between them and their magistrates.'[13]

The importance of the mayoral office to the city was shown in a number of different ways. The stipend provided by the city to outgoing lord mayors towards the cost of their socializing, discussed above, was one of these. There were many material displays as well, as the appendix of this book shows, including the provision of elaborate silver and gold ornamentation, which is discussed by Janet Redmond. As the centuries progressed so too did these trappings of office. From 1715 the lord mayor was provided with his own residence on Dawson Street, the Mansion House (see Clark in Appendix 2). From 1791 he had his own state carriage, which is discussed by Griffith (p. 91).

Apart from the material trappings of office there were some showy street displays that were intended to impress upon the population the importance of the office. The ceremony of riding the franchises took place every three years 'when the mayor, accompanied by four hundred citizens on horseback rode around the boundaries of the city'.[14] They were followed by the guilds; the

10 *Freeman's Journal*, 24 Sept. 1763.   **11** Lennon, *Lords of Dublin*, p. 48.   **12** *CARD*, x, p. 433.   **13** Ibid. **14** Mary Clark and Raymond Refaussé (eds), *Directory of historic Dublin guilds* (Dublin, 1993), pp 12–13.

merchants' guild rode immediately after the mayor as the oldest and most prestigious guild. The procession was intended to display guilds' ancient lineages, strength of numbers and the overall guild hierarchy. Another important ceremonial event was the day when the lord mayor was sworn into office, when the corporation would proceed in a cavalcade to Christ Church Cathedral. This was usually followed by a large entertainment at the end of the day provided by the lord mayor. These trappings of office were essential to impress upon the city that the office was significant. They were also important to entice freemen to undertake this expensive office.

RELIGION AND THE OFFICE OF LORD MAYOR, 1534–1829

Confessional faith became a central factor in the take-up of office from the sixteenth century right up to the first half of the nineteenth century. Of course this was not unique to the office; religion affected all aspects of Irish politics. Laws directly prohibiting Catholics from undertaking the office of lord mayor were, however, enacted quite late. In their essays, Colm Lennon and Patricia Stapleton show the effect this had on the office and those undertaking it. The main charge levelled against Catholics was that of recusancy. A recusant was someone who repeatedly failed to attend the established church which was, since Henry VIII declared himself supreme head of the church under the Act of Supremacy in 1534, the Anglican Church of Ireland. On the ground this split did not come about immediately, rather it emerged gradually as the reformation progressed, the impact of the king's actions became apparent, and the population began to assess what these new articles of faith meant to their own personal beliefs. Recusancy fines were introduced as a way of dealing with those who failed to regularly attend the new religious service, in the belief that such fines would add an incentive to the population to adhere to the new church. As these were seen as an adequate way of dealing with non-conformists, mayors were not required to take the oath of supremacy until 1604.[15] The oath stated that the monarch was the head of the church, thereby denying the authority of the pope in Rome. This would have been odious for any Catholic and to take such an oath would have meant they renounced their faith.

The 'new rules' enacted by Charles II in 1672 reinforced the requirement that the oath of supremacy be taken by the lord mayor, with an added

15 Lennon, *Lords of Dublin*, p. 48.

condition that the lord lieutenant also had to approve of the new mayor. Charles II was more favourably inclined to Catholics and he allowed that the lord lieutenant could exempt some individuals from taking the oath. However, the climate in Dublin was never relaxed enough during the reign of Charles II to allow for a Catholic to take the office and for his favourable attitude to be tested.

Further 'new rules' for the corporation were introduced by the Catholic monarch James II in 1687, when Catholics returned to civic government and ousted Protestants from office. This did not, of course, last long and these 'new rules' were rescinded by William and Mary in 1688.[16] After the Glorious Revolution that saw James II overthrown by Protestant William III, the Protestants would not forget that Catholics had once attempted to wrestle power from their hands. During the war Protestants who had been dismissed from office had continued to meet secretly in the city in Skinners' Alley (across from the city tholsel where the now-Catholic corporation would have met) where they continued the Protestant governance of the city. These aldermen were commemorated through an eighteenth-century city club called 'the Alderman of Skinners' Alley' which was made up of conservative Protestants.[17]

The penal laws, which were enacted from 1691, were the most comprehensive block on Catholic and Dissenter social and political advancement. From 1691 Catholics could not sit in parliament or hold public positions.[18] The franchise was completely withheld until 1793. Catholics could not become freemen, which blocked their entrance to guilds and therefore to the corporation. They could pay a fee to become quarter brothers, which allowed them to trade (guilds were not powerful enough to exclude non-quarter brothers from trading). Under the Test Acts, religious dissenters were forced to take an oath. While Quakers became members of guilds, they could not enter the corporation. Presbyterians took the oath and entered civic and national institutions, leaving Catholics and other dissenters on the outside.

When debate began in the 1780s and early 1790s about allowing Catholics enter guilds and corporations, the majority of corporation members proved they were against relief (see Griffith). However, the tide had turned against them and, in 1793, Catholics were once more given the right to become guild

16 Colm Lennon, *Dublin, Part II: 1610, 1756, Irish Historic Towns Atlas* (Dublin, 2008), p. 9.   **17** For more see Martyn J. Powell, 'The Alderman of Skinners' Alley: ultra-Protestantism before the Orange Order' in James Kelly and Martyn J. Powell (eds), *Clubs and societies in eighteenth-century Ireland* (Dublin, 2010), pp 203–23.   **18** 3 Will. & Mary, c. 2 [Eng.] (1691). It was not until 1728 that Catholics were explicitly prohibited from voting: 1 Geo. II, c. 9, s.7 (1727).

members and to sit on the corporation. They were also allowed to vote (although not to sit in parliament), to take degrees at Dublin University and to bear arms.[19] While this was a major step in the Catholic emancipation movement, the reality was that the Protestant guild and corporation elected its own members onto its council and they could simply refuse to vote for Catholics.

MUNICIPAL REFORM AND THE MAYORALTY FROM 1840

As discussed above, the corporation structures had evolved from medieval times and, by the early nineteenth century, were in significant need of reform. A modernized Dublin Corporation was established as a result of the Municipal Corporations Reform (Ireland) Act, 1840. In England and Wales, the system of municipal government was reformed by the Municipal Corporations Act, 1835, while in the same year significant defects were identified in the Irish system by commissioners appointed to inquire into municipal corporations.[20] Throughout the country, most corporations were self-perpetuating oligarchies devoted to protecting a narrow political and sectarian class.[21] In the case of Dublin, the corporation had gradually devolved its original responsibilities, such as paving, lighting and cleansing the streets, to other bodies, and was found to be wholly inadequate. The report concluded that complete reform of municipal government was required, ultimately leading to the act, passed in August 1840,[22] which abolished the existing sixty-eight borough corporations in Ireland and preserved borough councils in just ten locations, including Dublin. Intended to improve the operations and accountability of local government, the act gave these new councils strictly defined powers. The ten reformed corporations[23] were styled as mayor, aldermen and burgesses, with the exception of Dublin where the title right honourable lord mayor was retained.

Urban administration was now based on the principle of local democracy. All (male) ratepayers owning property with a yearly valuation of £10 were entitled to vote in civic elections and sit on the council, irrespective of their religious denomination. However, freemen, who were almost all Protestant, retained their municipal vote, and the lord lieutenant was given the power to

19 33 Geo. III, c. 21.   **20** First report of the commissioners appointed to inquire into municipal corporations in Ireland, HC 1835 (23), xxvii, 1.   **21** V. Crossman, *Local government in nineteenth-century Ireland* (Belfast, 1994), p. 75.   **22** The Municipal Corporations Reform (Ireland) Act, 1840 (3 & 4 Vict., c. 108), An Act for the Regulation of Municipal Corporations in Ireland.   **23** Belfast, Clonmel, Cork, Drogheda, Dublin, Kilkenny, Limerick, Londonderry, Sligo and Waterford.

appoint borough magistrates and sheriffs. Although the 1840 legislation increased the number of voters, it was far more limited than in Britain where the franchise had been granted to all ratepayers.

The new more democratic city council was now a single chamber body, presided over by the lord mayor. Each borough was divided into wards with three, six or nine councillors per ward and one alderman for every three councillors. One-third of the councillors were to go out of office each year, and one-half of the aldermen every three years. The quorum for council meetings was to be one-third of the whole, with matters being decided by majority vote.

When the Municipal Corporations Reform (Ireland) Act came into force in 1841, Dublin Corporation became the new municipal authority for the city of Dublin, replacing the Dublin City Assembly. In the local elections at the end of 1841, Daniel O'Connell was elected to the new Dublin Corporation and took office as lord mayor of Dublin. He was the first Catholic to hold this position since the reign of James II and the first democratically elected lord mayor of the city. The more democratic city council that replaced the ruling oligarchy included many representatives of the new business class in Dublin, many of whom were Catholics. In her examination of the attempts to commemorate Daniel O'Connell's mayoralty, Mary Clark considers the impact of municipal reform and the finely balanced nature of the city council in the period from 1841–71.

As the century progressed, Dublin Corporation's powers increased and became more streamlined. Under the Dublin Improvement Act, 1849, for example, it took over the duties of the Wide Streets Commission and the Paving Board. As the staff increased and more space was required, in 1852 the city council moved its headquarters from the City Assembly House on South Frederick Street to the larger Royal Exchange building, which was then renamed City Hall and became the centre of civic administration.[24]

Despite the reforms of 1840, Dublin Corporation continued to suffer from a poor reputation. The 1878 select committee on the local government of towns in Ireland criticized Dublin Corporation, referring to 'slack attendance at meetings, inattention to important duties such as the condition of the streets and sanitary matters generally, and criticizing a lack of proper control in dealing with officials and workmen'.[25]

24 Dublin City Public Libraries and Archive, 2006, *Serving the city, the Dublin city managers and town clerks, 1230–2006*, 2nd ed. (Dublin, 2006), pp 27–8. **25** Crossman, 1994, p. 81, from Report from the select committee on local government and taxation of towns (Ireland), HC 1878 (262), xvi, 11.

Clontarf Township

Drumcondra Township

Kilmainham Township

DUBLIN

Pembroke Township

Rathmines Township

Kingstown Township

Blackrock Township

Dalkey Township

Killiney Township

5 Dublin city and independently-governed townships in the late nineteenth century: courtesy of Joe Brady.

The status, income and political outlook of members of Dublin Corporation was to change significantly over the second half of the nineteenth century. In the late 1850s, the political balance of the corporation was evenly split between liberal and conservative, but by 1896 just eleven members out of a total of sixty were conservatives. Furthermore, the conservative business elite of the city were gradually replaced by nationalists of lower socio-economic status; by 1890 one-third of the total members of the corporation were either grocers or publicans or both.[26] Tension between the Catholic majority and the Protestant minority was evident in many acrimonious political debates within the corporation. The changes within the chamber reflected the fragmentation of Dublin's metropolitan area in the latter half of the century, as the middle classes increasingly moved to independently-governed townships just beyond the city boundaries (see fig. 5). As suburbs such as Rathmines, Ballsbridge

26 Mary Daly, 'Late nineteenth- and early twentieth-century Dublin' in Harkness and O'Dowd (eds), *The town in Ireland*, pp 228–30.

(Pembroke) and Clontarf became increasingly Protestant and middle class, the city area governed by Dublin Corporation became increasingly impoverished, with an imbalanced social structure and limited capacity to generate income from rates. In 1851, the population of the city was 258,369, while the suburban population was only 59,468; by 1891, the city's population had fallen to 245,001, while the suburbs had grown to 102,911.[27]

The next wave of local government reform in England and Scotland took place in the 1880s, with Ireland following in the 1890s. The Local Government (Ireland) Act passed into law on 12 August 1898, widening the franchise and designating the six largest municipalities, including Dublin, as county boroughs.[28] For the first time, women were entitled to vote. The new, more representative system also saw a decisive nationalist takeover of local government across the country. The impact of this change in a Dublin context is considered by Ciarán Wallace's essay on the mayoralty of J.P. Nannetti, which reveals the complex relationship between the different nationalist factions, as well as the challenge of retaining political integrity when faced with the competing demands and rewards of municipal office. As Lydia Carroll shows, there were times when, as leader of the city, the mayor was called upon to rise to exceptional demands. Thus it was for Lorcan Sherlock, whose three-term mayoralty was associated with a huge push towards home rule, the dramatic and sometimes violent events of the Lockout, and the start of the Great War.

As the essays in this volume suggest, political upheaval following the 1916 Rising impacted heavily on Dublin. The Local Government (Ireland) Act, 1919 introduced a system of proportional representation into municipal elections. Wards were replaced by electoral areas, and the entire council was to be elected triennially. Separate elections of aldermen and councillors were ended, with all members of the council elected by popular vote. The first candidate elected in each area was entitled to the title of alderman, while the remaining successful candidates were termed councillors. In the local elections of 1920, Sinn Féin gained a majority of seats. The members of the city council opposed to the Anglo-Irish Treaty of 1921 came into increasing conflict with the government of the Irish Free State. This situation culminated in the suspension of Dublin City Council by the minister for local government in May 1924, with three commissioners taking responsibility for the running of the city. Laurence O'Neill was the incumbent of the mayoralty in the aftermath of the Rising, serving from 1917 until the suspension of 1924. His careful negotiation of the

27 Mary Daly, *Dublin, the deposed capital* (Cork, 1984), Table I, p. 3.   **28** 61 & 62 Vict., c.37.

6 Early twentieth-century postcard (front and back) requesting signature of lord mayor, signed by Lord Mayor Joseph Hutchinson: reproduced courtesy of Ruth McManus.

role during troubled times deserves credit, but it is his involvement in attempts to resolve Dublin's appalling tenement conditions that is at the core of Ruth McManus' essay.

An elected local government was eventually restored to the city in 1930, at which time the office of lord mayor was filled once again. Under the Dublin Corporation Act of 1930, the city boundaries were enlarged to incorporate the former urban districts of Pembroke, Rathmines and Rathgar, while the position of town clerk, which had existed since 1230, was replaced by a newly styled Dublin city manager and town clerk, intended to reflect the role of a chief executive in a large company. The enlarged boundaries added significantly to the population for which the corporation was responsible,

which stood at 468,103 at the time of the 1936 census.[29] The last two mayors
considered in this volume were elected to this new, enlarged urban area. The
first is the charismatic Alfie Byrne, who is noteworthy as the longest-serving
lord mayor in the history of the office, and whose reputation as lord mayor
lives on in the public memory (see McEllin, pp 152–65). He was succeeded by
Mrs Clarke, the first woman to wear the chain of office and, indeed, the first
woman to serve as mayor or lord mayor anywhere in Ireland (see Litton,
pp 166–75).

THE MAYORALTY INTO THE TWENTY-FIRST CENTURY

Under the Local Government Act, 2001, Dublin Corporation, as with the
other county borough corporations, was abolished, to be replaced by a city
council. Thus the name Dublin City Council, which had been introduced
following the reform of the 1840s to refer to the assembly of elected
councillors, now came into use for the entire administration. This major
reform of local government saw the abolition of the 300-year-old title of
alderman and the 700-year-old title of 'town clerk' in Dublin, as well as the
abolition of the ancient name of Dublin Corporation.

Significantly, the 2001 legislation provided for a directly elected mayor for
Dublin City Council, although to date this has not been implemented. The
2007 Fianna Fáil/Green Party programme for government gave a commitment
to introduce a directly elected mayor for Dublin with executive functions by
2011. In a green paper entitled 'Stronger Local Democracy – Options for
Change', launched in April 2008,[30] the possible role, powers and geographical
remit of such a directly elected mayor were considered. The green paper
recognized the value of a directly elected mayor for Dublin City Council in
terms of bringing a greater democratic connection to city residents and
creating clearer accountability for the services delivered by the council. Such a
directly elected mayor would also have a high profile, both locally and
nationally, thereby raising the profile of Dublin. While the introduction of a
directly elected mayor for the city council area could be achieved without
disruption to the existing administrative and structural arrangements for the
Greater Dublin Area, it was suggested that a different model of mayor would

29 Table 8, Volume 1, Census of Population 1936, Central Statistics Office, 1938.   **30** Department of the
Environment, Heritage and Local Government (online), http://www.environ.ie/en/GreenPaper/html/
greenp_chapthree.html. Accessed 4 Aug. 2012.

be preferable in order to provide local leadership on major strategic issues facing the Dublin regional area. The green paper therefore proposed the introduction of a regional mayor covering the four Dublin local authority areas, to be directly elected by the people, and having a strategic role in areas such as regional planning, water services, waste management and housing.

How would the first citizen of the city be affected by this new structure? If strategic political leadership was to be provided by the regional mayor, the nature of the interaction between the regional mayor and county Dublin's four local authority areas, with their respective mayors, required further consideration. One possibility raised was whether or not the role of lord mayor of the city and regional mayor could be combined in one office. If the offices were to remain separate, it was recognized that 'both a city mayor and a regional mayor would have a particular status and importance which could potentially lead to conflict notwithstanding the different remits which would attach to those offices – not least in terms of ceremonial importance'.[31]

The commitment to holding a direct election for the Dublin mayor was maintained in the renewed programme for government in October 2009, which said that an election would be held the following year. In October 2010, the Local Government (Dublin Mayor and Regional Authority) Bill[32] was published by the Department of the Environment, Heritage and Local Government, providing for a directly elected regional mayor and for the establishment of a Dublin regional authority. The new mayoral office was to have some executive powers in areas such as housing, waste management and water services, while the mayor would also chair the Dublin Transport Authority. Intended to raise the profile of Dublin, enhance local democracy and accountability, and lead the provision of an integrated public service across the city and region, this role was envisaged as being entirely separate from the ceremonial position of lord mayor of Dublin. The regional mayor would develop and oversee policy for the region and would have the power to direct the authorities in Dublin in relation to policy issues. The mayor would be chairperson and head of a newly constituted sixteen-member regional authority, which would also include the four chairs of the local authorities, that is, the lord mayor of Dublin City Council, the mayors of South Dublin and Fingal County Councils, and the cathaoirleach of Dun Laoghaire–Rathdown County Council, among its members.

---

31 Ibid.   **32** Local Government (Dublin Mayor and Regional Authority) Bill, 2010, (online) http://www.environ.ie/en/Legislation/LocalGovernment/Miscellaneous/, accessed 4 Aug. 2012.

Though the legislation reached committee stage in November 2010, the Local Government (Mayor and Regional Authority of Dublin) Bill was scrapped by the new government when it came to power in March 2011. However, debate around the possibility of a directly elected mayor continues. In October 2011, the then lord mayor of Dublin, Andrew Montague, called for a directly elected mayor with executive powers and a regional authority to 'drive the urban and economic regeneration of the city'.[33] When the chain of office was passed to his successor, Naoise Ó Muirí, there were fresh calls for a directly elected lord mayor of Dublin.[34] In July 2012 an online campaign calling for a directly elected lord mayor was launched by a group of citizens from Dublin. 'Democratic Dublin', as the campaign is titled, suggests that 'A directly elected lord mayor would serve us by making sure that our services … are delivered in a cost effective manner that benefits us all. They could set out the vision for Dublin and would have the mandate from the people to see their vision implemented.'[35] Whether or not this will occur, and its likely impact on the existing centuries-old office of lord mayor of Dublin, remains to be seen.

33 *Irish Times*, 14 Oct. 2011.   **34** *Evening Herald*, 21 June 2012.   **35** http://democraticdublin.wordpress.com/2012/07/07/press-release-dublin-residents-launch-online-campaign-for-a-democratic-dublin/, accessed 4 Aug. 2012.

Mayor Francis Taylor (1595–6), the martyred mayor

COLM LENNON

The only early modern mayor of Dublin to be the subject of a printed biography is Francis Taylor, who held the office in 1595–6. Yet the *Idea togatae constantiae, [sive Francisci Tailleri praetoris in persecutione congressus at religionis Catholicae defensione interitus]* by John Mullan, which appeared in Paris in 1629, eight years after the death of Taylor, is no ordinary biography.[1] For one thing, it contains very few actual biographical details of the subject's life. For another, it is full of ardent Counter-Reformation polemic, conjoined with a catalogue of Roman Catholic martyrs who had triumphed over heresy. It is in this martyrological context that Francis Taylor emerges as a champion of Catholicism, a layman and urban patrician who suffered for his faith.

In any consideration of the role of the mayoralty of Dublin since the medieval period, the story of Francis Taylor's career represents a crisis in the relationship between the civic community of Dublin and the state authorities in Dublin Castle. His predicament appears to have arisen from a major politico-religious confrontation at the time of the 1613 parliament, which had serious (if delayed) implications for the established urban ruling elite of which he was a member, and apparently immediate and dire personal consequences for himself. This essay examines firstly the reasons why a conventionally successful ascent through the civic *cursus honorum* (or sequence of civic office-holding), culminating in the mayoralty and senior councillor status, was succeeded by a precipitous decline into humiliation and apparent disgrace, and secondly how this disaster came to be represented in the discourse of the Counter-Reformation as a triumph of religious constancy.

I

Francis Taylor, who was born about 1550, was a member of the gentry family which had its county seat at Swords in north Co. Dublin but which retained

---

1 The *Idea togatae constantiae [An ideal of civic constancy: or the persecution and destruction of Alderman Francis Taylor for the defence of the Catholic religion]* was part of a bipartite work, the other part of which under the same imprint was entitled *Epitome tripartite matyrum fere omnium qui in Britannicis Insulis nostra patrumque memoriade haeresi gloriose triumpharunt*. In some copies, two testimonial letters from leading

its active involvement in the municipal life of Dublin.[2] Many families which had grown wealthy through mercantile and commercial profits withdrew from the quotidian realities of urban life, preferring to live as rentiers in the countryside, but the Taylors continued to serve in a civic capacity. Taylor's nephew, George, was recorder, or principal attorney, of Dublin for twenty years in the late sixteenth century,[3] and Francis himself followed the traditional municipal pathway. In a typically endogamous arrangement, he married Genet Shelton, the daughter of Thomas, a leading merchant of Dublin, who was also engaged in civic politics.[4] The concerns of the mercantile community of Dublin were very much interwoven with those of the city council, and indeed the vast majority of aldermen and mayors in the early modern period were merchants.[5] Francis himself followed this career path, gaining his freedom of the city through the guild merchant and serving as a major figure in the guild throughout his adult life. His first civic posting was as one of the two sheriffs of Dublin in 1586–7, and he was elected to the bench of twenty-four aldermen, a life appointment, in 1589. Then, in 1595–6, came his turn to serve in the office of mayor of Dublin.[6]

During his mayoral year, Francis Taylor would have been surrounded by the trappings of his office, and his dignity and primacy were asserted through ritual pageantry. He was preceded everywhere by the swordbearer who carried the symbolic king's sword before him on all public occasions. He was also attended by mace-bearers, and had at his disposal a man of over twenty years of age to serve as a bodyguard. Also waiting upon the mayor and boarded by him were the city trumpeter and drummer, whose duties were ceremonial and functional. A team of civic officers helped the mayor carry out his administrative responsibilities. These honorific shows were a reminder of the importance of the chief magistrate as representative of royal government at local level.[7] Among the duties that attended his position were to serve as judge in the city court, to act as admiral of the port of Dublin, to be arbiter of weights and measures in the city markets, and to represent the city's interests before the state administration in Dublin and London. For Taylor and his fellow-incumbents, the mayoral year was an expensive one, most of the costs

Catholic clergymen were incorporated, giving the established facts about Francis Taylor's imprisonment. **2** For the main details of his civic background and career, see Colm Lennon, *The lords of Dublin in the age of Reformation* (Dublin, 1989), pp 271–2.   **3** See John D'Alton, *The history of County Dublin* (Dublin, 1838), pp 148–9.   **4** Genealogical Office, Dublin, MS 48, f.11.   **5** See Lennon, *Lords of Dublin*, pp 97–127.   **6** *CARD,* ii, pp 204, 231, 283; iii, p. 155.   **7** Lennon, *Lords of Dublin*, p. 52.

7 'Dublin martyrs', sculpted by Conall McCabe, 2001, depicting Mayoress Margaret Ball (née Birmingham) and Mayor Francis Taylor: reproduced courtesy of Ruth McManus.

of hospitality and entertainment having to come from the mayor's own
pocket. A subsidy of £50 was payable from municipal funds to defray these
expenses, later raised to £100 sterling, but this hardly compensated for the
suspension of his commercial dealings during the mayor's occupancy of his
position at the head of the municipal government.[8]

Among the principal concerns of the civic assembly during Francis Taylor's
year in office were the defence of the city (his term coincided with the early
phase of the Nine Years War) and the proper preservation of the civic records.
Anxiety about the security of Dublin in the event of outside attack gave rise to
proposals for the purchase of munitions for the city. Measures for the raising
and payment of a civic militia to be deployed in military campaigns were also
passed. Funds were to be collected for a proper system of fire prevention, with
the acquisition of fire-fighting equipment. Some reform of the administration
of the municipality was presided over by Taylor. Because of damage sustained
by the civic muniments due to unsuitable conditions for their storage, steps
were taken for their proper preservation by the city clerk. The new incumbent
of that office, William Gough, was ordered to file the records in a 'uniform
manner' and to keep them under lock and key. Taylor's previous experience in
the surveying of civic lands and the collection of revenues was reflected in
particular attention being paid to these facets of municipal administration
during his mayoralty.[9]

For a former mayor on the bench of twenty-four aldermen, the *cursus
honorum* demanded a progression through a series of interlocking offices on
the part of the now-senior councillor. For example, the outgoing mayor was
automatically appointed in the year following his incumbency as one of the
masters of the guild merchant or guild of Holy Trinity, and in subsequent years
he also served as mayor of the staple, and master of the guild of St George, the
civic community's religious fraternity.[10] It was also normal for a former mayor
to act as city treasurer on at least one occasion in the aftermath of his
magistracy. Exceptionally, not only did Francis Taylor fill the position before
his mayoralty in 1593, he also served several terms after 1596–7. In fact, he
seems to have been particularly important as a financial administrator on
behalf of the civic community, as he acted as auditor of the municipal accounts
on at least half a dozen occasions.[11]

---

8 Ibid., pp 48–9.   **9** *CARD*, ii, pp 283–97.   **10** Colm Lennon, 'Fraternity and community in early
modern Ireland' in Robert Armstrong and Tadhg Ó hAnnracháin (eds), *Community in early modern Ireland*
(Dublin, 2006), pp 174–5; idem, *Lords of Dublin*, p. 99.   **11** *CARD*, ii, pp 265, 321, 355, 465, 483; iii, pp
28–9, 59.

Upon him too fell the responsibility as senior civic figure to lead at least one delegation to court on behalf of the city. This was mounted in the spring of 1597 at an especially critical juncture in the history of the municipality. In March of that year a massive explosion had ripped through the central urban area, killing over 100 people and levelling a number of streets, houses and utilities. Coming as it did during a major wartime emergency, with attendant food shortages and infections, the blast was the culminating episode in a series of reverses of fortune that left the city vulnerable and dependent on state support. Thus, the quality of leadership of the 1597 embassy was of great importance and the citizens chose Francis Taylor, one of their most experienced political leaders, to head the delegation to the royal court, as well as the city clerk, William Gough.[12]

II

Social and economic difficulties at the end of the sixteenth century were compounded by political and religious challenges in the early seventeenth, all of which led to the imbroglio of which Francis Taylor was a victim. With the end of the war in 1603 and the beginning of the process of the centralizing of state governance, Dublin's position as seat of national administration was thrown into relief. It was considered essential to have a ruling aldermanic elite that was obedient in religion as well as politically loyal. In the context of the circumscribing of civic and guild privileges, the Reformation statutes of supremacy and uniformity, enshrining Anglicanism, began to be enforced seriously for the first time. The first major test case involved Francis Taylor's brother-in-law, Alderman John Shelton. When the latter refused to take the proffered oath of supremacy, he was debarred from the mayoralty in 1604–5, heavily fined and imprisoned at pleasure. This episode was followed by that of the 'mandates', which were decrees summoning named civic figures to Anglican services on pain of severe penalties for non-conformity. Twenty or so leading citizens were imprisoned, and, though Francis Taylor was not among them, there is little doubt that the period was one of severe testing for all of the aldermen. At issue were the limits of toleration of their liberty of conscience and of their municipal autonomy. Not surprisingly, plans for a national parliament in the early 1610s, the first such assembly for a quarter of

---

12 Lennon, *Lords of Dublin*, p. 126.

a century, were anticipated with foreboding as the state government aimed to make its military conquest of the island of Ireland a political reality.[13]

As part of the preparation for the parliamentary assembly, Francis Taylor sat on a committee of the civic corporation that met twice weekly from 1610 to discuss legislative measures pertaining to Dublin.[14] The aldermen knew that an opportunity would be afforded the city's members of parliament to speak out on behalf of the citizens who were increasingly conscious of the encroachment of central government on their civic privileges and religious beliefs. A contemporary chronicler was convinced that the Dublin community had no intention of choosing as member of parliament anyone who was not an 'open recusant', or Catholic dissident.[15]

In 1613 the body was summoned and elections of members were held. Dublin city borough was entitled to elect two MPs and the proceedings of that year proved to be chaotic. In the absence of the mayor, James Carroll, the burgesses selected Francis Taylor and Thomas Allen as MPs. Allen and Taylor were described by one hostile commentator as 'most Spanish' and 'seditious schismatiques', meaning presumably the most advanced in recusancy.[16] Francis Taylor's unmasking as a religious protagonist is something of a surprise, as there is no previous evidence of a firm creedal stance, yet his being chosen at this critical juncture by the citizenry should undoubtedly be seen as a symbolic gesture. The state authorities certainly thought so, as they demanded a re-run of the election, this one in the presence of the mayor, and the outcome in most contentious circumstances was the selection of two Protestants to sit in parliament for Dublin borough. The protests of the burgesses were part of the commission of enquiry into the holding of the 1613 elections in Ireland, but no determination could be reached in the case of Dublin, so vexed and controversial were the events.[17] The municipality had failed in its bid to be represented by Catholic aldermen but the most dreaded measures to do with strict religious orthodoxy were not proceeded with – a victory of sorts for the opposition.

---

13 Ibid., chapter 6, contains a survey of this period.   **14** 'Minute book of the corporation of Dublin, known as the "Friday book", 1567–1611', ed. Henry F. Berry in *RIA Proc.* 30, section C (1912–13), p. 513. **15** William Farmer's 'Chronicle of Lord Chichester's government of Ireland … for the years 1612–15' in John Lodge (ed.), *Desiderata curiosa Hibernica: or a select collection of state papers, to which are added some historical tracts*, 2 vols (Dublin, 1772), i, 156.   **16** *CSPI, 1611–14*, p. 305.   **17** Ibid., pp 360–1, 362, 436–8, 441–2, 445.

III

The years after 1613 until his death in 1621 were stressful ones for Francis Taylor. At some time during that period, he was imprisoned and apparently confined in captivity until his death.[18] This was an unprecedented ordeal for a senior alderman of Dublin Corporation and may reflect the seriousness of the rupture in city-state relations in the aftermath of the crisis of the earlier Jacobean period. There is no record of a trial in the court of castle chamber or other judicial forum. There are a couple of possibilities for the circumstances of his arrest and detention. As a result of the riotous events surrounding the disputed elections of 1613, a number of dissidents, possibly including Francis Taylor, were rounded up and jailed. The records of the castle chamber court are not extant for several months from the middle of 1613 onwards. It is more likely, however, that Taylor's capture came at a later stage, probably in connection with a serious clamping down on public dissent on the part of Catholics in 1616 and 1617.[19] During the 1610s it is clear that Francis Taylor was undergoing severe financial difficulties as the civic assembly rolls allude to his 'present troubles and weak ability' in 1617. In this connection, enquiries conducted by the city council revealed the indebtedness of Taylor to the civic purse, arising out of deficiencies in his accounts while mayor, treasurer and auditor of the municipality. The former mayor owed at least £100 Irish to the municipality, which he claimed to have been accumulated unwittingly, and for remittance of which he petitioned in the city assembly in July 1617.[20] In response, the city council alleviated a recognisance of £20 sterling in January 1618, but insisted on the payment of the balance of the account.[21] Fiscal distress and religious disaffection appear to have ensured his consignment to prison in his late sixties and his detention there until his death in January 1621.

The only extant reports of his demise, all from Catholic apologists, claim that Francis Taylor died on 30 January 1621.[22] His biographer claimed that the prison conditions endured for several years took their toll on an elderly man.[23] Mullan included the printed text of a letter from the leading Catholic clergy of the city of Dublin, dated 1629, to the effect that Taylor had spent seven years in prison, thereby suggesting that his internment began about 1614.[24]

---

18 Letters from Thomas Fleming, archbishop of Dublin, and others, 17 August 1630, 4 May 1630: Mullan, *Idea togatae constantiae*, addendum.   **19** Ibid., p. 96.   **20** *CARD*, iii, pp 82–3.   **21** Ibid., p. 89.   **22** Mullan, *Idea togatae constantiae*, p. 338.   **23** Idem, *Epitome tripartita martyrum*, p. 96.   **24** Letters from Thomas Fleming, archbishop of Dublin, and others, 17 August 1630, 4 May 1630: Mullan, *Idea togatae constantiae*, addendum.

John Lynch in his *Alithinologia*, which is largely based on Mullan, states that the confinement began about 1616, while Mullan himself claimed that Taylor's death occurred after a four-year period in jail.[25] There is corroboration of the date of death in the fact that Taylor's will, the text of which is extant, was drawn up three weeks before his death – on 4 January 1621. For a long-serving urban patrician who had reached the pinnacle of success in his municipal career, his bequests were decidedly modest. His son and heir, Thomas, was the principal legatee of his lands and tenements, while his wife, Genet, was provided for in the form of an income and continuing residency in a house on High Street. The sum of forty shillings was set aside for poor people who were to pray 'in way of devotion for my soul's health'. Taylor expressed a wish that he be buried in his parish church of St Audoen, Dublin, where his parents had been interred.[26] According to Mullan, Francis' sons were granted permission after long importunacy to take away their father's body from the prison to be buried in accordance with his wishes, with suitable funeral rites.[27]

IV

The reasons for the prolonged imprisonment of a civic leader in harsh conditions in Dublin remain puzzling. The Catholic martyrologists claim that Taylor suffered for his dedication to his faith, Mullan proclaiming that he was a noted protector of priests and that this was one of the reasons for his prosecution.[28] This is eminently possible, though even at the height of religious repression it was most unusual for jailings of recusants to last for more than some weeks. Taylor's being characterized as a 'Spanish and seditious schmismatique' person in a contemporary chronicle was fairly damning, but his fellow-MP and Catholic, Alderman Thomas Allen, elected in the overturned poll of 1613, does not appear to have suffered a similar fate.[29] It could be that the state exacted an exemplary punishment of a respected alderman in order to intimidate would-be dissenters and opponents, and that Taylor may have lacked persuasive friends within the civic community due to financial mismanagement or perhaps embezzlement.[30] It is quite conceivable that Taylor

---

25 John Lynch, *Alithinologia, sive veridica responsio ad invectivam mendaciis, falacis, calumnii, et imposturis foetam* (St Malo, 1664), p. 13.   26 Will of Francis Taylor, 4 January 1621: NAI, T.1747.   27 Mullan, *Idea togatae constantiae*, p. 338.   28 Ibid., pp 198–201, 267, 278.   29 Lennon, *Lords of Dublin*, p. 225. 30 *CARD*, iii, pp 82–3.

may have made enemies during his long-running management of municipal finances, being engaged in litigation against certain defaulters.[31]

Although confessional differences among the members of the aldermanic bench did not normally issue in public disagreements, the twenty-four preferring to present a united front in respect of civic policy, it is possible that Taylor fell foul of a Protestant coterie on the council. Perhaps there are factors that have not come to light due to lack of evidence, having to do with international conspiracy – his 'Spanishness' and 'seditiousness' – or the activities of a brother, Walter, a member of the Society of Jesus, who was a prisoner in the Tower of London during the Elizabethan period.[32] There were also signs of strong Catholic convictions on the part of Francis' nephew, George, whose residence in the city served as a mass-house, and his cousin, Michael, who gave over part of his mansion in Swords for the 'great concourse' of Catholics who attended mass there on Sundays around 1630.[33] Certainly the reputation of Francis Taylor in lay and clerical Catholic circles in the 1620s was potent enough for him to be presented in print as a martyr figure of the civic community by 1629.

Leaving aside the polemical dimension to the accounts of Taylor's death, there is no doubt that the prosecution of a senior civic leader who had defied the regime was reflective of a critical conjuncture in relations between city and state. Down to the 1600s, the affairs of the municipality, whether the selections of mayor, or the elections of MPs, were sacrosanct for the citizens and guild members. With the assertion of increasingly centralizing policies in church and state under the early Stuarts, however, the era of civic autonomy over which the mayors presided was doomed, and there was foreshadowed very clearly the intrusion of central government into the affairs of the civic body. The ordeal of Francis Taylor, a distinguished former mayor and, at the time of his death, the fifth-most senior councillor among the twenty-four aldermen, called into question the ability of the Dublin patricians thenceforth to maintain a cohesive platform of political and religious liberties, acceptable and tolerable in the eyes of the state.

31 See *CARD*, ii, p. 305, for example, for a reference to one such case. **32** Edmund Hogan (ed.), *Ibernia Ignatiana* (Dublin, 1880), p. 249. **33** 'Archbishop Bulkeley's visitation of Dublin, 1630', ed. Myles V. Ronan in *Archivium Hibernicum*, 8 (1941), 58, 63.

Sir James Carroll: a pragmatic Protestant mayor in the early seventeenth century

PATRICIA STAPLETON

The significance of Sir James Carroll's political career is that he was one of the first individuals to hold the position of mayor more than once, in 1612–13, 1617–18, 1624–5, 1634–5. Furthermore, Sir James Carroll, who was knighted and appointed chief remembrancer of the exchequer on 8 June 1609 by the-then lord deputy of Ireland, Sir Arthur Chichester, was one of many of his generation to adopt what could be termed a type of pragmatic Protestantism. He took this stance to ensure the succession of Catholic elites in civic government in the face of continuous English governmental directives. In the early seventeenth century the government aimed to erode the power and privileges of the civic elite and, more significantly, to exclude Catholics from positions of power and replace them with a Protestant, and increasingly English, civic government.

I

Sir James Carroll's career in civic government spanned twenty-three years from 1612 to 1635. He hailed from a family of Gaelic Irish origin and was the son of Thomas Carroll, an alderman of the city, and Alice Mountfield. James lived in Cook Street in the city and was a prosperous landowner with extensive landholdings in Wicklow and Wexford as well as in the eastern suburbs of Dublin, even before he became involved in civic politics. Sir James Carroll became a citizen of Dublin as 'son of a freeman' in 1613 and was elected to the board of aldermen in the same year.[1] He was appointed as mayor in the years 1612 to 1613, 1617 to 1618, 1624 to 1625 and from 1634 to 1635 and also served as mayor of the statute staple, an important arm of civic government which regulated all trade and finance, from 1618 to 1619.[2] Carroll was

---

1 James was elected mayor before he formally became a citizen when his father requested that James become mayor when he (Thomas) was removed from office for refusing to take the oath of supremacy. 2 Colm Lennon, *Lords of Dublin in the age of Reformation* (Dublin, 1989), p. 236; P. Stapleton, 'The merchant community of Dublin in the early seventeenth century: social, economic and political study' (PhD, TCD,

married three times, not an unusual occurrence in early seventeenth-century
Ireland. Indeed the Carroll family tree tells us that his father was married four
times.

In 1604, the taking of the oath of supremacy became a prerequisite to
holding civic office (as discussed by Lennon above). Many Catholic aldermen,
mayors and sheriffs-elect, were hard-line recusants who refused to conform to
Protestantism or to take the oath. This led to direct state action and many of
them were fined and imprisoned. The refusal of the recusant mayors to take
the oath, unsurprisingly, disrupted the pattern of elections to the mayoralty.
Sir James' father, Thomas, an ardent Catholic, was imprisoned 'at pleasure' in
1605 for his religious beliefs. When Thomas' turn came to serve his term as
mayor of the city, he asked that his son Sir James be instated in his place.[3]
Although Thomas Carroll was an uncompromising recusant who refused to
conform or take the oath his son, James, always presented himself as a loyal
and faithful Protestant. On the surface at least, it seemed that this was actually
the case.

In his will dated 2 October 1639 (a mere six days before his death) Sir
James made a specific stipulation that his daughter Amy should marry a
Protestant.[4] He said, 'I leave and bequeath to my daughter Amy for her
preferment the sum of one hundred pounds sterling ... And also I leave her
the sum of six pounds sterling now, upon condition that she marry, with the
consent of her mother, a Protestant'. He continued saying, 'the said six pounds
shall be made two hundred pounds sterling so that in all if she marry as
aforesaid she shall have three hundred pounds sterling to be paid to her with
as much expedition as possible may be'. Sir James' will begins with an
introduction commending his soul to God almighty and 'trusting through the
death of his dear son our Lord and saviour' the confession of all his sins. This
is fairly typical of other Protestant wills of the time. The introduction in this
will, however, is much shorter than those of other Protestants. Moreover, at
the end, it is simply dated 'this second day of October one thousand six
hundred thirty nine' unlike the usual Protestant ending to a will which always
mentioned the king both as defender of the faith and as king of England,
Scotland, Wales and France. Carroll's will reflects the ambiguity surrounding

2008), App. II, 'Civic government, 1620–1660', App. III A, 'Yearly franchise admissions, 1620–1690'; B.
Fitzpatrick, 'The municipal corporation of Dublin, 1603–40' (PhD, TCD, 1984), II, app. II.   **3** *CARD*,
iii, pp 23, 28.   **4** Will of Sir James Carroll, knight, the National Archives, Kew [TNA], Prob/11/205,
image ref. 93.

his religious conviction, similar to that of other Catholics, who presented public profiles as Protestant but most probably remained Catholic in private.

Sir James' public profile as a Protestant is upheld by the fact that he took the oath of supremacy and held the office of mayor on four separate occasions. Yet, he was reported to support and succor great numbers of priests in his house.[5] Similarly, other members of the city's municipal government upheld a Protestant profile in public while seemingly maintaining the Catholic religion in private. For example, the Arthur family was well established in the city by beginning of the seventeenth century when John, a descendant of the Old English Catholic Arthur family from Limerick, became sheriff in 1599. His sons, Robert and Thomas, were sheriffs in 1621 and 1636 respectively and his other son, Edward, was mayor in 1632. The Arthurs married into both Catholic and Protestant families and were directly linked through marriage to the Bysses, Cusacks, Goughs, Kennedys, Mapas and Seagraves. John Arthur was said to have 'conformed', albeit through official pressure, to the Church of Ireland. The Arthurs were most likely Catholic, however, as in 1641 Robert Arthur's mother-in-law, Lady Bathe (formerly Barbara Gough) of Drumcondra, left a chalice and vestments in her will to her daughter Catherine Gough. Moreover, Robert was accused of giving sanctuary to the Catholic rebels in 1641 and the wording of his will indicates the religious belief of a Catholic. Similarly, the religious convictions of the Duffe family are uncertain. Sir Thady Duffe was willing to serve as sheriff in 1603 as a substitute for a recusant, which indicates that he was a Protestant. Indeed, Sir Thady's son Richard, brother of Nicholas, declared himself a Protestant when claiming his father's properties in 1663. Richard Duffe, however, was accused of 'living amongst the rebels' in 1641 and had to 'account for his actions'.[6] Moreover, he was heir to Stephen Duffe, merchant of Dublin, who on his death in 1650 was said to have 'died a papist'.[7]

II

In the fifty years between 1580 and 1630, besides Sir James Carroll, only three individuals served as mayor on more than one occasion. Robert Ball, who

---

5 Lennon, *Lords of Dublin*, p. 236.   **6** Dermot MacIvor, 'Garrett Cooley of Ardee', *Irish Genealogist*, 3:7, (1962), 257–65; 'Deposition of Richard Duffe', 2 April 1642 (TCD, 1641 Depositions, MS 810), f. 210. **7** *Inquisitionum in office rotulerum cancellarie Hiberniae assorvataarum reportorium: abridgements of inquisitions* (2 vols. Dublin, 1826-9) [Inquisitions post-mortem], 1, no. 1, Car II.

served as mayor in 1604, replaced John Shelton who refused to take his position in 1609; Nicholas Barran, mayor in 1600, replaced both Thomas Plunkett and Edmund Purcell in 1607 following Plunkett's request to be exempt from office and Purcell's dismissal for refusing to take the oath; and Richard Browne served as mayor in 1614, 1615, and 1620. Yet in a sixteen-year-period between the years 1628 and 1646 no fewer than seven mayoral posts were held for a second time or more: Thomas Evans, who had replaced Walter Usher in 1628, was also mayor in 1630, Christopher Forster held the position in 1634, 1635 and 1638, Thomas Wakefield in 1640 and 1641 and William Smyth in 1643 and 1644, 1645, 1646. All of these individuals were Protestants. While Smyth's re-election as mayor in four consecutive years was undoubtedly due to the outbreak of rebellion and the subsequent decade of civil unrest in the city, it is significant that the replacements in the 1630s took place at the height of a hard line governmental directive against Catholicism and it indicates they were as a result of a similar crackdown to that of 1604.

Indeed the 1630s witnessed a cataclysmic change in the make-up of civic government in Dublin. After the arrival of Thomas Wentworth as lord deputy in 1633 he actively promoted a Protestant and loyal government in the city and used any opportunity to expel existing Catholic officials and ensure that those Protestants who remained in government were loyal to the crown. For example, in 1634 Christopher Brice was fined £600 and deprived of his office of sheriff for a 'great and heinous offence' in choosing citizens of the city of Dublin for the 'now intended parliament'.[8] Under normal procedure, the chancery issued writs for election to the sheriffs in each county, ordering them to hold election for the knights of the shire and to direct the chief magistrates of the cities and boroughs in their counties to elect their citizens and burgesses. Unfortunately no record of Christopher's actual offence survives amongst the court of castle chamber or other records but, presumably, he misdirected the citizens in some manner in relation to the elections. Whatever the reason, Brice's dismissal is significant because even if he did interfere in proceedings, the English administration was itself guilty of the same crime, in the first instance of which Carroll clearly displayed his loyalty to the English administration.

In 1613 two Catholic aldermen, Francis Taylor and Thomas Allen were elected as members of parliament [as previously discussed by Lennon]. James

---

8 *CARD*, iii, p. 291.

Carroll, as mayor, was absent from the city at the time of the election and on his return ordered a new election which he said should be open to non-native-born residents of the borough. This, unsurprisingly, provoked a riot in the city during which Carroll managed to save the king's sword from the rioters. Following the subsequent arrest of the main instigator of the riot, Carroll declared another election, disqualified the two Catholic members and, along with 'other the aldermen, his brethren and other good citizens' ensured the election of two Protestant candidates – Richard Barry and Thomas Bolton – at the instigation of the then lord deputy, Chichester. In 1634, the same year that Brice was dismissed, the corporation was prevented from electing candidates of whom Wentworth did not approve, but the lord deputy himself used his influence in favour of his own candidates, Richard Barry and Nathaniel Catelyn. He also supported the candidature of Sir James Ware and James Dongan to Trinity College, where members of parliament were elected by the university provost, fellows and scholars.

As Bríd McGrath has pointed out, the English administration had the power to issue and alter charters and therefore electorates.[9] They also strove to manipulate a Protestant majority in municipal government. Although Brice was a Protestant, his family had relatives and friends in both the Catholic and Protestant communities. Wentworth's centralizing policies ensured that established Protestants were increasingly losing their positions in the Irish administration, either to new arrivals who came to Ireland with the lord deputy or to those who he thought could be relied on to support his policies in government. Indeed, that Wentworth intended a Protestant re-edification of the city's government is evidenced the year after Brice's expulsion when James Carroll was also dismissed from his position as mayor. Ironically, it was Carroll himself who gave Wentworth the opportunity to do so when he misused his position as mayor to enhance his own personal profit.

III

Before Wentworth's arrival in 1633, the civic administration had looked forward to a reversal of attacks by state officials on local trading privileges and municipal customs exemptions. This curbing of civic power by Castle officials

9 Bríd McGrath, 'A biographical dictionary of the members of the Irish House of Commons 1640–41' (PhD, TCD, 1997), p. 31.

8 Golden Charter of Elizabeth I, 1582, which conferred title 'Admiral of the Port' on the lord mayor of Dublin: reproduced courtesy of Dublin City Library and Archive.

had provoked conflict between the royal administration and civic authorities in the previous two decades. Wentworth quickly made it clear, however, that he intended following these contentious policies that also threatened the standing of the Protestant members of the civic elite. At the trial of Thomas Strafford in 1641, Robert Kenney gave evidence against the lord deputy. He said that when Robert Dixon was inaugurated as mayor on 30 September 1633, just two months after the arrival of Strafford, he requested in his inaugural speech that the ancient charters and privileges of the city be reinstated. In reply, Strafford said that 'Ireland is a conquered nation … the king may do with them what he pleaseth: And speaking of the charters of Dublin … the charters are nothing worth, and binding the king no farther than he pleases'.[10]

City charters, the bedrock of Dublin's municipal government, basically granted recognition of specific rights including the right to all customs duties and other economic privileges. As the official head of city government and the only salaried member of the city assembly, the mayor's official functions included clerkship of the market, admiralty of the port and justice of the peace (fig. 8). He also had the final responsibility for regulation of internal trade, oversaw Dublin's shipping, maintained customs duties and had the final say on all matters relating to the port. The mayor also played a principal role in the governance of the statute staple, a body which was set up in 1326 to regulate the trade of basic or staple goods, which had evolved by the early seventeenth century as a sort of rudimentary bank and was *the* financial institution in Ireland. Thus the position of mayor was the real force of power both in the administration of municipal law and in the regulation of trade and finance. Moreover, the position provided mayors with the means to augment their personal wealth and they often used their position as clerk of the market to manipulate commodity prices for their own personal profit. In 1635 Wentworth directed the mayor, Sir James Carroll, be brought before the castle chamber for this very reason.

Following a proclamation by Wentworth in January 1634 which stated that coal should be sold to the poor of the city at a reasonable rate, Carroll was accused of selling coal at 16s. per ton, twice the normal rate of 8s. per ton, and pocketing the difference for himself.[11] This was not the first time that

10 J. Rushworth, *Tryal of Thomas earl of Strafford* (2nd edn, London, 1721), pp 156, 163. 11 'A proclamation concerning coales that none from henceforth be taken up at the king's rates, 16 January 1633/4', R. Steele (ed.), *Bibliotheca Lindesiana: a bibliography of royal proclamations of the Tudor and Stuart*

Wentworth ostensibly acted to defend the citizens of Dublin against inflated prices or duties. In 1633 the king had instructed that Dublin be charged an additional duty on coal as well as new duties on horses, cattle and sheep. Wentworth went to great lengths to ensure that the impositions were not introduced. The stance taken by Wentworth was not motivated by a desire to defend the rights of the citizens of Dublin, but was part of his strategic plan for newcomers from England to settle in Ireland. In a letter to the king defending his position on the duties he described Dublin as 'a growing people that would increase beyond all expectation if it were a little favoured'[12] and gave the imposition on coals, horses, sheep and cattle as an example of how Ireland was treated differently than England or Scotland. He argued that the impositions 'will be a great discouragement for any to transplant themselves and children into a country where they shall presently be dealt withal as aliens, and denied the favours and graces afforded to other subjects, and utterly quell and cut off any increase of trade'.[13] In short, Wentworth attempted to prevent the imposition as it would discourage new English settlers from coming to the city. The lord deputy was subsequently successful in his efforts to prevent the new impositions and thirteen months later wrote that 'this kingdom is growing apace'.[14] When James Carroll was accused of profiting from the sale of coal, he defended his position saying that he knew nothing about the proclamation and that as clerk of the market it was his privilege 'to take up coal by privilege and custom as he had done in the former times of his mayoralty'.[15] He was, however, duly convicted, fined £1,000 sterling, discharged from his office and imprisoned at Wentworth's pleasure.

V

While Wentworth's action against Carroll's breach of his proclamation on the price of coal cannot be morally reproached, it can be taken as a direct assault upon the ancient privileges of the city. After Carroll's trial, the lord deputy ordered that the sentence should be openly read in the city tholsel and remain on record there so that others that succeed him 'may take example thereby'.[16]

sovereigns, 1485–1714 (Oxford, 1910), II, pt 1, p. 39; *CARD*, iii, pp 307–8.   **12** Wentworth to Wandesford, 25 July 1636, William Knowler, *The earl of Strafford's letters and dispatches* (Dublin, 1740), II, p. 20. **13** Wentworth to Wandesford, 25 July 1636, W. Knowler, *The earl of Strafford's letters and dispatches*, II, p. 23. **14** Ibid., p. 89.   **15** *CARD*, iii, pp 307–8   **16** *CARD*, iii, p. 308.

By including this instruction, Wentworth gave himself the means to expel unwanted officials and thus ensure a loyal and Protestant city government. After Carroll's defeat, he was replaced by a Protestant newcomer, Sir William Blayden. Five Catholic aldermen were subsequently elected as mayor but not one of them served in the office up to 1641 and thereafter mayors of the city were all Protestant, with the exception of Walter Kennedy and Richard Barnewall who served in 1642 and 1647 respectively. It is notable that 1647, the year in which twenty-eight Catholic members were dismissed from the rolls of the city, was the last year in which Catholics appeared in any position in civic government. Another wave of new Protestant names entered civic government and thereafter no Catholics seem to have served in any capacity in the municipality up to 1660. Indeed, apart from a brief respite during the restoration years, the mayoralty and civic government remained predominantly, if not exclusively, in Protestant hands until Catholic emancipation.

Despite the best efforts of Sir James Carroll and others of his generation who adopted a public Protestant profile in order to protect their traditional role in civic government, they did not prevent their exclusion in the long term. In the first place, the English administration was well aware that these individuals upheld their Catholic convictions in private. More importantly, the English government, particularly after the 1630s, was intent on removing established Protestants (private and public) as well as Catholics from power. This was the case even when those individuals showed unmitigated loyalty as did Sir James Carroll when he manipulated the election of two Protestant members of parliament at the direction of the lord deputy in 1613. It is ironic, indeed, that the final downfall of Sir James Carroll, the pragmatic Protestant and loyal mayor, was effectively brought about by his own greed and misuse of the very privileges that he was empowered to protect.

Mayor William Smith (1642–7, 1663–5, 1675–6) and the building of the tholsel

RAYMOND GILLESPIE

Lord mayors of Dublin in the seventeenth century were a diverse group of men. Some were innovators while others simply maintained the status quo. Some were highly respected figures while others were reviled for their incompetence or lethargy. Peter Ward (lord mayor 1678–9) for instance was described by the earl of Anglesey as 'the dullest fool that ever was for lord mayor'. The duke of Ormond agreed, complaining 'if it be laid to my charge that my lord mayor has no more wit than God has sent him, I suppose the intelligencer is merry; he hath wit enough to be rich and an alderman and I think by those steps men get to be lord mayors'.[1] However one of Ward's predecessors, William Smith, was of a rather different character. He had a long history of involvement with the city during difficult times. In October 1642, at the height of the Irish insurrection, he became mayor, despite the fact that Walter Kennedy had been elected in June of the same year. The events were repeated the following year when John Carbery was elected but it was Smith who served in the office. It was not until 1644 that Smith's own turn to serve came round. Despite his willingness to serve he was only partly paid for his efforts, with arrears of £472 out of £600 due to him in 1645.[2] It might be presumed that the nerve of others failed during the years of crisis in the 1640s leaving Smith to step into the breech. After the Restoration, during the last of Smith's three prolonged periods in office (1675–6), the city took the decisive step of agreeing to rebuild the tholsel, or city hall, which stood until 1806. This decision was to have a profound impact both physically and symbolically on the city and its inhabitants. It served as a symbol of a new city rebuilding itself in the years after the restoration of Charles II when, as Maurice Craig puts it, the Renaissance arrived in Dublin with the newly elevated duke of Ormond.[3] Smith, during his final period as lord mayor, literally presided over the changing face of a city.

---

1 Historical Manuscripts Commission, *Calendar of the manuscripts of the marquess of Ormonde*, new series, 8 vols (London, 1902–20), iv, pp 242, 253.   2 *CARD*, iii, pp 391, 395, 405, 410, 423, 427–8.   3 Maurice Craig, *Dublin, 1660–1860* (Dublin, 1969), p. 3.

I

William Smith's appointment to the mayoralty took place, as was customary, on the third Friday after 29 September 1675, but it was a rather unusual affair.[4] He was by that stage a rather elderly man who had been admitted to freedom of the city at Easter 1628.[5] He had already been mayor during the traumatic years from 1642 to 1647 and again from 1663 to 1665. By the 1670s retirement might have seemed a more realistic prospect than the mayoral seat. On the eve of his election the Irish lord lieutenant, the earl of Essex, painted a pen picture of him:

> he is one aged near fourscore years, and has always been reputed a man of great integrity and loyalty; an eminent instance of the latter, he gave, as I am told, when my lord Ormond delivered up the sword to the parliament commissioners here [in 1647] he happened then to be mayor, came to the council table and acquainted my lord of Ormond that it was generally reported in the town and spread so far that no man doubted it, that his excellency intended to deliver up the government to parliament that he came to acquaint his lordship that himself was entrusted with the king's sword of the city and that he would not resign it to rebels. Whereupon my lord of Ormond gave him some check and ordered him to withdraw, but upon further consideration his lordship and the council though fit to call him in again and to commend him for the resolution he had showed in maintaining his majesty's authority and withal read the letter from his majesty requiring the lord lieutenant to deliver up the sword to the commissioners empowered by the parliament of England, whereupon he said he would submit.[6]

The tenor of this story is confirmed by what is known of the rest of Smith's life.

In 1662, for instance, when the administration feared the presence of Cromwellian sympathizers in Dublin Corporation and demanded that such potential dissidents be removed, it was Smith, with a few others, who was given the task.[7] While he had remained in Dublin during the 1650s, William Smith appears to have had little sympathy with the Cromwellian regime. At

---

4 *CARD*, v, p. 80.   5 *CARD*, iii, p. 214.   6 *Letters written by his excellency Arthur Capel, earl of Essex* (London, 1770), pp 344–5.   7 *CSPI, 1663–5*, p. 499.

the Restoration in 1660 he was felt to be a safe pair of hands and it was suggested that he be rewarded with a commissionership of customs and excise; he was duly appointed a commissioner in 1662, 1664, 1665 and 1667.[8] It was no doubt his credentials as a loyal subject that led to his election to the general convention that governed Ireland before the Restoration and he was appointed as one of the representatives of the city to wait on the future Charles II in 1660. In 1661 he was elected to the restoration parliament as MP for Dublin.[9]

Smith's sense of loyalty and duty can be attributed to his position as part of the Dublin civic elite in the seventeenth century. He may well have been born in the city about 1602 but if not he certainly served his apprenticeship as a merchant there and was admitted to freedom in 1628 by right of apprenticeship.[10] The name of his master was not recorded but it is likely to have been his uncle, Thomas Evans.[11] Evans himself was involved in city politics and served as mayor in 1626–7 and 1630–1. Thomas Evans had begun his involvement with civic politics at the level of the parish, being churchwarden of the parish of St John the Evangelist in 1618–19 and an auditor of the parish accounts almost every year until his death in 1634. William Smith followed the same pattern of advancement in the same parish. He was churchwarden in 1633–5 and subsequently acted as auditor of the parish accounts on a number of occasions. He returned as churchwarden in 1661.[12] In 1636 he entered civic politics becoming deputy sheriff and alderman of the city in 1636 and 1638, master of the city works in 1637 and finally mayor in 1642.[13]

Smith was also involved with other corporate bodies associated with the city. As a merchant he was a member of the Trinity guild and was master in 1648–9, as was usual for a former mayor, but also in 1659–60 when it was not his turn, probably to safeguard the guild's interests as the Cromwellian regime collapsed.[14] In addition, in 1645 he was master of St Anne's guild based in St Audoen's.[15] In this case his motives for joining this former Catholic guild that had survived the Reformation were probably financial since the guild was a wealthy body with substantial land holdings that were leased to members. Corporate bodies such as these provided the new Protestant elite, of which

8 *CSPI, 1660–2*, p. 71; Rowley Lascalles, *Liber munerum publicorum Hiberniae* (Dublin, 1824), pt 2, pp 131–2; Bodleian Library, Oxford, Carte MS 41, f. 125, MS 165, f. 157.   **9** Aidan Clarke, *Prelude to Restoration Ireland* (Cambridge, 1999), pp 199, 200–1, 294.   **10** *CARD*, iii, p. 214.   **11** *CARD*, iii, pp 238, 381.   **12** Raymond Gillespie (ed.), *The vestry records of the parish of St John the Evangelist, Dublin, 1595–1658* (Dublin, 2002), passim.   **13** *CARD*, iii, pp 316, 321, 334, 345.   **14** H.F. Berry, 'Records of the Dublin gild of merchants known as the gild of the Holy Trinity', *Journal of the Royal Society of Antiquaries of Ireland*, 30 (1900), 67.   **15** RIA, MS 12 O 13, ff 1, 4v, 9, 20v, 21, 21v, 22v.

Smith was a good example, with signs and ways of maintaining their newly enhanced status. Thus, any developments that might undermine the power and privileges of bodies such as Dublin Corporation were resisted by men such as William Smith.

Even at the height of the wars of the 1640s, Smith led a defence of civic privilege against what was seen as encroachment of the power of the state over the question of the defence of Dublin and the quartering of soldiers in the city.[16] A more dramatic instance of the same outlook occurred in November 1645 when the 'windows and doors were broken' of Smith's house in Fishamble Street by Lord Brabazon, an Irish privy councilor and son to the earl of Meath who owned the liberty of Donore, because Smith refused to hand over the keys of the city to him at midnight on the grounds that the keys were the property of the mayor.[17] The defence of urban privilege and institutions (including those of the parish) and the defence of the position of the urban elite, and the duty of that elite, were closely interlinked. William Smith's sense of achievement and identity was closely liked to both.

The second shaping factor in Smith's outlook was his religion. Unfortunately nothing has survived that would bare his soul but there are certainly hints that William's religious position was the sort of sacramental worship based on the parish associated with the Church of Ireland in the 1630s and again after the Restoration. St John's parish, where he lived for most of his life, was certainly of this tenor and he acted as churchwarden during the most significant reordering of the church in the 1630s. It was there William's mother was buried in 1638 and there he married for a second time in 1654, his first wife having died in 1650, probably of plague in the city. There too his children were baptized and in some cases buried.[18] His second marriage to the widow of Sir Arthur Leigh, who was the nephew of one of three brothers who had prospered in the Ulster plantation, provided him with a landed estate of 1,000 acres in Tyrone.[19] William, however, did not leave Dublin.

Within his parish his connections were with those who had resolutely supported Laudian reform. Jeremy Bowden, churchwarden of St John's from 1632 to 1634 and one of the main agents of Laudian reform, remembered

---

16 *CARD,* iii, pp 398–9, 401. For an episode the previous year HMC, *Ormonde,* n.s., ii, p. 167. **17** *CARD,* iii, p. 439.   **18** James Mills (ed.), *Registers of the parish of St John the Evangelist, Dublin, 1619– 1699* (rept Dublin, 2000), pp 81, 108, 265, 267, 268.   **19** George Hill, *An historical account of the plantation in Ulster* (Belfast, 1877), p. 265; R.C. Simington (ed.), *The civil survey, iii: counties of Donegal, Londonderry and Tyrone* (Dublin, 1937), p. 321.

William's daughters in his will suggesting connections between the families, perhaps originating in the fact that Smith and Bowden were both church-wardens in St John's in 1633.[20] There can be little doubt that Smith's religious inclinations, as with the political ones, lay with the local parish life of St John's with its brand of Laudian high churchmanship that carried with it ideas of the importance of social order and duty. Throughout the 1650s, when the Presbyterian minister Patrick Kerr held St John's, Smith continued to fulfill his duties as assessor of the parish cess and auditor of the parish accounts. One might not like what was preached on a Sunday but the duty of ensuring that the parish was respectably run by those who should undertake the task, by reason of their status, was at least as important as the theological hair-splitting of the 1650s. In that way William Smith's religion perhaps resembled that of the duke of Ormond who dominated the world of late seventeenth-century Irish government.[21]

II

It was this sense of civic loyalty and duty, associated with the social ideas of hierarchy and order embodied in the theology of the Caroline divines, that in 1675 probably impelled the elderly William Smith back into the tussle of civic politics. The source of the civic difficulties that required his political resurrection can be traced to the introduction in 1671 of rules for the government of Dublin, by restricting the franchise for elections to the most senior posts in the city. These arrangements proved difficult to implement and when Dublin Corporation was split on the issue, the corporation expelled the recorder, Sir William Davis, and seven aldermen, who were regarded by the commons as being responsible for the rules. The government declared this act illegal and in September 1672 the lord lieutenant, the earl of Essex, proposed to introduce 'new rules' for Dublin and other Irish cities that increased the power of government to control Dublin, required the taking of oaths of supremacy, allegiance and non-resistance to royal authority for all members of the corporation and increased the powers of the lord mayor and the aldermen at the expense of the common council. The guilds and the commons objected but the government proceeded and in order to demonstrate their determination

20 NLI, GO MS 290, p. 33.   **21** For this: Raymond Gillespie, 'The religion of the first duke of Ormond' in T.C. Barnard and Jane Fenlon (eds), *The dukes of Ormonde, 1610–1745* (Woodbridge, 2000), pp 101–14.

to carry out the proposals they imprisoned Dudley Loftus, one of the main opponents of the new rules in Dublin, and dismissed him from his legal post in 1673. Dublin Corporation was forced to fall into line but refused the government's demand that all references to the expulsion of William Davis and the seven aldermen should be removed from civic records.[22]

All this gave rise to considerable debate, not least about the legalities of the actions of the Dublin Castle administration particularly since the lord lieutenant, Essex, confessed that as a relatively recently arrived Englishman 'I do not enough understand the customs and constitutions of the city'. In the midst of these uncertainties, according to Essex, appeared 'a very ancient man, one Smith an alderman of about thirty or forty years standing, who saith there have several precedents been in his time when the commons have been refractory to the public authority, that upon these occasions the mayor, aldermen and sheriffs have done their duty'. Fearing that this advice was not enough, Essex invited a dozen or so of the aldermen of the city who had been least involved in the dispute to dinner and afterwards pressed them about their loyalty and their refusal to remove the records of the expulsion of the eight aldermen

> whereupon Alderman Smith, the most ancient among them told the rest it was his opinion that they should once more call an assembly and try if the commons would do what was fit and should they refuse, he conceived, that the aldermen, if the sheriffs would join therein, might in such a case perform their duty and not suffer the city to be undone through the stubbornness and faction of some few little people and offered several precedents when the like had been formerly practiced.[23]

An assembly was duly called, the appropriate pressure applied, and in June 1675 the government got its way thanks to Smith's advice and, presumably, some political manipulation by him.

There is little doubt that in the midst of a crisis over urban governance William Smith, with his knowledge of precedent and practice, was a formidable asset. For this reason he was prevailed upon to become lord mayor for one final term in an attempt to bring stability to the workings of the city's

22 For the outlines of this dispute see Sean Murphy, 'The corporation of Dublin 1660–1760', *Dublin Historical Record*, 38 (1984–5), 22–5; J.R. Hill, *From patriots to unionists: Dublin civic politics and Irish Protestant patriotism, 1660–1840* (Oxford, 1997), pp 48–58.   **23** *Letters written by his excellency Arthur Capel, earl of Essex*, pp 342–4.

government. In some ways it was a re-run of the lord mayoral election of 1663 when Richard Cook had been elected mayor on the second Friday after Easter. According to the assembly rolls, by early July the 'great confusions under which this city has laboured in several years past' was giving cause for second thoughts and a search for 'some able, loyal and well experienced person' to be chosen for the governing of Dublin. In all this it was made known that 'his grace the duke of Ormond, now lord lieutenant, and the council of this kingdom have a desire that Alderman William Smith should undertake the office of mayoralty of this city for the ensuing year'. Cook, probably with relief, petitioned to be exonerated from the office and this was duly accepted.[24] Smith took up the post and held it for two terms.

III

In the event, William Smith's last period in the lord mayoralty proved mainly uneventful. Most of what the assembly rolls record for that year was the routine life of a city: provisions for the guards, repairing broken pavements, water charges, property disputes, leases of land, unpaid debts and the city school for instance. There were some issues relating to disputes over the new rules that were tidied up, such as the requirement that men be free of the corporation rather than simply operate as quarter brothers or simply as members of guilds, in order to 'preserve the city's privileges, freedoms and immunities, to the great honour of the city' and against 'the charters, customs and laws of this city'.[25] It was perhaps characteristic of Smith that he would defend urban privilege by an appeal to the past. Somewhat out of the normal round, in January 1676 the assembly roll recorded that:

> Whereas also certain of the commons petitioned likewise unto the said assembly, showing that the tholsel of the city is so ancient and out of repair that besides the inconveniences and straightness of room, the same is so dangerously cracked that the city was fined in a thousand pounds, sterling, in his majesty's court of king's bench for not repairing thereof as by rule of that court did appear, and for that the building if repaired would be in no wise fit or suitable to the dignity and largeness of this city, most of the corporation of this kingdom being better accommodated with

---

24 *CARD*, v, pp 261–3.   **25** *CARD*, v, pp 84–5.

sessions houses, town halls and places of judicature and public
assemblies, the petitioners therefore humbly prayed that the assembly, in
consideration of the premises, that some course might be laid down in
this present assembly for the raising of money in order to erect a new
sessions house and a place convenient for the assemblies of the city and
that a place might be pitched on where to build the same.

The grand jury of the city was accordingly approached about the possibility of
finance.[26]

While the idea for the tholsel was only articulated in January 1676, by
March progress had been made and funding was in place from the grand jury
to create an 'ornamental sessions house and rooms fit for assemblies of this
city'. What the petitioners had in mind was clearly grander than what already
existed and moves were made to acquire additional property. By July,
consideration was being given to the question of where the corporation would
meet during the rebuilding and when Lord Aungier petitioned the city at the
same meeting to demolish two minor gates in the city the corporation, with
advance planning, declared that he was to allow the city 'such of the stones as
the workmen of the tholsel shall think fit to make use for the building of the
tholsel', which implies that some limited work may even have begun on the
new building before Smith left office.[27]

We must assume that William Smith had a considerable say in the design
of the new building to symbolize the dignity of the city. Unfortunately it is not
recorded who designed the tholsel but it may well have been the master
builder Thomas Graves. In January 1679 Graves petitioned the corporation
that 'this petitioner and his man have constantly attended the work of the
tholsel and new sessions house these two years and a half' and he claimed that
he had expended £20 on the project yet had received only £4 10s.
reimbursement, with no salary.[28] If Graves was not embellishing his story then
he had been employed on the work of the tholsel since the middle of 1676 or
about the time that the project was just beginning. Graves had long
associations with the city, being mace bearer in 1675.[29] There is therefore a
good case to be made that he was, in fact, the architect as well as the builder.[30]

26 *CARD*, v, p. 96.   27 *CARD*, v, pp 101, 109–10, 116. Ironically it was Smith who in 1663 had presided over the strengthening of the gates on Lord Lieutenant Ormond's instructions, Historical Manuscripts Commission, *Calendar of the manuscripts of the marquess of Ormonde*, old series, 3 vols (London, 1895–1909), i, p. 283.   28 *CARD*, v, p. 170.   29 *CARD*, v, p. 99.   30 Rolf Loeber, *A biographical dictionary of architects in Ireland, 1600–1720* (London, 1981), pp 55–6.

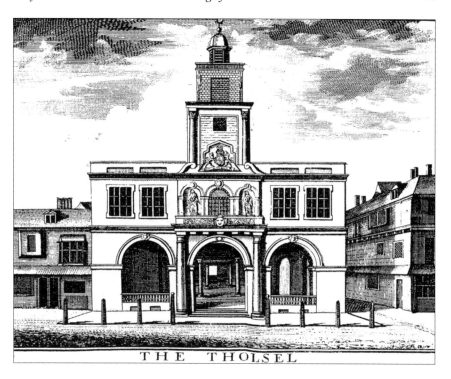

9 The tholsel; detail from Brooking's map of the city and suburbs of Dublin, 1728: reproduced courtesy of Dublin City Library and Archive.

The building was planned to reflect the outlook of men such as William Smith. Its scale and design were clearly meant to impress and reflect both the 'dignity' of the city and its new, modern values rather than the civic ideas associated with the old tholsel.[31] Dublin, after all, had become a lord mayoralty after the Restoration (see above, p. 20, and the following chapter by Redmond), had the gift of a cap of maintenance from the king and, from 1665, a grant of £500 a year to support the dignity of the lord mayor, a sum first collected by William Smith.[32] It was a city, as at least some contemporaries saw it, of European stature and the new tholsel was intended to signify that.[33]

31 For this Raymond Gillespie, 'Robert Ware's telling tale: a medieval Dublin story and its significance' in Sean Duffy (ed.), *Medieval Dublin V* (Dublin, 2004), pp 291–301. Dineley's view of the tholsel *c.*1681 is reproduced in Colm Lennon, *Dublin, Part II, 1610 to 1756, Irish Historic Towns Atlas* 19 (Dublin, 2008), plate 2(e). **32** Bodleian Library, Oxford, Carte MS 145, f. 271. **33** Raymond Gillespie, 'Dublin 1600–1700: a city and its hinterlands' in Peter Clark and Bernard Lepetit (eds), *Capital cities and their hinterlands in early modern Europe* (Aldershot, 1996), pp 84–9.

IV

William Smith's last term in office ended at Michaelmas 1676 when his successor, Christopher Lovett, was elected. It is clear that Smith was experiencing financial difficulties. At the beginning of his final lord mayoralty he had asked for a royal post in the customs. Although he claimed to be requesting this as 'a mark of his majesty's favour [that] may conduce much to the setting of the people in a good opinion' of him, it is clear from the petition that the income from such a lucrative post was at least as important as the status that it conferred.[34] By the end of the year his accounts were in some disarray. He may have been in dispute with the city over money as he refused to surrender the civic plate at the end of his mayoralty.[35] The mayoralty was an expensive office and for someone of Smith's age whose business was presumably not as thriving as it had been when he was younger, the office may well have cost him dearly. Moreover he seems to have been pre-deceased by his wife and all his children, leaving the problem of how he would be cared for in his old age. In 1679 the governors of the newly founded Blue Coat school at Oxmantown, who were in effect the corporation of Dublin, ordered that William should be accommodated in the school and would undertake the steward's role of the 'government of the house'.[36] In 1680 the English visitor Thomas Dineley noted of William (though confusing him with his successor but one in the mayoralty John Smith) that he was 'called the Beardless. He is said to have been lord mayor three years and mayor for seven years before, though now poor and full with age in Dublin hospital'.[37] He lived another four years, dying (according to his monument) on 31 October 1684, aged 82, his will being proved on 4 November. He was buried in the chapel of the Blue Coat school where he had spent his last years.[38] Fittingly the arms engraved on his monument included the arms of the city in whose service he had spent so much time and money, not least in the building of its new tholsel.

34 Bodleian Library, Oxford, Carte MS 218, f. 111.   35 *CARD*, v, pp 127, 135.   36 Leslie Whiteside, *A history of the King's Hospital* (2nd ed., Dublin, 1985), p. 21.   37 F.E. Ball, 'Extracts from the journal of Thomas Dineley', *Journal of the Royal Society of Antiquities of Ireland*, 43 (1913), 300.   38 Frederick Falkiner, *The foundation of the hospital and free school of Charles II, Oxmantown, Dublin* (Dublin, 1906), p. 77; NAI, Crossle Smith will abstracts, 7/781.

Sir Daniel Bellingham, Dublin's first lord mayor, 1665

JANET REDMOND

The office of mayor of Dublin was elevated to the rank of lord mayor by Charles I in 1641. Due to civil war and the subsequent Commonwealth regime it was not until the restoration that the office was first taken up by Daniel Bellingham, city goldsmith and loyal supporter of the crown. Bellingham was a powerful, civic minded and influential public figure in Ireland from the 1650s until 1667. A keen supporter of the duke of Ormond, this loyalty was richly rewarded with high offices, titles, land and great personal wealth. On the occasion of Bellingham's inauguration ceremony as lord mayor, he was described as a faithful and loyal servant who loved and was beloved of his fellow citizens.[1] Bellingham was lauded for his successful tenure as the city's first lord mayor, a role that he carried out with prudence, ability and faithfulness to the crown and the citizens.[2] However, from a position of power, trust, and great wealth, Bellingham was by 1667 burdened with massive debts and accusations of incompetence, abuse and corruption with regard to his handling of the Irish treasury. This essay will examine the development of the office of mayor of Dublin and its evolution in status and dignity. This elevation of office was motivated by the crown's desire to strengthen its hold on local government through direct royal intervention during the Restoration period.

I

Daniel Bellingham was born about 1620 into an old Norman family that had been resident in Kendal, Westmoreland, England, from the fourteenth century. Daniel's father, Robert, studied law at the Middle Temple, London, and, like many others, migrated to Ireland during the first years of the seventeenth century. This move may have been prompted by the fact that his sister, Grace, was married to Gerard Lowther, lord chief justice of the common

---

1 Speech made by the recorder, Sir William Davys to the duke of Ormonde on the occasion of Bellingham's inauguration as lord mayor. *CARD*, iv, pp 579–80.   2 A letter from the duke of Ormonde read to the city assembly members on the occasion of the election of the lord mayor for 1666. *CARD*, iv, pp 373–4.

people. Robert was high sheriff of Co. Longford in 1611 and was appointed attorney to the second remembrancer of the Exchequer from 1616 to 1620. He received a grant from James I of the wardship of Dominic Trant of Co. Kerry in 1620.[3] Robert married Margaret Whyte and they had two sons, Daniel and Henry, and three daughters, Jane, Margaret and Sarah.[4] Both sons were apprenticed as goldsmiths, a career that was seen as a gateway to wealth and political power.[5]

In 1637, Daniel commenced a seven-year apprenticeship with master goldsmith Peter Vanderoven.[6] He obtained the freedom of the goldsmiths' guild in 1644[7] and the freedom of the city of Dublin in 1648. Similarly, Daniel's younger brother, Henry, was granted the freedom of the city of Dublin in 1652;[8] he was high sheriff of Co. Kildare and then pursued a career in the army. He was a captain in a cavalry regiment in the army of the parliament and was subsequently rewarded for his loyalty with a grant of lands in Co. Louth (Gernonstown, now Castlebellingham) from Cromwell, which was confirmed afterwards by Charles II.[9]

Daniel Bellingham took premises in Castle Street, Dublin, and quickly built up a reputation for excellent work and craftsmanship. His maker's mark was heart-shaped bearing his initials 'D.B.'[10] The records of the Assay Office show that gold and silver plate was assayed for him from 1644 to 1649 (due to the loss of records at the Assay Office no further entries appear until 1694). Bellingham had a busy and extremely successful business and employed a number of apprentices including John Kinge (1643), John Partington (1651), John East (1656), Richard Webb (1656) and Abel Ram (1656). The successful careers of these apprentices give a clear indication of the high standard of

---

3 Wardships were an instrument of fiscal policy and a welfare organization for widows and children of the King's tenants in both England and Ireland (Victor Treadwell, *Irish Court of Wards under James 1, Irish Historical Society Journal*, 12:45 (March 1960)).   **4** *Burke's peerage, baronetage and knightage,* 103rd edition (1973), p. 220.   **5** From the earliest times of which we have any record, gold and silversmiths occupied leading positions; amassing great wealth, they became the bankers and money lenders; while monarchs looked to them at critical periods for supplies of money, necessary for the conduct of warlike or other enterprises, in which they happened to be engaged. Henry F. Berry, 'The Goldsmiths' Company of Dublin' (Gild of All Saints)', *Journal of the Royal Society of Antiquiries of Ireland,* 5th series, 31 (1901), 119. **6** Vanderhoven, a prominent Dublin goldsmith in the early sevententh century, was one of the first members of the Goldsmiths' Company of Dublin in 1637.   **7** Charles Jackson, *English goldsmiths and their marks, a history of the goldsmiths and plate workers of England, Scotland, and Ireland,* p. 364.   **8** Ibid., p. 364. **9** Thomas Bellingham, *Diary of Thomas Bellingham, an officer under William III* (1908), Anthony Hewitson (ed.), p. 45.   **10** 6. The maker's mark or, as it was designated in the Goldsmiths' Charter of 1637, 'the goldsmith's proper mark', was almost invariably found composed of letters, either separate or in monogram, indicating the Christian name and surname of the maker, until about the middle of the nineteenth century, Charles Jackson, *English goldsmiths and their marks, a history of the goldsmiths and plate workers of England, Scotland, and Ireland,* p. 585.

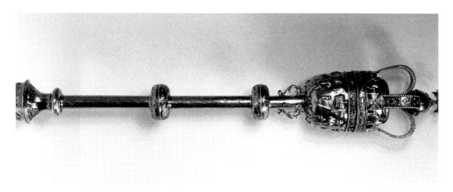

10 The great mace designed by Daniel Bellingham: reproduced courtesy of
Dublin City Library and Archive.

training they received; Abel Ram, in particular, had an illustrious career both
as a goldsmith and as a politician.[11]

There are only two known surviving examples of Bellingham's work, a
tablespoon and Dublin's great mace (fig. 10), but Dublin assembly roll records
show that he was commissioned by the city council to produce many pieces of
plate and important city regalia, including maces, swords and cups. In 1652
he was paid for six silver maces and the city sword and in 1656 there is a
request from Bellingham for monies owed to him for pieces of plate, a sword
and a large voyder of silver (a voyder is a tray or basket used for removing the
remains of a meal).[12] A noteworthy and prestigious commission for which
Bellingham was paid £350 sterling was for a golden cup and the earliest
known Irish gold freedom box which were presented as gifts to the duke of
Ormond on his arrival in Dublin in 1660.[13]

In Dublin, like other towns in medieval Europe, it was the wealthier
merchants and master craftsmen who supplied the majority of the members of
the civic governments, dominating the commercial and political life of the city
for almost seven centuries, from the late twelfth century until 1841.[14] Guilds
were legal recognition of the right of freemen to be organized into corporate
bodies thus enabling the most influential members of the community,
those connected with trade, to accustom themselves to collective action.
Membership of a guild was an essential first step for anyone contemplating a
career in municipal politics, as on completion of his apprenticeship a newly

---

11 As well as running a busy workshop in Castle Street from the early 1670s, Abel Ram was involved in
Dublin city affairs in many roles including sheriff, master of city works, alderman, auditor, city treasurer
and lord mayor.   **12** *CARD*, iv, pp 32, 104.   **13** Ibid., pp 243–4.   **14** The Municipal Corporations
Reform (Ireland) Act of 1840 removed the role of the trade and craft guilds in the city's government.

qualified craftsman became entitled to the franchise or freedom of the city and had the right to vote in municipal and parliamentary elections.[15] In Dublin, from the fourteenth century onwards, the guilds returned ninety-six representatives, called the commons, to the municipal governing body, the Dublin City Assembly. Members of the commons were then eligible for election as city sheriff, alderman and ultimately as lord mayor.

The goldsmiths' guild, the guild of All Saints, was established in Dublin during the fifteenth century; in 1637 it was granted a royal charter by Charles I, which allowed the guild the entire regulation of the trade in Ireland. One of twenty-four guilds in Dublin, the goldsmiths' guild was modeled on the same lines as the city council; headed by a master, the guild consisted of three wardens, freemen, quarter-brothers, journeymen and apprentices. The road to power in the council was similar to that in the guild; the master's position was similar to the role of the mayor, the wardens were equivalent to the sheriffs. As well as well as having control over its members, the goldsmiths' guild was entitled to appoint four members to the common council of Dublin. Frequently its members were elected to high office, most notably Daniel Bellingham, Abel Ram and Thomas Bolton, all of whom served as lord mayor.

In addition to running his business, Bellingham became involved in the goldsmiths' guild; he was warden from 1648 to 1649 and again from 1656 to 1657. Over a twenty-year period he served the city on numerous committees and in many important roles including sheriff, master of city works, alderman, major in the city militia, lord mayor, auditor and treasurer. One of the earliest recorded entries was in 1653 when he was appointed to a committee set up to 'state the accounts of such moneys as were borrowed for the supply of the army and for the use of the Commonwealth.'[16] In 1656 Bellingham received an order to furnish all the non-commissioned officers of the newly formed regiment of Irish Guards and men with a red cassock together with cloth breeches, two shirts, one pair of stockings and one pair of shoes.[17]

II

The restoration of King Charles II to power was widely welcomed and supported by the mayor, sheriffs and municipal council who willingly and enthusiastically co-operated with the officers of the army who seized Dublin

---

15 M. Clark and R. Refaussé (eds), *Directory of historic Dublin guilds* (Dublin, 1993), p. 12.   **16** *CARD,* iv, p. 54.   **17** C. Litton Falkiner, *Illustrations of Irish history and topography, mainly of the seventeenth century*

Castle in December 1659. The city leaders, looking forward to increased prosperity following the period of civic poverty associated with the civil war, held a lavish reception for the viceroy, the duke of Ormond, on his triumphant return to Dublin in May 1660.[18] Ormond was in the fullest sense a resident viceroy; he returned to Ireland with a desire to give back prosperity to the country. He was anxious to emphasize Dublin's importance and status as the capital city and he exercised his authority by providing finance for the civil and military needs of Ireland. The new administration replaced known Cromwellian supporters, giving lucrative contracts and positions to their most loyal supporters. The Irish budget had a political as well as a monetary significance, and the management and control of Irish revenues was seen as a political prize.

Charles II began reconstituting the Irish exchequer in August 1660 and the earl of Anglesey, a loyal supporter of the king's administration in parliament, was appointed as vice treasurer for Ireland.[19] Bellingham, who had maintained contact with the exiled Ormond, was appointed as deputy receiver general to Anglesey. Despite the importance of Anglesey's role as vice treasurer he was absent for long periods and was more concerned with enhancing his position in court; as a result the day-to-day control of the country's finances was left to Bellingham. In September 1662, Bellingham was knighted by Ormond, alongside his brother-in-law, Alderman Sir George Gilbert, as a tribute to his skills and loyalty to the King.[20] Bellingham received lucrative parliamentary commissions including the supply of clothing for the army in Ireland in 1661 and in 1662 he was appointed to the office of alnage of cloth. The holder of this title was the official responsible for supervision of the shape and quality of manufactured woollen cloth.

The establishment of a mint for coining small silver coins in the city of Dublin was recommended by the lord justices in 1662 and the sole right of working the mint was granted to Sir Daniel Bellingham, Sir Thomas Vyner and Robert Vyner who were described as having 'served our cause loyally'.[21] Bellingham petitioned and received forfeited lands in Co. Kildare in 1662 and during the 1660s he was granted lands on Oxmantown Green and St Stephen's Green, as well as acquiring large tracts of land around Finglas and Blanchardstown. It is difficult to estimate the exact financial gain, however, as his personal accounts have not survived.

(London, 1904), p. 81. **18** Ibid., pp 360–1. **19** Seán Egan, 'Finance and the government of Ireland, 1660–85' (PhD, TCD, 1983), p. 22. **20** *CARD*, iv, p. 246. **21** *CSPI, 1662*, pp 515–16.

The charter of 1229 gave Dublin the right to appoint a mayor but in 1641 King Charles I had decreed that the mayor was to be styled lord mayor and his wife, lady, madam or dame. This was not officially used or adopted for twenty-four years. Alongside the important civic duties of the office of lord mayor, the main burden of administering justice within Dublin and its liberties devolved upon the mayor. J.T. Gilbert, editor of the voluminous city corporation records, discusses how the official duties of the mayor developed and expanded. His duties included the power to grant license to Irish tenants and servants for temporary stay in the county of Dublin with Protestant employers. In his presence, in public parts of the city, marriages were solemnized. He had authority to act judicially in admiralty cases and he was entrusted with funds for Trinity College Dublin.[22]

During the early to mid-seventeenth century, the custom of the course of succession for the position of mayor declined and the post was made elective. However in 1657, in order to avoid differences and inconveniences, it was agreed to return to 'the ancient and laudable custom of succession' for the office of mayor and provision made was for each alderman to succeed in turn to the office of mayor of Dublin in order of seniority.[23] The position of mayor was a prestigious one and it was also one reserved for the wealthy, as in order to be considered for the position one's estate had to be valued in excess of £500 sterling.[24] Charles II, anxious to reward and maintain the loyalty of the city council, declared that the mayor should assume the title and the dignity of lord mayor that was granted in 1641.[25] The mayoral insignia was enhanced, royal grants were increased and honours were extended to the city, putting it on a footing with London. It was stated that 'the mayoralty of this city should be supported and maintained with that dignity and splendour which is suitable to the said gracious concessions of his majesty'.[26]

In 1661 Charles II directed that the lord mayor had the right to wear a great chain and as proof of royal esteem he sent a chain to the corporation together with a cap of maintenance. He also provided for the right for the mayor to have a 'certain sword gilted with gold' borne before him.[27] The chain, in the form of a gold collar of SS, was composed of links in the shape of the letter S, alternating with Tudor roses and trefoil-shaped knots with a portrait bust of Charles II.[28] This style of chain was up to this time a mark of special

22 *CARD*, iv, p. ix.   **23** *CARD*, iv, p. 113.   **24** *CARD*, iv, p. 353.   **25** Ibid., p. 351.   **26** Ibid., p. 359. **27** *CARD*, i, pp 42–3.   **28** Patrick Meehan, 'The civic regalia, insignia, charters and manuscripts of Dublin' (1931), NLI MS 5789, pp 3–4.

favour reserved for senior officials of the crown. This very striking chain can be seen on portraits of Christopher Lovett (lord mayor 1676–7) and Humphrey Jervis (lord mayor 1681–3). The chain disappeared after the Battle of the Boyne and was replaced by the present chain given to the city by King William III in 1698. The dignity of the mayor was further enhanced in 1662 when he was given the command of a company of foot soldiers. A master of civic ceremonies and yeomen of the lord mayor's wardrobe were also appointed.[29]

III

In his position as deputy receiver general, Bellingham spent long periods away from his family and in a petition to Charles II he stated that this 'was to the great damage and ruin of himself and many others, whose estates are in his hands'.[30] Bellingham was proposed for the position of lord mayor in 1662 and again in 1664, but he was excused on both occasions as a result of a royal request to dispense with the custom of succession.[31] In 1665, despite the unsettled condition of the Irish revenue and the continuing absence of the earl of Anglesey, Bellingham was appointed as Dublin's first lord mayor at the insistence of Ormond. On his appointment to the office Bellingham was commended as 'a person great in his experience, wary in his resolves and resolute in his undertakings, loyal to the Duke of Ormond, faithful to Charles II, a lover and beloved of his fellow citizens.'[32] A contemporary portrait (by an unknown artist) of Sir Daniel Bellingham depicts him in formal robes, with his wand of office (fig. 11). The chain shown in the portrait is not the gold collar sent by Charles II, but may be the insignia of the old office of the mayor of Dublin.

Maces were carried alongside the city sword in ceremonial processions; however the city does not appear to have had a great mace until the mayoralty of Bellingham. This magnificent mace, designed and made in Bellingham's workshop, is described as a fine example of Restoration craftsmanship. The shaft of the mace is original and is ornamented with a chased floral design and has two knops elaborately ornamented in a similar manner (fig. 10). The head was re-fashioned in 1717–18 by Dublin silversmith Thomas Bolton and is ornamented with the Rose and Thistle for Great Britain, the fleur-de-lis for France and the harp for Ireland. The letters G.R. stand for Georgius Rex and

29 *CARD*, iv, p. 44.   **30** *CSPI, 1663–65*, p. 500.   **31** *CARD*, iv, p. 387.   **32** Ibid., p. 340.

11 Portrait of Sir Daniel Bellingham, first lord mayor of Dublin, artist unknown:
reproduced courtesy of Dublin City Library and Archive.

indicate allegiance to the house of Hanover. The orb and the cross were added in 1807 by Mathew West of Dublin.[33] The mace remained Bellingham's personal property until 1667 when the city council bought it from him at a cost of £93 18s. 6d.[34]

Bellingham spent a large sum of money building a house that was described as a 'large elegant structure' at the ancient entrance to Cow Lane at the corner of Fishamble Street and Castle Street. He was resident there from 1665 with his wife Jane, daughter of Richard Barlow of Little Toghill, Cheshire, his son Richard and six daughters, Sarah, Hester, Alice, Rebecca, Mary and Jane.[35] The house contained ten hearths, a clear indication of its size and importance.[36] Bellingham's wife, Jane, died in 1668 and was buried at St Werburgh's Church; he seems to have married a second time as in a codicil to his will dated 27 April 1672, he wrote, 'I do give and bequeath unto my dear and loving wife one trunk of linen now in a little room with the nursery in my house in Castle Street'.[37] In 1680, Lady Bellingham was recorded as the owner of this house.[38]

During his term as lord mayor, members of the commons petitioned the assembly stating that they observed the prudent care and affection that Bellingham had for the city and they expressed particular gratitude for his procurement of a royal grant of £500 sterling for the better support of the dignity of the office.[39] Lauded for his loyalty and commended for his hospitality Bellingham seemed indispensable to Ormond, who described him as 'trusty and well beloved'.[40] Bellingham hosted a lavish reception, at a cost of £100 sterling, to mark Ormond's arrival back to Dublin in 1665.[41] In discussing the splendid welcome that he received, Sir Nicholas Armorer described how 'our new lord mayor outdid even Sir John Robinson in all things except in talking of it himself.'[42] Richard St George, Ulster king of arms, confirmed the ancient arms of Bellingham to Daniel in 1665, with the motto *ainsi il est amicus amico* (friendly to a friend). Bellingham displayed notable civic spirit; he gave several sums of money for the paving of Smithfield and for the erection of a staircase in the tholsel.[43] He was also involved in taking care of the clock at the tholsel.[44]

33 P. Meehan, 'The civic regalia, insignia, charters and manuscripts of Dublin', pp 3–4.   34 *CARD*, iv, pp 423–4.   35 *CARD*, iv, p. 376.   36 F.J. Holden, 'Property taxes in old Dublin', *Dublin Historical Record*, 13 (1953), 137.   37 Representative Church Body Library, p. 326/14.   38 M. Clark, 'Dublin City pipe water accounts, 1680', *Irish Genealogist*, 7:2 (1989), 201–4.   39 *CARD*, iv, p. 367.   40 Ibid., p. 373. 41 Ibid., p. 360.   42 *CSPI, 1665*, p. 654.   43 *CARD*, iv, p. 385.   44 Ibid., p. 397.

Ormond was anxious that Bellingham be re-elected as lord mayor for another year and in support of his recommendation he stated 'what prudence, faithfulness and ability Sir Daniel Bellingham has proved himself to his majesty and his people in the discharge of that office … conceive it may be for his majesties service and the good and safety of the kingdom if such a magistrate were continued for one more year'.[45] However, Bellingham was excused following a request from Anglesey, who stated that 'it would be a great hindrance to his majesty's service if he should be continued lord mayor another year'. Bellingham, despite his commitments with the exchequer, was then elected as city treasurer in 1666.[46] As a further sign of his loyalty and the esteem in which he was held, Bellingham was created first baronet of Dubber, Co. Dublin, in March 1667.

V

Complaints against the Irish treasury steadily multiplied after 1667, with the accounts described as being in a terrible state. Anglesey, as vice treasurer, and Bellingham, as his deputy receiver general, both resigned amid allegations of negligence, corruption, abuse and severe criticisms of the way in which they handled the Irish finances.[47] A London treasury investigation in 1668 blamed Bellingham for the unsatisfactory state of the Irish finances and described him as 'a negligent and grossly inefficient officer.'[48] In his defence, Bellingham stated that 'he has been purely my Lord Lieutenant's martyr, for had he listened to Orrery's persuasions, and brought accusations against the duke & against Lord Anglesey, he would have escaped all trouble.'[49]

By 1670, Bellingham was burdened with debts of over £14,000 and he faced threats of arrest unless they were cleared.[50] Proceedings for the recovery of the money he owed continued against Bellingham for the remainder of his life and upon his son Richard, the second and last baronet of Dubber, following his father's death in 1672. Throughout his lifetime, nevertheless, Bellingham remained civic minded and faithful to the citizens of Dublin. A good example of his commitment to the city was the bequest he made in his will of two lots of land in St Stephen's Green to the King's Hospital at

45 *CARD*, iv, pp 373–4. 46 Ibid., p. 387. 47 S. Egan, 'Finance and the government of Ireland, 1660–85', p. 24. 48 Ibid., p. 24. 49 MS Carte 68, fol(s), 180–81, Aungier to Ossory: written from London, 19 September 1668, www.bodley.ox.ac.uk/dept/scwmss/projects/carte (Bodleian Library, University of Oxford). 50 *CSPI, 1666–69*, Charles II (3), p. 593.

Oxmantown Green and to the poor of St Werburgh's parish. He also bequeathed certain lands near Finglas for the relief of poor debtors confined in the city and Four Courts marshalseas.[51] Bellingham's career as a politician ended with a dramatic fall from grace for a man who, as a renowned goldsmith and loyal supporter of Charles II and Ormond, was on his appointment as lord mayor described as 'an able and trustworthy magistrate'.[52]

51 Certified copy of codicil of will of Sir Daniel Bellingham, Public Records Office of Ireland–National Archives of Ireland.   **52** *CARD*, iii, p. 580.

John Exshaw: champion of Dublin's merchants

MÁIRE KENNEDY

John Exshaw held the uncommon distinction in the eighteenth century of being twice elected lord mayor of Dublin. He was a successful businessman coming from a substantial family of booksellers.[1] Members of the book trade were represented by the guild of St Luke the Evangelist, which was the guild of cutlers, painter-stainers and stationers. Part of the merchant sector, booksellers also held an important position due to their role in the dissemination of information through print. Because of the skills required for the practice of their trade, levels of literacy among members of the book trade and their families were among the highest at this social level. Exshaw was active in municipal politics from an early age, holding a number of important posts in the city. Admitted free of the guild 'by birth' in 1779, he became an alderman in 1782, aged 31, going on to hold the positions of sheriff, high sheriff, coroner, police magistrate, and lord mayor. However, his hopes to win a seat in parliament were dashed in 1790. A loyalist throughout his life and a prominent member of the establishment, he opposed the union with Great Britain considering it would have a detrimental effect on the trade and manufactures of Ireland. His career was long and distinguished, and he remained in business until 1822.

I

John Exshaw's uncle, Edward, the founder of the business, was an energetic and innovative bookseller, who had a bookshop known as 'the Bible' on Cork Hill from 1732. Much of his prosperity was due to the reprint trade in books, which ensured the success of the Dublin book trade throughout the eighteenth century. The absence of copyright legislation in Ireland meant that Irish booksellers could legally reprint any new publication from England or Scotland without having to pay for copy. Production costs were also less in

---

1 For a fuller treatment of John Exshaw's business and family connections see Máire Kennedy, 'Printer to the city: John Exshaw (1751–1827), printer, bookseller and lord mayor of Dublin', *Long Room*, 52–3 (2007–8), 15–25.

Ireland resulting in substantially lower prices for the reprints than for London originals, causing British booksellers to label the Irish 'pirates'. Edward Exshaw imported the monthly *London Magazine* from the mid-1730s, but in 1741 he began to issue an Irish edition. This was not merely a reprint of the London edition but, like some contemporary newspapers, it involved reprinting most of the original content of the magazine, while including additional material of Irish interest such as news items, listings of new Irish books, and notices of births, marriages, deaths and promotions.[2] John senior, father of the John Exshaw who became lord mayor, joined Edward in business in 1745. In 1748 the two brothers published the first issue of the annual *English Registry*, a list of English members of parliament, officers of the army and navy, of the law and trade, which was issued to accompany Watson's *Almanack*. These two publications were to sustain the firm throughout most of the eighteenth century by bringing in an assured income. In addition to providing regular finance, the sale of these publications allowed the Exshaws to build up a network of contacts throughout Ireland for the sale of books and patent medicines. When Edward died in December 1748, John (senior) went into partnership with Edward's widow, Sarah, for the publication of the *English Registry* and Exshaw's *London Magazine*. From 1755 the title was changed to Exshaw's *Gentleman's and London Magazine* as material from the *Gentleman's Magazine* was now being included in the reprint. John's business included a bookbinding workshop and records show that he was responsible for a major rebinding project of Trinity College's manuscripts.[3] In 1754 he moved his bookshop to a more prominent location at 86 Dame Street, at the corner of Crampton Court. John senior died on 9 March 1776, and was survived by his third wife, Dorcas, formerly Wilkinson.[4]

John Exshaw the younger was born in 1751, the second son of John and his first wife Faith Walker. He was apprenticed to his father, and took over the thriving family business in March 1776 at the age of 25, on the death of John senior. John married in May 1776. Finn's *Leinster Journal* reported the marriage of 'John Exshaw, an eminent bookseller to Miss Wilkinson, a most

---

2 *The London Magazine and Monthly Chronicler [or Gentleman's Monthly Intelligencer]* (Dublin, 1741–54), *The Gentleman's and London Magazine* (Dublin, 1755–95); Geraldine Sheridan, 'Irish literary review magazines and enlightenment France: 1730–1790' in Graham Gargett and Geraldine Sheridan (eds), *Ireland and the French enlightenment, 1700–1800* (Basingstoke, 1999), pp 26–8. **3** W. O'Sullivan, 'The eighteenth century rebinding of the manuscripts', *Long Room*, 1 (1970), 19–28. **4** John married Mrs Dorcas Wilkinson, a widow from Anne Street, Linen Hall in 1772. *Reports of the Deputy Keeper, Appendix to the 26th report*, p. 287. *Hibernian Chronicle*, 3 Sept. 1772. *Hibernian Magazine*, 6 (1776), 216.

amiable young lady with a considerable fortune'.[5] John's wife, Angel Wilkinson, was the daughter of his father's third wife, Dorcas, from a previous marriage.[6] In October 1787 Angel died aged 32 years.[7] John remarried in the mid-1790s and was married for the third time in 1805.[8] Women played an important role in the business of bookselling, performing such tasks as press correcting and proof reading, accounting and selling.[9] The many attested instances of women taking over businesses on the deaths of husbands and fathers point to a high degree of literacy among wives, daughters and sisters of booksellers. Sarah Exshaw, widow of Edward, took over his share of the business when he died in 1748. It is known that Angel Exshaw was highly literate; a manuscript book of poetry survives which she commenced in 1767, when she was aged 11, and which ends with her marriage in May 1776.[10] John Exshaw lived and worked in prosperous circumstances, he succeeded to a profitable business at a young age, and his first wife brought a large fortune to the marriage. He lived at Roebuck, Co. Dublin, and had his bookshops successively at prestigious addresses at 86 Dame Street, 98, then 103, Grafton Street.

II

When John junior took over the family business in 1776 he inherited a well-run, expanding enterprise, with many publications such as Exshaw's *Gentleman's and London Magazine* and the *English Registry* ensuring a regular income. Advertising the business after his succession he announced: 'he intends carrying on the printing, bookselling and stationery business in the same extensive manner as his late father did'.[11] John Exshaw built on the contacts with English colleagues set up by his uncle and father. John junior was clearly groomed for succession by his father, although he is not listed as an apprentice. By 1774 he was already managing part of the business as he advertised a variety of patent medicines, including Dr James' Fever Powder,

5 *Finn's Leinster Journal,* 22–5 May 1776.   **6** DCLA, Dublin MS 101, '"Poems and sentiments, &c. selected from several authors" by Miss Wilkinson, folio manuscript book written by Angel Wilkinson, July 25th 1767', inscription on final leaf.   **7** *Dublin Chronicle,* 25 Oct. 1787; Parish registers of the Church of Ireland parish of St John, Clondalkin, Dublin Heritage Group (DHG) database (DCLA).   **8** Kennedy, 'Printer to the city', pp 15–16.   **9** Vincent Kinane, 'A galley of pie: women in the Irish book trades', *Linen Hall Review,* 8:4 (Dec. 1991), 10–13.   **10** Wilkinson, 'Poems'. The final entry is a poem by her cousin, James Whitelaw, statistician and historian of Dublin, on the occasion of her marriage, addressed to Mrs Exshaw, and dated May 1776.   **11** *Hibernian Journal,* 22–5 Mar. 1776. *Freeman's Journal,* 23–6 Mar. 1776. *Hibernian Journal,* 15–17 Apr. 1776.

imported from Newbery in London.[12] In the 1780s he had a correspondence with the London bookseller John Murray. One of the leading English booksellers, Murray was keen to establish trading connections with the Dublin book trade for the sale of London publications and to negotiate the publishing of London editions of books newly printed in Dublin.[13] Exshaw became printer and stationer to several official bodies, he printed schoolbooks, university textbooks, trials, speeches, sermons and plays. His publications were made up of a mix of low-cost works of current interest and educational textbooks, and works that required more investment with a slower return.

With many of his high-cost publications Exshaw worked in co-operation with other Dublin booksellers in order to spread the risk. In 1776 and again in 1779, in association with William Hallhead, he published the English translation of the Abbé Raynal's *A philosophical and political history of the East and West Indies* in four volumes, and a new enlarged edition of the same work in six volumes was issued with Luke White in 1784.[14] The six-volume octavo set, printed on superfine paper, was selling for two guineas bound.[15] These editions are finely printed on good quality paper with well-executed engraved plates and maps, and their cost to the reader was high. Another major work, William Guthrie's *A new geographical, historical, and commercial grammar*, was published in different editions by the Exshaws from 1771, with the thirteenth edition coming to over 900 pages of text, with plates and maps, in 1789.[16]

The cheaper publications were printed in large numbers for a countrywide readership. Exshaw used his country network, established for the sale of the *Gentleman's and London Magazine* and the *English Registry*, to promote sales. Plays had a wide audience; they reflected fashionable taste and were reprinted to coincide with theatrical performances. Costing about one shilling, they were within the reach of many readers. For the printer, they meant a rapid turnover; they were short and did not constitute a major commitment of standing type or paper supplies, so they were very cost-effective to produce. Exshaw printed plays for a group of Dublin booksellers, the Company of Booksellers, during

12 *Hibernian Journal*, 25 Jul. 1774.   **13** William Zachs, *The first John Murray: and the late eighteenth-century London book trade* (Oxford, 1998).   **14** Abbé Guillaume Raynal, *A philosophical and political history of the settlements and trade of the Europeans in the East and West Indies* (Dublin, printed for John Exshaw and William Halhead, 1776), ESTC T65482; (Dublin, printed for John Exshaw and William Halhead, 1779), ESTC T72764; (Dublin, printed for John Exshaw and Luke White, 1784), ESTC T125367.   **15** *Volunteer's Journal*, 21 June 1784. *Freeman's Journal*, 30 Nov.–2 Dec. 1784.   **16** William Guthrie, *A new geographical, historical, and commercial grammar* (Dublin, for J. Exshaw, B. Grierson, and J. Williams, 1771), ESTC N20123; (Dublin, for James Williams and John Exshaw, 1780), ESTC T212578; (Dublin, for J. Exshaw, 1789), ESTC T186615.

the 1770s and 1780s.[17] He undertook a more significant project in 1794 when he printed *The plays and poems of William Shakespeare* in sixteen volumes, royal duodecimo, printed on a fine wove paper, with notes by Edmond Malone. This luxury set sold for three guineas in boards.[18] Speeches and trials were current, up-to-date publications, which needed to be issued while interest was at a peak. Exshaw reprinted several speeches from the British Houses of Lords and Commons associated with the debate on the proposed union. These pamphlets, selling for about sixpence, had an immediate audience. For example, on 14 February 1799 he printed 1,500 copies of the first edition of British Prime Minister William Pitt's speech of 31 January in the House of Commons, with 500 copies of a second edition printed less than a week later.[19] Even though he was personally opposed to the union, his publication of pro-union pamphlets showed that his personal stance did not interfere with business. He printed a range of law books, including legal case books, Irish term reports and reports of trials, including some of the major trials for high treason which were taking place after the 1798 rebellion. His is the imprint on the reports of the trials of Oliver Bond and Robert Emmet.[20]

The sale of schoolbooks was one of the most profitable activities for a bookseller. A report published in the *Freeman's Journal* in 1773, opposing the proposed Stamp Act, stated that 'the greatest consumption of books, here, is in our public-school'.[21] The provisions of the Stamp Act proposed to apply duties to books, newspapers, pamphlets, and advertising. The inclusion of schoolbooks caused an outcry, so when the act came into force the following year schoolbooks and books of devotion were exempt. Exshaw issued text-books and grammars for students of French, Latin and Greek. The publication of French-language readers for the use of schools was another staple of the Exshaw list. *Les avantures de Gil Blas*, used in Irish schools for the teaching of French, was reprinted in different editions by John senior and John junior in 1763, 1784 and 1796.[22] A range of other readers for students of French, such

17 Richard B. Sher, *The Enlightenment and the book: Scottish authors and their publishers in eighteenth-century Britain, Ireland, and America* (Chicago, 2006), pp 473–82. Exshaw printed at least ten plays for the Company of Booksellers between 1777 and 1787.   **18** *The plays and poems of William Shakespeare* (Dublin, John Exshaw, 1794), ESTC T138592; *Freeman's Journal*, 10 Apr. 1794.   **19** TCD, MS 10,315, Ledgers of D. Graisberry (1777–85), f. 22, 14 Feb., 18 Feb. William Pitt, *Speech of the Right Honourable William Pitt, in the British House of Commons, on Thursday, January 31st, 1799* (Dublin, John Exshaw, 1799), ESTC T56438; T202914.   **20** *Report of the trial of Oliver Bond, upon an indictment of high treason* (Dublin, printed by John Exshaw, 1798), ESTC T176181. *A report of the proceedings in cases of high treason at a court of Oyer and Terminer* (Dublin, printed by John Exshaw, 1803); *Freeman's Journal*, 22 Sept. 1803.   **21** *Freeman's Journal*, 27–30 Nov. 1773.   **22** Alain René Le Sage, *Les avantures de Gil Blas* (Dublin, chez

as *Dialogues moraux et amusants* by Madame Fauques de Vaucluse (1777), and *Fables, lettres, et variétés historiques* (1778), formed part of his output for schools.[23] A Latin textbook, Cornelius Tacitus, Opera, printed by Exshaw in 1788, was used as a school and college text and Trinity College recorded receipt of 950 sets in July of that year.[24] Another copy has a prize binding which shows that it was presented as a premium by Ennis School in 1790.[25]

Becoming official printer or stationer to a municipal, government or religious body was an advantageous appointment as it ensured a guaranteed amount of work and income in the course of a year. Exshaw was named stationer to the lottery commissioners in 1780, printer and stationer to the Society for Promoting Christian Knowledge in 1787, printer to the University Press in 1787–8, and stationer to the post office and the police in 1792.[26] He worked with the grand juries of Dublin city and county from 1810 to 1813, and was paid for printing work and the supply of books and stationery.[27] He carried out printing work for Dublin city from 1804, becoming official printer to the city from 1818 to 1820. He was not succeeded by any of his family, and the Exshaw family bookselling business, which had begun in 1732, ended with John's retirement in 1822. He died on 6 January 1827, at his seat in Roebuck, aged 74 years, and is buried at St John's Cemetery, Clondalkin, with his first wife, Angel, and three of their daughters.[28]

III

Exshaw's political career was played out on the municipal stage, although he had higher ambitions. He ran for a parliamentary seat in 1790 in opposition to Henry Grattan and Lord Henry Fitzgerald, but was unsuccessful in his bid. His position within the guild of St Luke was strong from the beginning. Coming from a family of active members and having a considerable business behind him, his rise within its ranks was swift. Admitted free 'by birth' in

Jean Exshaw, 1763), ESTC T153213; (Dublin, de l'imprimerie de Jean Exshaw, 1784), ESTC T120539; (Dublin, de l'imprimerie de Jean Exshaw, 1796), ESTC T201177. **23** Marianne-Agnès Pillement dame de Fauques, *Dialogues moraux et amusants* (Dublin, Jean Exshaw, 1777), ESTC T183751. *Fables, lettres, et variétés historiques* (Dublin, Jean Exshaw, 1778), ESTC T184573; *Freeman's Journal*, 7–9 May 1782. **24** TCD, MUN/LIB/2/1. M. Pollard, *A dictionary of members of the Dublin book trade, 1550–1800: based on the records of the Guild of St Luke the Evangelist Dublin* (London, 2000). **25** *C. Cornelii Taciti Opera* (Dublinii, Johannes Exshaw, 1788), ESTC T96043, DCLA copy. **26** Pollard, *Dictionary. Dublin Chronicle*, 22 Mar. 1792. **27** *Freeman's Journal*, 12 June 1810; 3 June 1812; 12 June 1813. **28** Michael J.S. Egan, *Memorials of the dead, Dublin city and county*, 8 (Dublin, 1995), p. 16.

1779, his first post was that of sheriff, to which he was elected for the year
1779–80.[29] He became an alderman in 1782 and in October of the same year
was sworn warden of the guild.[30] He was elected coroner for the city in 1784.[31]
In 1788 he resigned as divisional justice of police, an action which gained
widespread approval. The *Dublin Chronicle* commented: 'for nearly two years
he acted as a Divisional Magistrate to an institution that was confessedly
unpopular, with judgement, temper, perspicuity and candor, in the various
situations of that arduous duty'.[32] In 1789 he was presented with the freedom
of the Trinity guild of merchants, as a mark of 'approbation of his conduct in
resigning' from the police.[33] However, he later resumed this position after the
passing of the Dublin Police Magistrates Act of 1808,[34] and remained a
magistrate until his death in 1827, when the post was abolished. The Trinity
guild was the most powerful in the city, and the first in order of precedence,
therefore his admission was a promotional step. He became warden of that
guild in 1799, junior, then senior, master in 1801 and 1802 respectively.
Exshaw was captain of the First Regiment of Royal Dublin Volunteers in
1797. He commanded the 1,000-strong Stephen's Green yeomanry in 1797
and 1798, and was adjutant-general to the entire yeomanry forces of the Dublin
district.[35] A ceremonial sabre, made by Archer of Dublin, was presented to
Exshaw in 1797 by his regiment, and it is still in the possession of his
descendants. It is inscribed: 'Presented by the Non Commissioned Officers
and Privates of the First Regt. of Royal Dublin Volunteers to Alderman John
Exshaw, their Captain Commandant. Dublin 1797'.[36] The *Gentleman's Magazine*
printed an obituary in which his career was outlined and praise lavished on
him for his command of the yeomanry 'during the disturbances of 1797 and
1798'.[37] According to the obituary, he published *Hue and Cry*, the police
gazette; however, no copies of an Irish edition for this period have survived.

IV

Exshaw's first term as lord mayor occurred in 1789–90. Alderman John Sutton
was chosen to be lord mayor of Dublin for that year but he asked to be
excused due to ill health. Alderman John Exshaw was elected in his place on 8

29 *CARD*, xiii, pp 52, 64–5.   **30** *CARD*, xiii, p. 235.   **31** 15 Oct. 1784, *CARD*, xiii, p. 523.   **32** *Dublin Chronicle*, 23–26 May 1789.   **33** *Dublin Evening Post*, 14 July 1789.   **34** 48 Geo., III, c.140, Dublin Police Magistrates Act, 1808.   **35** *Gentleman's Magazine* (Jan. 1827), 94.   **36** I am very grateful to Mr John Exshaw, John Exshaw's descendant, for this information.   **37** *Gentleman's Magazine* (Jan. 1827), 94.

12 Lord Mayor John Exshaw, artist unknown: reproduced courtesy of E. Exshaw, copyright Dublin City Library and Archive.

May 1789 and he took up his position after the Michaelmas assembly on 16 October. The *Dublin Chronicle* commented that Exshaw would be the youngest 'Chief Magistrate' to govern the city of Dublin.[38] He had as his sheriffs Charles Thorp, painter and plasterer, and James Vance, a grocer.[39] To celebrate his appointment he gave 'a sumptuous entertainment to several of the nobility, gentry and citizens at the Mansion House'.[40] During his term in office the main matters for consideration were the extension of the pipe water system to various areas in the city, the regular management of the city leases, and the initiation of a project to raise a fund for the rebuilding of the Tholsel in a new location (see above, Gillespie, pp 53–62).[41] He was succeeded as lord mayor by Alderman Henry Howison, who was elected on 5 August 1790 (see Griffith, p. 94).[42]

Exshaw's second term as lord mayor came in 1800 when on 24 February he was elected in mid-term on the death of the sitting lord mayor, John Sutton. He held office for the remainder of the year, until Michaelmas when the new lord mayor, Charles Thorp, was sworn in.[43] His second term was marked by a very bad economic phase with high inflation and scarcity of provisions. The over-riding political debate concerned the proposed legislative union with

38 *Dublin Chronicle*, 23–6 May 1789.   **39** *CARD*, xiv, pp 113, 121.   **40** *Freeman's Journal*, 29 Sept.–1 Oct. 1789.   **41** *CARD*, xv, p. 154.   **42** *Freeman's Journal*, 7 Aug. 1790.   **43** *CARD*, xv, p. 140.

Great Britain. A series of objections to the proposed union was undertaken by the city assembly. On 17 January 1800 the sheriffs and commons requested the lord mayor, John Sutton, to appoint a committee to 'draw up resolutions expressive of our entire disapprobation of the destructive measure of a Legislative Union between this Country and Great Britain' to be published in the *Freeman's Journal* and *Anti-Union Evening Post*.[44] The publication of the resolutions was followed at the end of the month by the drafting of a petition to parliament against the proposed union, which they considered to be 'so destructive to the interest, so fatal to the independence, and so pernicious to the tranquillity of Ireland' (see also Hill, pp 98–106).[45] The petition, unanimously agreed, was ordered to be 'engrossed, put under city seal, and presented to Parliament by the city representatives, and that the corporation with the Regalia do attend the delivery'.[46] The death of the lord mayor occurred during this process, and Exshaw acted 'locum tenens' from early February until his election on 24 February, and he continued the anti-union campaign. In early February addresses were drafted and presented to those members of parliament who had commercial interests in the city, most notably David Latouche, banker.[47] In April, Lord Mayor Exshaw, with the board of aldermen, drafted a petition to the king, arguing against the union on the basis of the 'destructive consequences that must arise to the trade and manufactures of this kingdom'. A deputation, comprising Alderman Henry Howison and Nathaniel Hone Esquire, was sent to London to present the address to the king. On the return of the delegation the address was ordered to be printed in the *Freeman's Journal*.[48]

The assembly vehemently opposed the union, which it considered to be a 'national calamity', fearing the erosion of the 'commercial privileges' of the city, and the destruction of the 'chartered rights' of its citizens.[49] But its opposition followed strict protocol, its petitions advancing up the scale until finally being presented to the king. The assembly exerted its authority to the best of its ability, engrossing petitions and giving them the authority of the city seal. Presentation to parliament was done with full honours, accompanied by the city regalia. In particular they noted that they were not just defending their own rights and privileges as businessmen, but defending those of all citizens. The loyalty of the petitioners was stressed at all times: their affection for the

---

44 Ibid., pp 127–8. *Freeman's Journal*, 18 Jan. 1800.   **45** *CARD*, pp 135–7.   **46** Ibid., p. 137.   **47** Ibid., pp 137–8.   **48** *CARD*, xv, pp 143–4, 156, 160, 165. The delegates were paid £300 expenses for the trip. *Freeman's Journal*, 5 Apr. 1800, 27 May 1800.   **49** *CARD*, xv, pp 136–7.

crown and their support of the constitution. In May, after the attempted assassination of George III, an address of congratulation on his 'providential escape' was drafted by the assembly and was presented to the lord lieutenant to be sent to his majesty.[50]

V

The Act of Union had two major consequences on Exshaw's business interests as a bookseller. The first concerned the extension of copyright to Ireland, the second the loss of a significant portion of the market for books as the parliamentary elite and fashionable society moved to London. As noted above, Irish booksellers had benefited throughout the eighteenth century from the lack of copyright legislation in force in Ireland. The provisions of the Copyright Act (Great Britain) of 1709 were not considered by the Irish parliament and were not adopted as law.[51] Consequently, Irish booksellers could reprint any new title from England or Scotland without having to pay for copy. Critically, they were able to supply the Irish market with new and bestselling books, undercutting London prices and thus depriving English booksellers of Irish customers. Accusations of piracy from the London book trade failed to have any damaging effect on the Irish trade, which blossomed during this period. The market for books changed significantly after the union and successful booksellers targeted the literate sections of the public with less expensive books, placing less emphasis on the latest trends in reading. Book auctions, arising from the closure of many elegant town houses, meant that an important range of second-hand and antiquarian books was available at reasonable prices. Many of Dublin's booksellers who held radical political views had already emigrated to the United States after the 1798 rebellion. Among the most successful were Patrick Byrne who set up business in Philadelphia and John Chambers in New York. Booksellers such as Exshaw, who were loyal subjects and who had a diverse range of publications and a countrywide marketing network, were able to weather the inhospitable conditions.

John Exshaw came from a successful and forward-looking family of merchants in Dublin city. His father's bookselling business in Dame Street and his first wife's large fortune set him up financially early in life. This enabled

---

50 Ibid., pp 158–9. **51** 8 Ann, c.19, Great Britain. Came into force on 10 Apr. 1710. M. Pollard, *Dublin's trade in books, 1550–1800* (Oxford, 1989), pp 69–70.

him to expand his business and gave him the opportunity to serve the city
with distinction in several different roles. He lived and worked through
turbulent times, commanding a battalion of yeomanry during the 1798
rebellion. He was a strong supporter of government in all matters, but he was
vehemently opposed to the union as he considered it would be harmful to
trade. John Exshaw remained in Dublin after the union and despite reverses
to the bookselling business he continued to prosper, sustained by the diversity
of his printing and publishing projects, and in particular by his role as official
printer and stationer to official and public bodies, until his retirement from
business in 1822.

Henry Gore Sankey: the portrait of a perfect mayor, 1791–2

LISA-MARIE GRIFFITH

On completion of his term as lord mayor in 1792, Alderman Henry Gore Sankey was bestowed some very special honours by the upper chamber of the corporation, the alderman board. He was given not just an address of thanks but also a gold box, and was requested to sit for his portrait which would then 'be placed in a conspicuous part of the Mansion House' so that it would set an 'example to future lord mayors to emulate his merits'.[1] It was common for aldermen who had navigated the office without offending too many civic officers to be voted an address of thanks, less so to be granted a gold box, and highly unusual for their portrait to be requested (fig. 14). Indeed this request marks Sankey's one-year term out for special mention. The corporation hoped future lord mayors would emulate his term. The portrait of the lord mayor no longer hangs in the Mansion House. Today it is given a special honour as it hangs with portraits of several other eminent mayors in the council chamber of Dublin City Hall.

On an examination of his career as a civic representative, however, Sankey does not seem like an obvious man to be chosen for such a special honour. While he was clearly an active member of the corporation, it is difficult to see why he was elevated above other active corporation members who were not shown the same gratitude. He was not a celebrated city patriot. Indeed he does not seem to have been popular in the wider city. The editor of the *Freeman's Journal*, Francis Higgins, described Sankey's citywide support in 1797 (after his term as lord mayor) as follows:

> He has interest at the board of alderman when coupled with Alexander, in the common council scarcely none. Among the corporations he is looked upon as a person of great hauteur, holding a variety of places under government – in the coal yards (against which the lower orders make great complaint), also at the paving board and lottery commissioners

1 Lady Gilbert (ed.), *Calendar of ancient records of Dublin,* 18 vols (Dublin, 1902) [hereafter *CARD*], xiv, p. 289.

etc. etc. From these and other circumstances the bulk of the corporation
would rather vote for the Wooden man [the pillory] in Essex Street.[2]

The alderman board supported him, but few other city factions seem to have
backed him. Sankey placed advertisements with the *Freeman's Journal*. This is
not a very complimentary picture of Higgins' customer.

   A review of Sankey's career is needed to understand why a man with so little
city-wide support could have so many honours bestowed upon him. It will
show that these honours were prompted more by civic politics and factions
rather than by Sankey's own popularity. Sankey's civic career, and the episodes
in which he became embroiled, shed light on the politics of the office of lord
mayor, the alderman board and the corporation, as well as highlighting how
political factions outside the corporation shaped politics within the civic
institutions.

I

Henry Gore Sankey became a freeman of the city of Dublin by birth, or as the
son of a freeman, in 1768.[3] He joined his father, Edward Sankey, in business
at 77 Grafton Street once Henry Gore was made free of the merchant's guild
(although more than likely Henry Gore trained with Edward). Henry Gore
traded with his father at these premises until his father retired in 1779.[4] He
had acquired premises at 9 Clare Street by 1783, a move probably influenced
by the relocation of the Custom House to the east of the city, particularly as
Sankey sat as a commissioner for the Wide Streets Commission.[5] Wine
merchants were, for the most part, absent from the Committee of Merchants
and Chamber of Commerce, which objected to the Custom House's relocation
from Essex Quay to a new location on the north side of the Liffey and to the
east of the city. This address change suggests that Sankey was not reluctant to
embrace the change.[6] This new site gave easier access to the north side and the
Custom House as well as additional access to the Merrion Square and Baggot
Street developments built up in the following two decades. By 1812 Sankey

2 Francis Higgins to 'Dear Sir' [Edward Cooke], 11 July 1797 (Thomas Bartlett (ed.), *Revolutionary Dublin,
1795–1801, the letters of Francis Higgins to Dublin Castle* (Dublin, 2004), p. 174).   **3** Gertrude Thrift (ed.),
'Roll of freemen; city of Dublin 1468–1485, 1575–1774', iv (NLI, MS 79).   **4** *Wilson's Dublin Directory*,
1776.   **5** Henry Gore Sankey (representative of Thomas Pilkington), Wide Streets Commission, 27 July
1786 (Registry of Deeds, 376.479.252102).   **6** The foundation stone for the new Custom House was laid

had acquired a house on one of these new developments and lived at 6 Rutland (now Parnell) Square.[7] The account books of the Bank of Ireland give glimpses of a proportion of his wealth and by 1801 Sankey held £7,215 in bank stock.[8] This figure represents only a portion of his wealth at this time. David Dickson estimates that 'in 1791–2, 11 per cent of the Irish population had a gross per capita income in excess of £20 p.a., while 59 per cent were surviving with less than £5 p.a.' In contrast there was a considerable 30 per cent in the middle of these income brackets surviving on between £5 and £20.[9]

Sankey took over his father's position of superintendent of the city coal yard on his father's death, which gave him additional income to his business profits of £200 per annum.[10] The office required him to stockpile coal when the market was flooded, in anticipation of periods of scarcity.[11] Coal was a commodity with a constant demand in the capital, and the 'absence of any regulation of the trade encouraged the periodic glutting of the Dublin market'.[12] During the coldest months, crisis could ensue in the city, as poorer citizens could not afford the inflated prices of coal caused by seasonal scarcity. While the coal yards were supposed to ensure that there was enough coal in the city, this was not always possible, and commissions of 1761, 1791 and 1796 suggested that the lord mayor should be vested with greater power to deal with the scarcity and abuses within the coal trade, such as hoarding, overpricing[13] and a prevalent fraudulent practice known as the 'Old Man'.[14] In 1793 Sankey, acting in the capacity of ex-lord mayor and superintendent of the city coal yards, was called to a House of Commons commission to investigate the abuses in the coal trade. Under oath he testified that he had made fines in the city amounting to £99 during his mayoralty. He further

---

in August 1781 and the building opened for business a decade later, in November 1791.   **7** *Wilson's Dublin Directory*, 1812.   **8** Bank of Ireland Stock Book, 1783–1800 (Dublin City Library and Archive, MS 9, f. 104).   **9** David Dickson, *New Foundations: Ireland 1660–1800* (Dublin, 2nd ed., 2000), p. 110.   **10** He replaced Timothy Allen (*Freeman's Journal*, 4 Sept. 1764).   **11** House of Commons, *Report from the committee to whom it was referred to inquire into the causes of the excessive price of coals etc.* (Dublin, 1761).   **12** Louis Cullen, *Anglo-Irish trade* (Dublin, 1968), p. 122.   **13** Reports of the commissions that sat to deal with coal prices in the city are in no way complete or detailed but do shed some light on the abuses and activity of lord mayors in this area (House of Commons, *Report from the committee to whom it was referred to inquire into the causes of the excessive price of coals etc.* (Dublin, 1761), NAI, Coal records, 1a–46–46 Public Coal Yard Commissions 1769–96).   **14** A piece in the *Freeman's Journal* defined the practice of Old Man in 1771: 'What is meant by the OLD MAN, is a sum of money, from one often to five shillings per ton, which is returned by the captains out of the price they receive from the public for their coals; the higher the coals are, the greater the OLD MAN; at a time when the coals are sold to the public for a guinea per ton, the humane factors often have whole cargoes from the captains at the markets for 19s. 6d. or 20s. per ton. The remainder they are content with for their trouble; indeed those factors are sometimes obliged to allow the loaders 6d. or 9d. per ton, out of that for their services.' (*Freeman's Journal,* 1 Jan. 1771).

testified that the actions of two coal vendors in particular, Toole and Sutherland, were responsible for driving up prices in parts of the city, which indicates he had an extensive knowledge of the market.[15] Six days later W. Reilly, a city coal factor, gave evidence that on one occasion Sankey had summoned and fined three coal factors a total of £16.[16] The testimonies indicate that individual lord mayors, Henry Gore Sankey included, did attempt to regulate the coal trade but that it was difficult to ensure that these reforms were observed consistently.

While there is a natural progress through the civic hierarchy, Sankey's civic career mirrored his own father's in many respects. He followed him into the corporation as well as the coals yards, and the similarities in progression and rank show the continuity of families in the corporation. Edward was sheriff in 1759–60, appointed alderman in 1761 and lord mayor in 1766–7. By 1773, his son Henry Gore was serving for the merchants' guild on the common council of the corporation.[17] In 1777 he was appointed high sheriff, and was particularly active. For example, he suppressed a 'notorious' gambling establishment on Essex Street called Morris' Café in November 1777.[18] When the house was re-opened a few weeks later, Sankey made a further attempt to have it shut down. He entered the house, identified some of the clientele, and had the market cryer, Daniel Crinnigan, imprisoned in Newgate for gambling.[19]

Edward Sankey's death in March 1784 created a vacancy on the board of aldermen. Edward's death notice stated that he was a 'most distinguished' alderman. He had a 'refined elegance of manners', which 'were happily blended in this Gentleman's character'.[20] The death notice went on to acknowledge that in his son there was a ready replacement for Edward. While his death would be 'an irreparable loss to his friends … the congenial disposition of his son Henry Gore Sankey Esq., [would] ensure the continuance of those many amiable qualities'.[21] Sankey took the opportunity to forward his ambitions with the corporation and to be elected to his father's seat. The election of Sankey to the position of alderman, and the office of superintendent of the city coal yard shows the continuity of particular families to higher corporation offices.[22]

In 1790 Henry Gore Sankey ran for one of two parliamentary seats of Dublin city. His popularity as a city sheriff and the ease with which he

15 Committee on the state of the coal trade, 1793 (NAI, Coal records, 1a–46–46, f. 6).   **16** Ibid., f. 38.
17 He is certainly on the council by 1773 but it is difficult to discern when he first sat on it (*Dublin Directory*, 1773).   **18** *Dublin Journal*, 4 Nov. 1777.   **19** Ibid., 20 Dec. 1777.   **20** Ibid., 18 Mar. 1784.
21 Ibid.   **22** *CARD*, xiii, p. 356.

acquired a seat on the alderman board confirm that the upper ranks of the corporation held him in great esteem. He had been nominated by the alderman board with outgoing Lord Mayor John Exshaw (see p. 79) as 'a fit and proper person to represent this city in the ensuing parliament'.[23] Sankey and Exshaw united for the course of the election campaign, advertising together in February, March and April.[24] In addition, Dublin Castle and the conservative newspapers the *Dublin Journal* and the *Freeman's Journal* supported their campaign. Support for aldermen in parliament had declined greatly after the Lucas affair of 1749. While the common council was elected directly by the freemen of the city, the alderman board was a body that was selected from the common council but by its own members, which made the voting very unpopular in the common council and ensured the membership of the alderman board remained conservative. Throughout the 1740s a common councillor, Charles Lucas, spoke out about what he saw as the corruption in the upper chambers of the corporation. His chance to rival their power came during the election of 1749, when Lucas and his running mate, James La Touche, stood against the two alderman candidates. The election of 1749 became a monumental event in civic history. The election prompted 150 pamphlets to be written, and Lucas even produced his own paper, *The Censor*. When Lucas turned his focus from the corporation to the national government and to insulting government supporters, he was accused of libel, labelled in parliament an enemy of the country and forced to flee Ireland. This was not the last of Lucas, however, and he returned to Ireland to be elected as a city MP in 1761. He was a constant and steady reminder to the Dublin electorate that city aldermen were conservative. A vote for an alderman was considered to be a vote for the Dublin Castle administration. The election of Alderman William Alexander to parliament in 1783 must have raised the hopes of the alderman board of having a further candidate elected. However, the support of the alderman board for the administration contrasted with city liberals' determination to repeal the much-hated Police Act. The Police Act was passed in 1786 in response to the Gordon riots in London. It created a full-time, salaried, uniformed and regulated police force in Dublin for the first time. To pay for this force additional taxes were imposed on the citizens of Dublin. The force was resented not just for this additional tax but because it was believed that a full-time paid force of this nature would impose on

23 *Dublin Journal*, 13 Feb. 1790.   **24** *Dublin Journal, Freeman's Journal, Saunder's Newsletter,* Feb., Mar., Apr. 1790.

the liberties of the population.[25] The election was 'well-orchestrated and sustained … against the [Police] Act, which secured the support of those concerned for civil liberty'.[26] Despite the unpopularity of this act within the corporation and the city at large, Exshaw and Sankey supported the police force. Their opponents were Henry Grattan and Lord Henry Fitzgerald, two popular city patriots whom they could not defeat.

II

The high point in Sankey's public career came while he was lord mayor in 1791–2. His term began with ceremony and display, and throughout the year he worked hard to enhance his profile, particularly with city Protestants. Sankey used the discussion concerning Catholic relief and the consolidated Protestant ascendancy in the corporation and city guilds to build on his popularity. A consolidated Catholic Committee fronted by successful merchants, prominent city traders and professionals was making great headway in Dublin, demanding relief from the penal laws. Catholics were denied entrance to guilds and the corporation of the city. Denied the title of freeman from the late seventeenth century, it was requested that they pay a fee for the privilege of trading in cities, and they were granted the title of 'quarter brother'. This gave them access to guilds in name only, and they could not participate in any civic structures. This was a sorely-felt restriction. Catholic businessmen refused to pay the fee and traded regardless, outside the bounds of the guilds. They wanted a say in the civic government, however, and were eager to become involved. Most Protestants wanted to hold on to their monopoly within civic and political institutions, and they pointed to the wars of the seventeenth century as evidence that Catholics could not be trusted and should not be allowed entrance to civic associations on an equal footing. The debate about Catholic entrance to the corporation was intensifying when Sankey took office.

At the beginning of his term he held a large dinner at the Mansion House and provided a turtle that reportedly weighed 179 pounds for his guests. The lord lieutenant attended and sat at the right hand of the mayor,[27] and Sankey was joined by some of the most important individuals in the country.[28] While

---

25 J.R. Hill, *From patriots to unionists: Dublin civic politics and Irish Protestant patriotism, 1660–1840* (Oxford, 1997), pp 183–5.   **26** R.B. McDowell, *Grattan: a life* (Dublin, 2001), p. 106.   **27** *Dublin Journal*, 6 Sept. 1791.   **28** 'The right honourable Major Hobart, Lord Donaghmore, Baron Hamilton, Mr Justice Boyd, the honourable Mr Packenham, the honourable Mr Jocelyn, the honourable Mr Cockayne,

13 The lord mayor's state coach which made its first appearance on the streets of
Dublin in November 1791, during the mayoralty of Henry Gore Sankey:
reproduced courtesy of Dublin City Library and Archive.

this event was a corporation ceremony (although not an annual occasion), the
appearance of so many high-ranking officials and nobility at the table of a
merchant was significant. It showed that, through his work in the corporation,
Sankey had opportunities to socialize with the upper class.[29]

Sankey was the first lord mayor to ride in the new state coach, a highly
publicized occasion. The coach was unveiled for the annual celebration of the

Mr Secretary Hamilton, Major Freemantle, General Ward and his Aide-de-Camps, Dean Wetham, Mr
Borough, Mr Meck, Capts Finch and Mitche, Aide de Camps in waiting to his Excellency, the surgeon
general, Mr Quinn, several of the board of aldermen, members of the common council and a number of
respectable citizens' (ibid.). **29** Municipal records do not record social activities but corporation traditions

birth and landing of William of Orange (4 November). Traditionally a cavalcade of civic and national figures went in state to the castle so this was an important corporation event that was covered in the press, with Sankey mentioned several times. The *Dublin Journal* reported with much pleasure that the carriage built 'to enable the chief magistrate to appear with splendour proportionate to his rank and authority' was almost ready for its appearance at the annual celebrations.[30]

January 1792 provided further opportunities for Sankey to cast himself as a civic leader. The year opened with a public address by the Catholics associated with the Catholic Committee to the lord lieutenant, Westmoreland, which was printed in the national press, and demanded 'further repeal of the laws affecting the Roman Catholics of Ireland'.[31] It was indicative of the heightened tension over the issue of religious freedom which lingered all year. A Catholic relief act was passed and achieved more than any other repeal to date. On 20 January 1792 the corporation drew up an address of loyalty to George III stating that as they were 'sensibly impressed with the value of our excellent constitution' they hoped the king would 'preserve the Protestant ascendancy in Ireland'.[32] This statement was supported by an address drawn up in the same assembly to the city MPs, Lord Henry Fitzgerald and Henry Grattan, which expressed the corporation's fear of Catholic enfranchisement: 'At times like the present when we see the newspapers filled with resolutions of different associations expressing discontent and urging … alterations in the happy constitution under which we have lived and prospered' they wanted their city MPs to defend their constitution.[33] The MPs had claimed during the election that they would uphold the wishes of their constituents so the corporation wanted them to object against any further relief for Catholics which they believed would 'subvert the Protestant ascendancy'.[34] The addresses became popular within and outside the corporation and Sankey, as the lord mayor and signatory, received much of the thanks by those opposing Catholic enfranchisement. He was becoming a figure to represent and lead their beliefs.

The heightened political atmosphere within the city and the subsequent printed addresses from guilds and the corporation show that as chief magistrate, Sankey was sought out to become the civic defender of Protestant ascendancy. In September the corporation drew up a letter addressed 'To the

can be identified from some records such as the annual oyster day (Lady Gilbert (ed.), *Calendar of ancient records of Dublin,* 18 vols (Dublin, 1902), viii, p. xxi).   **30** *Dublin Journal,* 22 Oct. 1791.   **31** *Dublin Journal,* 1 Jan. 1792.   **32** *CARD,* xiv, p. 241.   **33** Ibid., 243.   **34** Ibid.

14 Portrait of Henry Gore Sankey by William Cuming (1769–1852), erroneously attributed to H.D. Hamilton: reproduced courtesy of Dublin City Library and Archive.

Protestants of Ireland' in response to the pamphlet *An address from the general committee of Roman Catholics, to their Protestant fellow subjects, and to the public in general*.[35] The letter asserted that Dublin Corporation believed in a Protestant ascendancy that consisted of 'a Protestant king of Ireland – a Protestant parliament – a Protestant hierarchy – Protestant elections and government … by a connection with the Protestant realm of Britain'.[36] Almost a week after Sankey's successor took office, the *Dublin Journal* reported that among Sankey's qualities, such as his hospitality and concern for the poor, were that he was 'warmly attached to the constant in church and state' and that his 'manly spirit stood forth in … support' of this cause.[37] The passage portrayed Sankey as a loyal defender of the Protestant faith. Furthermore, the address of loyalty had been a popular move within the corporation: 'The committee that drew up the address included besides two police commissioners and John Giffard on the castle side, one of the most popular opposition aldermen (Henry Howison), and the Presbyterian alderman, William Alexander, it was therefore broadly representative of all shades of opinions in the corporation'.[38] The address further offered civic support to those within parliament who sought to defend the Protestant faith on similar lines. While parliament had eroded the powers of the corporation between 1760 and 1790 (including the establishment of the police force from 1786), in matters of religious policy they were 'prepared to back the guilds and corporations'.[39]

III

The addresses that Sankey received at the close of his term as lord mayor illustrate how popular he had become over the course of the year. The guild of felt-makers, guild of smiths and the guild of brewers printed a thanks, with a response from the outgoing lord mayor, three times in the *Dublin Journal*.[40] The guild of felt-makers, which presented the longest of the addresses, thanked Sankey in a general manner for the 'attention which … [he] paid to every department of office', and drew particular attention to his attempts 'to suppress the immoderate use of spirituous liquors amongst the lower order of

---

35 General Committee of Roman Catholics of Ireland, *An address from the general committee of Roman Catholics, to their Protestant fellow subjects, and to the public in general* (Dublin, 1792).   **36** *CARD*, xiv, p. 287.   **37** *Dublin Journal*, 6 Oct. 1792.   **38** Hill, *From patriots to unionists*, p. 221. **39** J.R. Hill, 'The shaping of Dublin government in the long eighteenth century' in P. Clark and R. Gillespie (eds), *Two capitals: London and Dublin, 1500–1840, Proceedings of the British Academy*, 7 (2001), p. 165.   **40** *Dublin*

people'.[41] Through licensing, regulation and inspection of the city public houses, Sankey may have attempted to enforce serving hours and to eradicate the illegal alcohol trade in the city. The guilds painted Sankey as an active and reforming lord mayor and yet during his term he received more press coverage for socializing and for his comments against Catholic equality than for his reforms. Indeed these reforms were really nothing very new, and other mayors had gone further and been more active during their own terms.

In addition to an address of thanks, as previously mentioned, the corporation gave Sankey a gold box and asked him to sit for his portrait. This is quite remarkable. The corporation voted to pay £100 for the portrait. However, by April 1793 the budget had increased to £500. After visiting an exhibition of paintings displayed at a museum in Mary Street, they chose the young portrait painter William Cuming of Crow Street. Justin Pope was commissioned to make the frame at a cost of ten guineas.[42] In Sankey's response to their address he stated that he hoped the corporation would 'continue happy and united, a glorious example of loyalty and patriotism to a great and prosperous nation'.[43] Sankey's 'loyalty' address suggests that defence of Protestant ascendancy was a key issue with Protestant freemen and coming at this time he was linked with the cause. This ensured that his term had a dramatic effect on his profile with the Protestant freemen.

His portrait as lord mayor depicts him standing in the Royal Exchange overseeing the city and its interests. The portrait was hung within the Mansion House and suggests that the aim was to create a memorial to a mayor who defended the Protestant faith and the Protestant ascendancy.[44] While the corporation never explicitly stated any reason for Sankey being given this special honour, it is clear that the most significant event of Sankey's career was his defence of the Protestant ascendancy in the corporation. More than his reforming initiatives or socializing, even more than using the state carriage for the first time, this marked him out. It brought him into the public eye for his political opinions and allowed him to be leader of a cause that most of the Protestant corporation supported. It is for this reason he was asked to sit for his portrait. He was a man of his times. He did not initiate the Protestant address but he took it up as his cause, defended it and spread it. It certainly bolstered his public career, and the portrait was a great honour. Because Sankey's reforms had limited impact, his term is no longer remembered or

Journal, 20–5 Oct. 1792.   **41** Ibid., 25 Oct. 1792.   **42** Ibid.   **43** Ibid., 312–13.   **44** *Dublin Journal*, 27 Apr. 1793.

marked out for special attention. The main significance of Henry Gore Sankey's mayoralty is the way in which this episode, and his defence of the Protestant monopoly in the corporation, reveals the nature of civic politics in the 1790s and the extent to which Irish society was divided.

IV

By the close of his term Sankey was undoubtedly a popular civic figure among freemen supporters of Protestant ascendancy. In 1797 the alderman board put him forward for parliament again. This attempt was doomed from the beginning. The election was the first that allowed Catholics to benefit from repeal of the penal laws which had disqualified all Catholics from voting. A staunchly Protestant figure was never likely to be a popular candidate with the new electorate. Francis Higgins commented on the problems of Sankey's candidacy in a letter of 8 July 1797: 'government knows from the experienced expenditure of a large sum that aldermen cannot carry their election'.[45] Aldermen were too conservative and hugely unpopular. It was Higgins' belief that Sankey did not have enough support to carry an election and prompted him to comment that Sankey 'has interest at the board of aldermen when coupled with [Alderman] Alexander, in the common council scarcely any'.[46] By 25 July it was reported that Sankey had declined an offer by the alderman board of nomination for election to a city seat. Higgins' paper the *Freeman's Journal*, by now a Castle paper, publicly supported his claim to election whatever doubts Higgins may have had privately: 'It is but fair to say this gentleman had a strong claim on his fellow citizens; he served the various offices of trust and importance with so much impartiality and vigilant conduct'.[47] Sankey's failed parliamentary endeavour did not cause him to break from his urban connections. In 1811 Sankey sat once more for a portrait by William Cuming, this time as colonel of the militia,[48] a position he held from 1793. Though he retired from business in 1794, his retirement was filled with corporation duties until his death, and he remained extremely proud of his position in the Dublin militia.

45 Francis Higgins to 'Dear Sir' [Edward Cooke], 11 July 1797 (Thomas Bartlett (ed.), *Revolutionary Dublin, 1795–1801, the letters of Francis Higgins to Dublin Castle* (Dublin, 2004), p. 173). **46** Ibid. **47** *Freeman's Journal*, 25 July 1797. **48** The city militia was a voluntary armed guard that was raised during war time to defend the country against attack, it was considered a measure of popularity and respect to be appointed to senior positions within the militia.

In 1791–2 the majority of those within the civic government were resisting attempts to reform and open up the institution to Catholics. The episode of the corporation's Protestant ascendancy address suggests that the office of lord mayor reflected the opinion of civic officers and many of the Protestant freemen. Sankey was not acting independently or leading civic opinion. He was briefly made popular by supporting the Protestant ascendancy, a cause which was already popular among freemen. In following up the 'Protestant ascendancy Address' with a well-publicized thanks to the lord mayor who had presided over it, the corporation was reminding the public of its commitment to the Protestant ascendancy. Sankey was simply a temporary and convenient figurehead. Although his portrait still hangs in the council chambers, the cause of his erstwhile fame has long been forgotten.

Lord Mayor Thomas McKenny and Catholic emancipation, 1818–19

JACQUELINE HILL

Despite a wealth of studies on the subject of Catholic emancipation,[1] the significant role played by liberal Protestants in the campaign is still not fully appreciated. During the 1820s Catholics came to realize their own political strength when the Catholic Association (founded in 1823) successfully harnessed Catholic voting power to return pro-emancipation candidates to parliament. This was to transform the campaign's prospects for a speedy resolution. Before that time, however, the successive organizations formed to lobby on Catholics' behalf relied mostly on petitioning parliament and making overtures to ministers and other key figures. Such strategies rendered them heavily dependent on the support of liberal Protestants. Not all Protestants, of course, were sympathetic to Catholic aspirations for political equality. Many urged Catholics to remain content with the political rights conferred on them in the 1790s, and hard-liners gave support to organizations such as the Orange Order, founded in 1795. This highlights the importance of those Protestants, including the majority of Irish MPs by the mid-1820s, who were able to look beyond the traditional assumptions of the confessional state and envisage a fully inclusive political system.[2]

Thomas McKenny, who was lord mayor of Dublin in 1818–19, was one such liberal Protestant, and during his mayoral year he was to make a significant contribution to the emancipation cause. This was despite Dublin Corporation's role at the forefront of the anti-emancipation campaign (1792–1829). In defying the views of most of his colleagues in the corporation, McKenny not only testified to the divisions among Protestants on the subject, but – given that this was in a period before parliamentary reform – demonstrated the potential of the old regime for adopting a reformist agenda. The fact that only a few years later reform from within would be overtaken by the juggernaut of the Catholic Association does not detract from the

---

1 Among the more important are: J.A. Reynolds, *The Catholic emancipation crisis in Ireland, 1823–1829* (New Haven, 1954); Fergus O'Ferrall, *Catholic emancipation: Daniel O'Connell and the birth of Irish democracy, 1820–30* (Dublin, 1985); Thomas Bartlett, *The fall and rise of the Irish nation: the Catholic question, 1690–1830* (Dublin, 1992). 2 See O'Ferrall, *Catholic emancipation*, pp 114–20.

significance of figures such as McKenny, and understanding his contribution to emancipation seems all the more important given that within a decade increasingly assertive Catholic leaders were becoming openly impatient with what they saw as the inadequacy of Protestant support.[3] It will be argued in this contribution that Thomas McKenny's liberal outlook needs to be seen in the context of his business occupation, and also that an understanding of the workings of the civic hierarchy is crucial to revealing how a man of such views could have had the opportunity to make his contribution to the emancipation campaign.

I

Thomas McKenny was born in 1770, to a James and Jane McKenny, then living at 63 Stephen Street, close to St Stephen's Green. James McKenny is described in the Dublin *Directories* as a haberdasher. He appears to have died during the 1780s, and his business was taken over by Jane McKenny, described as a 'hosier and haberdasher'. By the late 1790s Thomas was running the business in Stephen Street on his own account, and had been selected by his guild (the guild of hosiers and knitters) to serve as one of its representatives on the lower house, or city commons, of Dublin Corporation.[4]

In the early nineteenth century McKenny seems to have been prospering (as were other McKenny relatives, also Protestant business people)[5] and the business moved around the corner to 47 South Great George's Street. According to a survey completed in the 1830s, he was at that time one of the chief employers in the hosiery trade, employing about one hundred journeymen, each of whom would have had their own frame for the manufacture of either silk, or cotton and worsted, stockings, and all earning about £1 per week in wages.[6] McKenny's status is suggested by the fact that in 1805 his name was proposed, by the city commons, as one of eight resident freemen from whom the aldermen were obliged to choose two to serve as sheriffs for the ensuing year. It was a requirement for filling that office that the individuals concerned should be worth at least £2,000.[7] At all events, he was selected for the office by

3 Daniel O'Connell to Lord Cloncurry, 24 Sept. 1828, in O'Connell, *The correspondence of Daniel O'Connell*, ed. Maurice R. O'Connell, 8 vols (Dublin, 1972–80), iii, letter 1489.　**4** *CARD*, xv, pp 533, 535, 537, 539.　**5** See Linde Lunney, 'James McKenny (1844–1917)' in *DIB*.　**6** 'Reports on trades and manufactures, Dublin, 1834' (RIA, MS 4.B.31), pp 209, 213.　**7** *CARD*, xv, p. 411; Jacqueline Hill, *From patriots to unionists: Dublin civic politics and Irish Protestant patriotism, 1660–1840* (Oxford, 1997), p. 123.

the aldermen. However, rather than take on the burden and responsibility of the position – no doubt the business needed his attention – he did what was not infrequently done in such circumstances: paid a fine of three hundred guineas (a sum that would have taken one of his journeymen approximately six years to earn).[8] This entitled him, without having to serve the office, to become a 'sheriffs' peer', which bestowed life membership of the city commons. It also made him eligible, at some time in the future, to be chosen a member of the more select aldermanic board.

For some years, nothing was heard of McKenny. Presumably he was still preoccupied with his business, from which he retired in 1817, selling it as a going concern to a William Ring, hosier.[9] By that time he had begun to be listed in the Dublin *Directories* as 'Thomas McKenny, Esquire', with an address at 25 Lower Fitzwilliam Street, off Merrion Square. Although less than a mile from South Great George's Street, this represented a move away from the world of trade to the world of the gentry and professions. By that time, too, in 1811, on the death of Alderman John Rose, McKenny had been one of four sheriffs' peers selected by the aldermen to fill the vacancy on the aldermanic board, and he was chosen by the lower house for the position. Seven years later, the board chose him as lord mayor elect, and he was confirmed in this position by the lower house.[10]

II

In view of McKenny's very public stance some years later in support of Catholic emancipation, it is natural to look for signs of such views at an earlier period. In order to rise in the civic hierarchy, Thomas McKenny had to have been a Protestant or Protestant dissenter, but his surname suggests that the family had at one time been Catholic (the 'O', 'Mc' or 'Mac' prefixes were very rare among those who were lord mayors in the period of the penal laws). The only McKenny listed in the convert rolls (a list of Catholic converts to the Church of Ireland, mainly covering the period 1760 to 1790) is a Dennis McKenny (a Catholic priest), so the conversion may have occurred before 1703, the earliest year covered by the rolls.[11] In this respect, it is noteworthy

8 *CARD*, xv, pp 411–12.   **9** 'Reports on trades', p. 213.   **10** *CARD*, xvi, p. 261, xvii, p. 204. The vote in the city commons was 76 for McKenny, and 34 against: Journal of sheriffs and commons, Easter assembly, 3 April 1818 (Dublin City Archives, CI/JSC/10, fo. 155r-v).   **11** Jacqueline Hill, 'Mayors and lord mayors of Dublin from 1229' in T.W. Moody, F.X. Martin & F.J. Byrne (eds), *A new history of Ireland*, ix (Oxford,

that McKenny's guild, serving the hosiers and knitters, was one of only two of the twenty-five Dublin guilds to have been founded by a charter from the Catholic King James II (1688) (and the other guild, the tanners, claimed an earlier origin).[12] Given the Catholic resurgence in Dublin civic life by 1688, it is reasonable to surmise that Catholics would have been prominent among the early guild officials and members. After the Williamite revolution, a new set of oaths required by statute excluded Catholics from full membership of guilds, but towards the end of the eighteenth century, when what had been essentially a dynastic question became 'the Catholic question', the hosiers' guild, along with a few others, had a record of taking a liberal stance on the subject. In 1784 the guild expressed support for the principle of Catholics obtaining 'every privilege that is consistent with a Protestant government and constitution', and in 1793 its representatives in the city commons voted in support of the admission of a Catholic merchant to the freedom of the city.[13] After the passing of the Act of Union, the guild maintained this stand. When in the early months of 1818 O'Connell secured a writ of mandamus (a judicial remedy requiring a subordinate body to take – or not take – a specific action), directing the corporation to admit a Catholic guild-member to the freedom of the city, the tradesman in question was a member of the hosiers' guild.[14] And at parliamentary elections most hosiers supported pro-emancipation candidates, as can be seen from surviving poll book evidence. McKenny himself is recorded as voting decisively for pro-emancipation candidates in 1806.[15] Given that the ballot was not secret, his liberal views (and those of his guild) would have been well known. Indeed, the Whiggish *Freeman's Journal* noted the popularity of his selection as lord mayor elect among the people of the city.[16]

The corporation in general, however, had a very different political outlook: from 1805, any sign of activity on the part of the Catholic Committee or its successors to petition for emancipation had prompted a counter petition.[17] Given the outlook of most corporation members, it may be asked, how did a man with such views come to achieve the highest civic office? Several factors are worth noting. The first was the seniority principle commonly observed in respect of the mayoralty. Other things being equal, the most senior alderman by date of appointment to the board would be chosen to fill the office, an

1984), pp 547–64; Eileen O'Byrne and Anne Chamney (eds), *The convert rolls* (Dublin, 2005), p. 165. **12** Mary Clark and Raymond Refaussé (eds), *Directory of historic Dublin guilds* (Dublin, 1993), pp 22, 30. **13** Hill, *From patriots to unionists*, pp 181, 233, n. 83, 245, 275.   **14** *Freeman's Journal*, 28 Jan., 17 April 1818.   **15** *The poll for electing two members to represent the city of Dublin in the imperial parliament ... 1806* (Dublin, n.d.), cols 27–8.   **16** *Freeman's Journal*, 7 Oct. 1818.   **17** *CARD*, xv, p. 404; xvi, pp 19–20;

ancient custom that continued, with few exceptions, after the passing of the 1760 Dublin Corporation Act, which gave members of the city commons a say in the selection of lord mayors: of four names selected by the board, the lower house was obliged to select one. At Easter 1818 when the selection was due to be made for the ensuing civic year, McKenny was the most senior alderman, and as a major corporation bondholder he had helped reduce the interest on the corporation's debt from six to five per cent.[18] Having retired from business the previous year he was well placed to devote time to the office, and as an added attraction to the cash-strapped corporation (the treasurer had defaulted on the accounts in 1814) he indicated his willingness to serve the office without seeking emoluments, thus suggesting that he would forgo the usual payment of £1,000 as compensation for expenses incurred in office. (It is worth noting, however, that he was appointed without any financial conditions.)[19] Lastly, had either house of the corporation been disposed to block McKenny's selection on the grounds of his political views, the fact was that since 1813 (coinciding with the chief secretaryship of Robert Peel (1812–18)), supporters of Catholic emancipation were divided and demoralized over issues such as the veto, thus allowing their opponents to take the initiative.[20] In those circumstances the likelihood that McKenny's liberal views would have any significant political effect during his mayoral year must have seemed remote.

III

The timing of these events, however, was significant. McKenny was chosen lord mayor elect at Easter 1818, but was not due to be sworn in until Michaelmas (29 September). In the meantime an important political development had taken place. Robert Peel had ceased to be chief secretary in August (his place was to be taken by Charles Grant, a Scot, and a known supporter of emancipation). This altered the political climate, and at an election for a new alderman that took place in July, when Peel's forthcoming transfer back to England had become known, there was considerable debate in the city commons about the political views of the prospective candidates.[21] When McKenny came to be sworn in, the *Freeman's Journal*, a pro-

68–71, 324–7, 380–2, 388, xvii, pp 52, 111, 155, 198. **18** *Freeman's Journal*, 20 Oct. 1819. **19** See McKenny's speech at Sheriff White's dinner, *Freeman's Journal*, 8 Oct. 1818; for debate on whether to restrict his remuneration, see DCA, C1/JSC/10, fo. 155r-v. On the corporation's financial problems, see the address from certain aldermen of Dublin to the lord mayor, sheriffs, commons and citizens of Dublin, *Freeman's Journal*, 29 March 1819. **20** Bartlett, *Fall and rise*, pp 304–11. **21** *Freeman's Journal*, 18, 23 July 1818.

emancipation newspaper, noted approvingly that in the procession to Dublin Castle for the event, McKenny's coach carried no 'party colours' (by which was meant that there was no sign of the orange or purple that would have suggested support for ultra-Protestant or Orange views). At the lord mayor's dinner for the lord lieutenant, McKenny intervened to forbid the band to play the tune 'Croppies lie down' (a loyalist anti-rebel folksong dating from the period of the 1798 rebellion).[22] Some days later, at Sheriff White's dinner for the new lord mayor, a row broke out when hard-line ultra-Protestants demanded the usual toast to the glorious memory of King William *before* the toast to the new lord mayor (an inversion of the usual practice). McKenny made his position clear: he had no objection to the toast to William's memory being proposed – the principles of the glorious revolution of 1688 were entirely commendable – but because of the significance being placed on the toast by the hard-liners, he would decline proposing it himself. As lord mayor, he intended to act impartially.[23]

Meanwhile, buoyed up by the prospect of a Whiggish chief secretary (Grant arrived in Dublin to take up the post in January 1819), Daniel O'Connell planned to revive the petitioning campaign. He was particularly keen to encourage Protestant support.[24] That significant Protestant goodwill existed is reflected in a series of meetings, at parish level, held by sympathetic Dublin Protestants to support their Catholic fellow citizens.[25] This initiative culminated in late January 1819 in a numerously signed requisition to the lord mayor to convene a general meeting of Dublin Protestant freemen, freeholders, and householders to petition parliament in support of emancipation.[26] Alarmed at such a prospect, the corporation had already drawn up a petition of its own, challenging the view that the Protestants of Ireland were favourably disposed towards emancipation, and urging parliament to maintain the existing constitution. The corporation's advice to the lord mayor was to disregard the requisition.[27] But even had he wished to do so, the prominence of some of the names attached to the requisition would have made that very difficult. Among the signatories were the duke of Leinster, the earls of Meath and Charlemont, Lords Cloncurry, Downshire, Donoughmore, Clifden, and Cremorne, Henry Grattan, MP for Dublin city, three other MPs, and several leading mercantile figures.[28] As McKenny said, given

22 Ibid., 1, 3 Oct. 1818.   **23** Ibid., 8 Oct. 1818.   **24** Oliver MacDonagh, *O'Connell: the life of Daniel O'Connell, 1775–1847* (London, 1991), p. 165.   **25** *Freeman's Journal*, 16, 20, 23, 25, 26, 28 Jan. 1819. **26** O'Connell to Owen O'Connor, 6 Jan. 1819 (*O'Connell correspondence*, ii, letter 756); *Freeman's Journal*, 15 Jan., 8 Feb. 1819).   **27** Petition dated 22 Jan. 1819 (*CARD*, xvii, pp 255–6); *Freeman's Journal*, 23 Jan. 1819. **28** *Freeman's Journal*, 8 Feb. 1819; William Drennan to O'Connell, 30 Jan. 1819 (*O'Connell correspondence*,

the standing of such figures, how could he refuse to allow the meeting to go ahead? What sealed his unpopularity in corporation circles was that not only did he agree that the meeting could be held, but that he himself would chair it.

Efforts to prevent the meeting being held were unsuccessful, and it took place at the Rotunda on 11 February 1819. Described as a meeting of Protestant freemen, freeholders, and householders of Dublin, an estimated 3,000 people attended, including the duke of Leinster, the earls of Meath and Charlemont, Lord Cloncurry, and several MPs, including Grattan, Sir Marcus Somerville, and William Parnell. A minority of those present, led by barrister Thomas Ellis (a future MP for the city) and some of the aldermen, sought an adjournment, but they were greatly outnumbered, and eventually withdrew. Thereafter all went smoothly, and a resolution to petition parliament was passed 'with acclamation', stating that 'the emancipation of our brethren the Roman Catholics … would prove highly conducive to the tranquillity of Ireland … and essentially necessary for the permanent prosperity of the United Empire'. Protestants in the rest of Ireland were called on to follow Dublin's example, and copies of the petition were left at the Commercial Buildings for additional signatures.[29] Opponents organized a counter-petition, but this backfired when the organizers left copies at the royal barracks for signature: an unwise move, because members of parliament were becoming concerned at the presence of Orangeism in the army, and in the event on 26 February a regimental order was issued, forbidding the soldiers to sign.[30]

The upshot was that McKenny became even more popular with Dublin Catholics. Several parishes held meetings to thank him, and an aggregate meeting of Catholics, chaired by the earl of Fingal, also expressed its gratitude. On the other side, both houses of the corporation censured him for holding the meeting.[31] There was a particularly heated exchange in the city commons, during which John Giffard, sheriffs' peer and acting grand master of the Grand Orange Lodge of Ireland, was reported to have declared that 'since the last day they had met … the WORLD WAS TURNED UPSIDE DOWN', with 'the Protestant people of this City' being 'bullied by a Popish rabble!'[32]

Some of the heat engendered by the meeting evaporated in May, when in the House of Commons Henry Grattan's attempts to obtain a committee to consider the laws affecting the Catholics failed, and emancipation seemed to

ii, letter 762, n. 4). **29** *Freeman's Journal*, 12, 20 Feb. 1819; see also *Dublin Evening Post*, 11, 13, 16 Feb. 1819. **30** *Freeman's Journal*, 26 Feb., 1 Mar. 1819. **31** Ibid., 22 Feb., 4, 6, Mar. 1819; corporation meeting of 19 Feb. 1819 (*CARD*, xvii, p. 261). **32** *Freeman's Journal*, 20 Feb. 1819; for Giffard, see *DIB*,

15 Portrait of Lord Mayor Thomas McKenny, engraving drawn by
William Brocas (*c.*1794–1868): reproduced courtesy of Jacqueline Hill.

be no further forward. But public gratitude was again expressed at Michaelmas
1819, when McKenny relinquished office: there was another round of parish
meetings, in which there was some Protestant involvement.[33] There was also a
call in McKenny's own guild, the hosiers, for an address to him, and an
engraving of the lord mayor, holding the requisition for the Protestant
meeting, went on sale and sold very well.[34] By this time, the corporation itself
had softened: a vote of thanks to the outgoing lord mayor was carried in the
affirmative (to cheers from a crowded public gallery), though by only one vote,
and a vote to grant him the usual £1,000 payment was negatived by 58 to 20
votes.[35] However, some apathy set in among liberal Protestants, and efforts,
again spurred on by O'Connell, to prompt Protestant notables to set on foot
a subscription to express gratitude to McKenny for his services to the
emancipation cause were somewhat slow to get under way. A dinner in his
honour, urged by O'Connell in November 1819, was not held until May 1820

Jacqueline Hill, 'John Giffard (1746–1819)'.   **33** *Freeman's Journal*, 1, 4, 5, 7, 8, 11, 15, 19, 25 Oct. 1819.
34 Ibid., 19 Oct. 1819. For the engraving, drawn by William Brocas, 5 Henry St., Dublin, see *CARD*, xvii,
plate vi.   **35** *Freeman's Journal*, 16, 20 Oct. 1819.

(though McKenny had been ill in the meantime). And it was not until May 1822 that the duke of Leinster, the earl of Meath, Lords Cloncurry and Killeen, as well as O'Connell, presented McKenny with 'a service of plate' in appreciation of his contributions to the cause.[36]

But in fact, parliamentary opinion was changing, and the show of Irish Protestant support for the cause was having an effect. In 1821, for the first time, a bill for Catholic emancipation passed the House of Commons, although it failed in the House of Lords. Had emancipation been granted before the Catholic Association developed its ground-breaking tactics, there must have been a possibility that it would have been received by Catholics as a boon, granted by Protestant wisdom and liberality, rather than forced on parliament by the harnessing of the Catholic vote. This point was made in London by sixty-five Protestant peers, all with property in Ireland, who in June 1825 drew up resolutions in support of emancipation, arguing that it would be prudent 'to confer with advantage what cannot be refused with safety and to adopt in peace a measure which may be forced upon us in war'.[37] Such a timely concession could have had far-reaching implications for Catholic-Protestant relations in the decades to come.

IV

In conclusion, following his mayoral year, McKenny remained an alderman, but seems to have played a relatively minor part in the board's activities. He continued to support Catholic emancipation, and was among those who formed an 'Irish Club' in Dublin to support liberal causes. In 1831 he was raised to the baronetcy by the Whig government of the day, and his name was among those that O'Connell considered proposing to stand for the representation of Dublin city in parliament.[38] He went on living in Fitzwilliam Street until his death in 1849, though he also acquired a country residence, Mount Rothe, in Co. Kilkenny. By the time of his death he had been made a justice of the peace. The story of his mayoralty reveals how even an ultra-Protestant body such as Dublin Corporation could harbour liberal elements, and shows how important the role of liberal Protestants was to the emancipation campaign before the ground-breaking changes of the mid-1820s.

36 *O'Connell correspondence*, ii, letters 805, 958; MacDonagh, *O'Connell*, pp 165–7. 37 Cited by O'Ferrall, *Catholic emancipation*, p. 115. 38 *O'Connell correspondence*, ii, letter 907, iii, letter 1278, iv, letters 1834, 1854, n. 4.

Daniel O'Connell and Dublin's quest for a new mayoral image, 1841–71

MARY E. CLARK

Daniel O'Connell was elected as lord mayor of Dublin at 12 noon on 1 November 1841. Triumphantly, he donned the traditional red robes trimmed with fur, along with the gold mayoral chain, a gift to the city from William of Orange in 1698. With the lord mayor's tricorne hat cocked on his head, O'Connell displayed himself at the window of the City Assembly House in William Street to the cheering crowds below. '"Boys, do ye know me now?" cried O'Connell, while his supporters, thrilled by his unfamiliar finery, answered fervently "Sure, aren't ye our own darling Liberator?"'[1]

Although O'Connell bedecked himself with the established trappings of his new office, he was lord mayor for a democratic age, and his election transformed Dublin's mayoralty, to the extent that it had to be re-shaped to fit his stalwart frame. The first Roman Catholic to hold the post since the reign of James II, O'Connell was the first lord mayor to have no connection with the city's ancient trade guilds, and the first to be elected by a franchise which, though limited, was democratic. This new type of lord mayor – modern but traditional, national but local, patriotic but subversive – called for a fresh language and innovative forms of expression in projecting and promoting the office. For thirty years, from 1841 until 1871, Dublin City Council wrestled with the problem of devising a public image for O'Connell, which would express every facet of his complex public persona, and would breathe renewed life into the traditional image of the Dublin mayoralty. This struggle called for a re-evaluation of accepted forms of portraiture, in painting and in sculpture. Although the manifold character of the Liberator proved to be too elaborate for expression in a single medium, a partial solution was found through the presentation of a multiplicity of images, each redolent of a particular aspect of his heroic character. For O'Connell was truly larger than life, a characteristic that had never previously graced the Dublin mayoralty and which eventually proved to be beyond the municipality's powers of exposition.

---

1 Sean O'Faolain, *King of the beggars* (London, 1938), p. 321.

I

A factor governing and controlling the municipality's freedom of expression in the period 1841–71 was the finely balanced nature of the city council. O'Connell had been instrumental in securing the passage in 1840 of the Municipal Corporation Reform (Ireland) Act, which brought a restricted but democratic franchise to existing local government. The principal effect in Dublin was the abolition of the centuries-old system of civic government by the ancient trade guilds.[2] Until 1840, the trade guilds had successfully preserved the Protestant ascendancy, claiming that their charters required new members to subscribe to the oath of supremacy and to the oath repudiating transubstantiation, thus effectively excluding Roman Catholics.[3] In this way, the guilds avoided the liberal effects of the relief acts which abolished the penal laws in 1793, while their charters also kept them outside the scope of Catholic emancipation, passed in 1829. To O'Connell, it was insupportable that Roman Catholics could qualify for the parliamentary franchise but not for the municipal franchise, dependant as the latter still was upon membership of a trade guild. This exclusion from civic government was especially offensive to the emerging Catholic merchant class, which lent its support to O'Connell's cause. But municipal reform was more than the completion of Catholic emancipation: for O'Connell it was also a necessary step towards repeal of the Act of Union. His words struck terror into the hearts of the beleaguered members of the Dublin City Assembly: 'Give me Reform and I will get everything else!' After all, this was the desperado who in 1815 had killed one of the Assembly's members in a duel, when the hapless alderman John Norcot D'Esterre attempted to avenge O'Connell's insulting description of Dublin Corporation as 'beggarly'.[4] Throughout the 1830s the Dublin City Assembly attempted in vain to preserve its Protestant character, and constantly presented petitions to parliament, which were valiantly and successfully opposed by O'Connell. Tenaciously and successfully, the Liberator fought for reform of the Irish corporations, and for the removal of the self-perpetuating Protestant oligarchies which still monopolized civic government.

The 1840 Reform Act introduced a new municipal franchise, which depended, not on religion, but upon ownership of property with a rateable

2 Fergus A. D'Arcy, 'The trade unions of Dublin and the attempted revival of the guilds', *JRSAI* 101:2 (1971), 113–27.   **3** Jacqueline R. Hill, 'The politics of privilege: Dublin Corporation and the Catholic question, 1792–1823', *Maynooth Review*, 7 (Dec. 1982), 17–36.   **4** O'Faolain, *King of the beggars*, pp 219–22. A contemporary engraving, entitled 'Shooting of D'Esterre' records the event. National Gallery of

valuation of at least £10 per annum. This measure allowed for the enfranchisement of a sufficient number of Catholics to create a power base for O'Connell
in Dublin, although even then he was obliged to choose his constituency with
caution. O'Connell had lost his seat as MP for Dublin city in the summer of
1841, and he had been obliged to withdraw to Cork, where he had been
returned to parliament.[5] In the municipal election held on 25 October 1841,
the first after the passage of the Reform Act, O'Connell stood for the Four
Courts ward, the scene of his numerous triumphs as a barrister.[6] A second
defeat in Dublin could not be endured, but O'Connell's success was
guaranteed by a local supporter, Thomas Arkins, a well-known tailor who
generously gave up his candidacy in the adjoining Linen Hall ward to allow
the Liberator to take his place. O'Connell was accordingly elected for both
wards, and just one week later, he was elected as lord mayor at the inaugural
meeting of Dublin City Council, held on 1 November 1841.[7] Tom Arkins
then compounded his magnanimity by making a set of mayoral robes for
O'Connell and presenting them to him as a gift.

But in politics, a gift can incur obligations. As lord mayor, O'Connell tried
to maintain a neutral stance, which was intended to soften the impact of the
emerging power of the Catholic mercantile class upon the erstwhile Protestant
ascendancy. He even established an informal but effective 'mayoralty compact'
whereby 'the lord mayor is alternately selected from one particular political
party and religious denomination in one year and from another … in the next
following year.'[8] Accordingly, when O'Connell completed his term of office,
he was succeeded by one of his supporters, the Protestant George Roe, a
distiller whose firm was later to finance the restoration of Christ Church
Cathedral. This effectively established a confessional partnership that ultimately
led to enhanced political power for Dublin City Council. But O'Connell's
neutrality as lord mayor had not prevented a re-distribution by Dublin City
Council of the political patronage enjoyed by its predecessor body, the city
assembly. During March and April 1842, incumbent civic officials were
systematically removed from their posts and replaced with loyal O'Connell
supporters, often to the detriment of the city. The outstanding John Semple
(see pp 192–3) was dismissed as city architect and replaced with the lesser
talent of Hugh Byrne. Robert Dickinson and George Archer were dismissed

Ireland, cat. ref. 11,241.   **5** O'Faolain, *King of the beggars*, p. 317.   **6** *The Citizen, or Dublin Monthly
Magazine*, 4:25 (November 1841).   **7** O'Connell was proposed by Councillor J.L. Arabin, and was
seconded by Alderman George Roe. Dublin City Archives, manuscript minutes of Dublin City Council,
vol. 11, p. 2 (henceforth, City Council manuscript minutes).   **8** City Council manuscript minutes, vol. 25,

as town clerks and were replaced by William Ford, a solicitor who later acted for O'Connell in his 1844 trial for conspiracy, while Tom Arkins was rewarded with the lucrative post of city sword-bearer[9] – a post which included responsibility for the sale of unredeemed pawnbrokers' pledges, from which he drew a commission.[10]

O'Connell managed to escape opprobrium for this naked political trafficking. When he retired from the mayoralty in November 1842, the city council passed the following resolution: 'That we cannot separate without expressing our unanimous approbation of the impartial manner with which Alderman Daniel O'Connell has discharged the duties of lord mayor of Dublin during the past year.' Two weeks later, the city council unanimously agreed 'That Alderman O'Connell, the late lord mayor, be requested to sit for his Portrait for the purpose of having it placed in the Assembly Room.'[11] A portrait committee was set up to give effect to this resolution, consisting of three Catholics and three Protestant members of the city council, including the new lord mayor, George Roe. Three proposals were submitted to the city council for consideration, from James J. Stephens, Robert Lucius West and Joseph Patrick Haverty, whose portrait of the Liberator in the guise of an Irish chieftain was well-known from a contemporary engraving.[12] No decision was made, and the matter was allowed to lapse.[13]

When the city council proved to be tardy in commissioning an image of O'Connell as lord mayor, the artist William Henry Holbrooke moved to fill the gap, by producing a lithograph. This had the endorsement of the sitter, giving it a quasi-official status, since it bore O'Connell's signature along with his crest, and the legend: 'The First Catholic who attained that Office after an interval of One hundred & 50 years'. Not surprisingly, Holbrooke employed the traditional emblems of mayoralty as a means of emphasizing O'Connell's

---

pp 53–6. Although the mayoralty compact was informal it was respected and enforced at least until 1864, when it was challenged by A.M. Sullivan, who was then a member of the city council. Because it was an unofficial arrangement, there is no documentation relating to it from O'Connell's day, and the description quoted above is taken from an account of the practice, given by Sullivan to the city council in 1864. **9** City Council manuscript minutes, vol. 11, pp 94, 104–5; also Mary Clark and Gráinne Doran, *Serving the city: the Dublin city managers and town clerks* (Dublin, 1996), pp 28–9. **10** The sword bearer's right to this commission was confirmed by Section 208 of the 1840 Municipal Corporations Reform (Ireland) Act. **11** City Council manuscript minutes, vol. 11, pp 258, 279. **12** National Gallery of Ireland, cat. ref. 10,000. The portrait was engraved by W. Ward. See also Fergus O'Ferrall, 'Daniel O'Connell, the Liberator, 1775–1847: changing images' in Brian P. Kennedy and Raymond Gillespie (eds), *Ireland: art into history* (Dublin, 1994), pp 91–102 (henceforth, O'Ferrall, 'O'Connell: changing images'). **13** Ibid., vol. 11, pp 283, 294; vol. 12, p. 2.

achievement. He is depicted wearing official robes, along with the lord mayor's great chain (a gift to Dublin from William of Orange) and the chief magistrate's chain (worn by the lord mayor in his capacity as president of the court of conscience, a forum for the settlement of small debts). O'Connell is seated in the very chair that had been featured in portraits of lord mayors How, French and Cooke during the 1730s and 1740s. The city sword and mace are notable omissions, with their connotations of subservience to the crown; although he was personally devoted to Queen Victoria, O'Connell considered himself to be the equal of any crowned head. His position, face on to the viewer as in pictures of enthroned monarchs, rather than seated to one side as was usual in mayoral portraits, gives a sense of openness and frankness to O'Connell's image, while reinforcing his quasi-royal status. The Liberator's prestige was reinforced by his choice of residence and mode of transport as lord mayor, preferring his own house in Merrion Square and his triumphal chariot to the Mansion House and mayoral coach, which had been sullenly surrendered in a dilapidated state by the outgoing Dublin City Assembly.

O'Connell remained a member of Dublin City Council to the end of his life and continued to enjoy the confidence of his fellow-councillors. When he was imprisoned in 1844 on a charge of conspiracy, the city council prepared an address of support, along with petitions to the queen and to parliament, seeking his liberation. When the House of Lords quashed his conviction, the council prepared an address of congratulation for presentation outside the prison gates on O'Connell's release.[14] On receiving news of O'Connell's death at Genoa in May 1847 on his way to Rome, the city council unanimously agreed to adjourn for three weeks as a mark of respect: the minutes of this meeting are written on black-edged paper.[15] This grief persisted: as late as the following November, the city council unanimously decided 'to pay a marked and enduring compliment to the memory of the great emancipator of our fellow-countrymen, by placing a full-length portrait of the successful champion of the glorious principles of civil and religious liberty in this hall.'[16] A sum of 150 guineas was voted for the purpose, and a committee of seven members was established 'to procure the painting of a portrait of the late Daniel O'Connell MP dressed in his robes as lord mayor, by an Irish artist'. Once again, the proposal did not proceed beyond the establishment of this portrait committee.

---

14 City Council manuscript minutes, vol. 13, pp 33–40, 94–5.   15 Ibid., vol. 14, p. 67.   16 City Council manuscript minutes, vol. 14, p. 123.

II

The transformation of Dublin civic politics wrought by O'Connell continued after his death. The orderly and peaceful inclusion of middle-class Catholics in the civic franchise allowed for the gradual transfer of real power to Dublin City Council. Under the Dublin Improvement Act, 1849, two unelected bodies, the Wide Streets Commission and the Paving Board were abolished, and their responsibilities for the planning and paving of new streets were transferred to the municipality, along with their property. The City Assembly House was now perceived to be too small to house an enlarged municipality and in 1851 the city council purchased the neo-classical Royal Exchange as the city hall. The exchange's coffee room, with exquisite eighteenth-century plasterwork by Charles Thorp, now became the council chamber, with a minimum of adaptation. However, new furniture was required for the chamber, and this afforded an opportunity for the city council to express its identity. A superb ceremonial chair was commissioned for the lord mayor, featuring symbols of Irish nationalism entwined with established emblems of the Dublin mayoralty.[17] The chair is surmounted by the lord mayor's official coat of arms, adorned with a garland of shamrocks instead of a scroll and flanked by two pillars, each one festooned with shamrocks and topped with a Grecian urn surmounted by the cap of maintenance.[18] Two Irish harps adorn the front of the chair, each decorated with shamrocks, while the arms are formed by two magnificent carved Irish wolfhounds, representing Bran and Sceolán, the hunting dogs of the legendary giant Fionn Mac Cumhal. The size and scale of the chair indicate that its occupant was a personage of immense stature and great importance, reflecting the status conferred on the office by O'Connell.[19] Nationalist symbolism was extended into brass railings supplied for the council chamber, which were lavishly decorated with shamrocks. The lord mayor's chair was an ambitious attempt to harness existing nationalist iconography to the Dublin mayoralty, which until then was wholly reliant upon a symbolism expressive of the city's dependence upon the crown.

---

17 The lord mayor's chair was carved in Irish oak by J. Kerr and Co., cabinetmakers, 42–43 Stafford Street, at a cost of £25 10*s*. and was inspired by a design from the noted furniture-maker Arthur Jones.   **18** The cap of maintenance (from the French, *chapeau de maintenance*) was carried in front of the lord mayor during public processions. For a discussion of its origins and significance, see pp 61 and 68.   **19** The lord mayor's chair is 76 inches high by 32 inches wide and the seat is 32 inches deep, while the back of the seat is 51 inches in height.

In purchasing the Royal Exchange, Dublin City Council also acquired a series of portrait sculptures, including a statue of O'Connell by John Hogan, displayed in the circular entrance hall, or rotunda. This had been commissioned by the Repeal Association in 1843, at the height of O'Connell's series of monster meetings which, it was confidently expected, would culminate in repeal of the union.[20] The statue is on a majestic scale, being twelve feet high, and shows O'Connell in his role as orator, with his right hand raised in an emphatic gesture. However, the statue was not completed until 1845, two years after all hope of repeal had vanished with the cancellation of the monster meeting at Clontarf. When Dublin City Council acquired the statue six years later it had become a monument to a great man who had failed to achieve his final goal. But it could also be seen as a symbol of hope for the future, and the eventual achievement of repeal. This interpretation was reinforced in 1854, when the municipal franchise was extended to include owners of property with a rateable valuation of £4, who were now eligible to vote in local elections.[21] In practice, this meant the enfranchisement of an increased number of Catholics which in turn led to the expansion of constitutional nationalism and to a reappraisal of the historic role of O'Connell in developing this movement.

III

In 1862, a project to raise a national monument to O'Connell was instigated by John Gray, a member of Dublin City Council and an advocate of constitutional nationalism, a cause that he advanced as proprietor and editor of the *Freeman's Journal*.[22] The city council quickly declared its support for Gray's new proposal and allocated a site at the end of Sackville Street for the O'Connell monument, which was 'about to be erected by the Irish Nation and the Catholics of the World.'[23] When John Henry Foley was commissioned in 1866 to design the monument, the city council decided that the time had come to give increased importance and visibility to Hogan's statue of O'Connell in City Hall and moved it to the centre of the rotunda, displacing

---

20 F.E. Dixon, 'Dublin portrait statues', *Dublin Historical Record,* 31:2 (1978), 60–9; John Turpin, 'John Hogan in Dublin', *Dublin Historical Record,* 34:1 (1980), 2–14.   **21** 17 & 18 Vict., c. 103, enacted on 10 August 1854.   **22** Paula Murphy, 'The politics of the street monument' in *Irish Arts Review* (Yearbook, 1994), pp 202–8; and 'John Henry Foley's O'Connell monument' in *Irish Arts Review* (Yearbook, 1995), pp 155–6.   **23** City Council manuscript minutes, vol. 23, p. 121.

a bronze statue of George III by Jan van Nost. O'Connell's superiority to the ousted royal was affirmed when the sculptor James Cahill was commissioned to prepare a square pedestal for the statue in polished Dalkey granite, to be 9 feet 6 inches high.[24] An inscription recording the birth, death and burial of O'Connell was carved on the pedestal in four languages, one on each side, in English; in Irish, which O'Connell spoke in his youth; in French, the language of his schooldays in St Omer; and in Latin, the universal language of the Catholic Church.[25] The statue had been removed to its new and dominant position within City Hall by July 1864, just one month before the lord mayor of Dublin, Peter Paul McSwiney, laid the foundation stone for the O'Connell monument in Sackville Street.[26]

To mark the twentieth anniversary of the Liberator's death in 1867, the city council carried out yet another review of his statue in City Hall.[27] The statue was still invisible from the street, and at best it was in a semi-public position. The council now instructed James Cahill to move the statue outside, where it was placed on its plinth of Dalkey granite at the top of the steps leading to the entrance of the building. This re-positioning of the O'Connell statue was seen by the council as the culmination of a two-year project to re-build the balustrade and entrance to the City Hall, to a design by architect Thomas Turner.[28] However, the removal of the statue caused immediate controversy on architectural grounds, which was heightened by concern for its preservation from the elements. The *Irish Builder* thundered 'We cannot call to mind an example of a barbarism more incongruous than … placing this statue in a position so utterly opposed to all ideas of art.'[29] The lord mayor, William Lane Joynt, was concerned for the physical welfare of the marble statue, and sought the expert opinion of George F. Mulvany, who was both director and founder of the National Gallery of Ireland. Mulvany was gratified that this figure of 'the great Irish tribune' was now for the first time 'in a suitable position of elevated dignity and publicity' which did justice to 'this truly heroic work'. Its new location in front of City Hall, 'one of our many architectural monuments

24 Ibid., vol. 25, p. 74. Cahill was paid £140 sterling for supplying the pedestal and moving the statue to its new location.   **25** The inscription in English reads: 'O'Connell. Born at Carhan, County of Kerry, on the 6th day of August, AD 1775. Died in the city of Genoa, on the 15th day of May, AD 1847. Entombed in the cemetery of Glasnevin, near Dublin, on the 5th day of August, of said year.' The inscription in each of the other three languages is a translation of the English text, the Irish version being especially badly translated.   **26** City Council manuscript minutes, vol. 25, pp 161, 231.   **27** City Council manuscript minutes, vol. 27, pp 420–2, 518.   **28** James A. Culliton, *The City Hall*. Eason's Irish Heritage Series, 34 (Dublin, 1982), pp 21–2.   **29** Quoted in Culliton, op. cit., p. 22.

16 Collage of photographs of former lord mayors, with Daniel O'Connell at the centre, prepared in 1867: reproduced courtesy of Dublin City Library and Archive.

of a past century', was appropriate for 'a man who pre-eminently drew great inspirations from the past [but] based his action on the present'.[30]

Mulvany's report was sufficient to keep the statue in its new location for the time being, but public dissatisfaction continued. In 1869 the city council called for a second opinion from a quartet of experts: the sculptors Joseph Kirk and Thomas Farrell, who had previously advised on re-positioning of the statue within City Hall; the city architect John Stirling Butler; and the city marshal Michael Angelo Hayes, an artist by profession. These four experts disagreed with Mulvany concerning the new position of the O'Connell statue in front of City Hall, describing it as 'injudicious in an architectural and artistic point of view'. They also expressed concern for its long-term preservation since 'the arm is fastened by an iron dowel and will inevitably exfoliate and burst the joint, and the rust from it will be likely to permanently stain the statue'. They advocated returning it indoors to the rotunda, placing it on a lower pedestal, and locating it at the foot of the south staircase.[31] These recommendations were now carried out by the city council, just before O'Connell's mortal remains were exhumed and laid to rest under George Petrie's round tower at Glasnevin, in May 1869.[32] The lord mayor, Sir William Carroll, and the city councillors attended the Glasnevin ceremony in their official robes as a gesture of support, unperturbed by their recent demotion of the O'Connell statue, and satisfied that they had acted correctly on the advice of leading experts.[33] The plinth of Dalkey granite, originally provided to give additional grandeur to the statue, remained outside the entrance to City Hall. It is there to this day as an empty but eloquent testimonial to Dublin City Council's unsuccessful attempt to express the heroic stature of the man who had been the city's first democratically elected lord mayor.

The removal of O'Connell's statue to the front steps of City Hall was not the only project undertaken by the city council to mark the 20th anniversary of the Liberator's death. An ambitious collage of photographs of former lord mayors of Dublin was assembled in the form of a family tree, with O'Connell at the centre, symbolizing his position as the originator of the modern mayoralty (fig. 16). This collage adorned the frontispiece of a volume listing property owned by the municipality, which was prepared in 1867 by the law agent, Francis Morgan.[34] The photographs were supplied for inclusion in the

---

30 City Council manuscript minutes, vol. 28, pp 36–7.   **31** City Council manuscript minutes, vol. 30, pp 3–5.   **32** Ibid., vol. 30, p. 143.   **33** Ibid., vol. 30, pp 180–1.   **34** Dublin City Archives, 'Morgan's Rental', dated 1867.

17 Portrait of Daniel O'Connell by Stephen Catterson Smith the elder (1806–72);
note the ornate frame by Thomas Cranfield: reproduced courtesy of
Dublin City Library and Archive.

collage by former lord mayors, or by their families if they were deceased, and they form a gallery unique in Ireland of early civic images produced by this then-recent invention.

IV

In 1870, Councillor John P. Norwood launched a successful attempt to revive the long-standing proposal to obtain a portrait of Daniel O'Connell for display in the council chamber. Two nationalist members of the city council, A.M. Sullivan and Peter Paul McSwiney, assisted him in this enterprise. They first attempted, but without success, to acquire 'an exceedingly fine painting of O'Connell' that belonged to the National Bank and had been removed to its head office in London.[35] Ironically, this was the iconic portrait by Haverty, whose submission to paint the Liberator from the life as lord mayor had not been accepted in 1842. Meanwhile, Norwood had discovered that Stephen Catterson Smith the elder was already working on a posthumous portrait of O'Connell. Catterson Smith had executed several portraits of the Liberator during the latter's lifetime, beginning with a rather poor likeness carried out in 1825, which was nevertheless engraved and published by Robins of London.[36] A second engraved portrait, dated 1830, was distributed as a free insert in *Carpenter's Political Letter*.[37] Catterson Smith had also painted the Liberator for Waterford City Council and now, in the twilight of his career, he had returned to this theme. Dublin City Council decided to purchase this portrait from Catterson Smith and to obtain a frame for it from Thomas Cranfield.[38] The portrait was delivered in 1871 and it was duly hung in the council chamber.

It had taken Dublin City Council thirty years to obtain its planned portrait of Daniel O'Connell, but the final result was disappointing. Thomas Davis, in his essay 'Hints for Irish historical painting', had identified 'The Corporation Speech' as a suitable theme for an O'Connellite painting, which he hoped to see realized.[39] This theme might have provided an imaginative and dramatic canvas for Catterson Smith, and could have inspired a truly original work. Instead, the artist reproduced the stock image of the Dublin mayoralty, using all the traditional iconography in a conventional way – such was his anxiety for accuracy that he even borrowed the lord mayor's great chain of office (the

35 City Council manuscript minutes, vol. 31, p. 259.   **36** NGI, cat. ref. 10,981. See also O'Ferrall, 'O'Connell: changing images', p. 95.   **37** NGI, cat. ref. 10,977.   **38** City Council manuscript minutes, vol. 31, p. 360.   **39** D.J. O'Donoghue (ed.), *Essays literary and historical by Thomas Davis* (Dundalk, 1914), pp 112–15; also O'Ferrall, 'O'Connell: changing images', p. 97.

collar of SS) from the incumbent lord mayor, Patrick Bulfin.⁴⁰ The new nationalist iconography, developed in 1852 to adorn the lord mayor's chair, was totally ignored by Catterson Smith, while O'Connell's heroic nature is indicated only by his massive girth and by his gaze, which is fixed firmly on the future. Cranfield's frame, which he designed in consultation with Catterson Smith, is equally disappointing, since its series of carved shells and floral garlands relate more to the existing Georgian plasterwork in the council chamber than to any symbolism associated with the Liberator. O'Connell had been reduced to the status of just another lord mayor, with the dangerous elements of his radical vision air-brushed out of history. Catterson Smith's portrait received due regard when the Royal Hibernian Academy (RHA) asked the city council for permission to include it in its exhibition of 1872. The RHA president, Colles Watkins, described the O'Connell portrait as 'a most attractive picture' and assured the council that 'every care will be taken of it'.⁴¹ Satisfied with these assurances and with this trite accolade, the city council duly agreed to lend the portrait to the Academy.

V

For thirty years, the city council had struggled to give artistic expression to the transformation which Daniel O'Connell had wrought on the Dublin mayoralty. Time and again, the council had retreated from the contest, finding itself unequal to the challenge. On other occasions, it had engaged its energies in a protracted repositioning of an existing statue of the Liberator, convinced that by so doing it was contributing significantly to the enhancement of his reputation and posthumous influence. By purchasing a conventional portrait of O'Connell, which repeated the traditional mayoral iconography without developing it in any way, the city council had finally admitted defeat, and abandoned its search for a challenging image of its founding figure. This challenge was taken up by the O'Connell monument committee, which brought John Henry Foley's unfinished work to completion and its ultimate unveiling in 1882. It is this monument which provides the defining image of O'Connell as he guards the entrance to Dublin's premier street, re-named in his honour by a city council which had finally learned to cherish his memory.

---

40 City Council manuscript minutes, vol. 32, p. 136. Lord Mayor Bulfin died during his term of office, and Dublin City Council immediately voted to commission his portrait as a posthumous memorial. The proposal got no further than the formation of a committee and the portrait was never realized. City Council manuscript minutes, vol. 32, pp 163–4.   **41** City Council manuscript minutes, vol. 32, p. 506.

'A rather mild sort of rebel': J.P. Nannetti

CIARÁN WALLACE

J.P. Nannetti appeared on the Dublin political scene at the end of the nineteenth century, his successful public career lasted until the First World War. Beginning as a young Fenian and labour activist, he went on to become the workers' lord mayor of Dublin and a prosperous MP for the Irish Parliamentary Party (IPP). His career illustrates the IPP's broad appeal, but it also suggests the mercenary nature of the politician. Nannetti's former supporters in the ranks of radical labour loudly condemned his financial success. Was J.P. Nannetti truly Dublin's first labour lord mayor, was he an example of the IPP's ability to absorb and employ its opponents or was he simply a politician with an eye to the main chance?[1]

The first decade of the twentieth century in Ireland can appear tranquil when compared to the tumultuous years from 1912 to 1922, yet important political and social changes were underway. The development of organized labour, the evolving role of women and the emergence of Sinn Féin all had a profound effect on politics in Dublin. In 1898, parliament radically enhanced the significance of local government in Ireland through the Local Government (Ireland) Act. A far wider electoral mandate, accompanied by increased powers and responsibilities, led to greater public and press interest in Dublin City Hall. The new legislation lowered the qualification threshold for tenants, women and workers; as a result the municipal electoral roll increased almost fourfold.[2] Standing for election also became far easier, admitting a new type of working-class candidate into the political arena. The IPP, as the permanent majority on the municipal council, expected to harness the diverse strands of political energy in the city. At the first reformed local elections in January 1899, however, the new political force of labour posed a serious challenge. Temporarily weakened by the Parnellite split of the 1890s, the IPP struggled to regroup, but the world was changing and the old party was no longer the sole prophet of Ireland's future. Nannetti's shifting allegiance, and the response

---

1 This article is based on original research funded by the Irish Research Council for the Humanities and Social Sciences.   2 Ciarán Wallace, 'Local politics and government in Dublin city and suburbs, 1898–1914' (PhD, TCD, 2010). The electorate in Nannetti's Rotunda Ward increased by 237%, while eligible voter figures in Inns Quay and Trinity Wards increased by over 520%.

which it evoked, show the fluid political climate during this period; they also point to a weakness at the heart of established nationalism.

I

Joseph Patrick Nannetti was born in Dublin in 1851 to Joseph Nannetti, an Italian immigrant sculptor and modeller, at 6 Great Brunswick (now Pearse) Street. He was educated at the Convent of Mercy on Baggot Street, and with the Christian Brothers on North Richmond Street. A printer by trade, Nannetti joined the Liverpool Typographical Society trade union during a period spent working on Merseyside; he also helped to found the city's first Home Rule Society.[3] Back in Dublin by 1873, Nannetti married Mary Egan, daughter of a railway engineer, and raised a family. His labour activism continued. He was a founding member of the Dublin Trades Council (DTC), serving as its secretary and president. He became a foreman printer with the leading nationalist newspaper, the *Freeman's Journal*, and still found time to write for the *Labour Gazette* and the *Evening Mail*.[4] Even before he stood for local election, Nannetti had been involved in low level political activity. He was a committee member of the United Irishmen's Centennial Association, a nationalist organization which worked to promote events commemorating the rebellion of 1798.

Interestingly, J.P. Nannetti also had a brief fictionalized existence. In Joyce's *Ulysses*, Leopold Bloom calls to the office of the *Freeman's Journal*, where he meets Nannetti to negotiate the placing of an advertisement. The two men represent starkly different possibilities for immigrants to Dublin, Bloom as a Jew who struggles to establish his Irish identity, and Nannetti as an Italian who is fully assimilated into the heart of the nationalist establishment.

At the time of Nannetti's first election in 1898, the family lived at Hardwick Street, in the Rotunda Ward that J.P. represented. Over the following years the family had a succession of homes, each slightly more respectable than the last.[5] Elected on the old franchise, Nannetti was supported by the skilled craftsmen of the DTC. In 1899, in the first reformed local elections, workers' candidates

3 James McConnel, 'Fenians at Westminster: the Edwardian Irish Parliamentary Party and the legacy of the New Departure', *Irish Historical Studies*, 34:133 (May 2004), 42–6.   4 Marie Coleman, 'Nannetti, Joseph Patrick ('J.P.')', *Dictionary of Irish biography*, vol. 7 (Cambridge, 2009).   5 From Juverna Terrace on the Finglas Road they went to St Anne's Terrace, Clontarf, which belonged to Mary Nannetti, and finally to 47 Whitworth Road, Drumcondra.

performed well, taking nine of the sixty seats on the council. The Labour Electoral Association (LEA), a broad campaigning alliance which was newer and more radical than the DTC, could take much of the credit for the success. J.P. Nannetti was frequently counted as the tenth member of this team of workers' representatives. This new political force of organized labour caused much consternation among newspaper editors and the authorities in Dublin Castle. In police reports detailing the composition of the municipal council, labour was divided into subcategories of nationalist, extremist and unionist; officialdom, it seems, could only conceive of labour in terms of green or orange.[6] The *Irish Times* reproduced articles from the London papers; *The Times* described the labour candidates as 'without exception, extreme Nationalists, not to say Fenians … the city council of Dublin, [has] passed into the hands of revolutionaries, avowed or unavowed'.[7] *The Globe* was no less alarmist, calling Dublin's new labour councillors 'Jacobins'.[8]

There was some substance to these allegations. Nannetti claimed to have been a member of the secret Irish Republican Brotherhood (IRB) since 1867, and to have been trusted in the inner ranks of that organization.[9] This might account for his determination to campaign under both nationalist and labour banners during his political career. From the 1870s, advanced nationalism had a policy of contesting elections for any and all electoral offices on whatever boards, councils and authorities became available.[10] At a time of increasing democratization in Ireland, the growing power of boards of Poor Law Guardians, rural and urban district councils and county councils provided fertile ground for such political infiltration.[11] Nannetti's early involvement with the DTC was possibly also an element of this strategy, gaining control of part of the labour movement.

II

As a labour councillor, Nannetti was immediately involved in an embarrassing U-turn on the subject of lord mayors sitting for a second term. In the local election campaign, labour candidates had condemned this practice, not for

6 Dublin Metropolitan Police District. 'Numerical return of results of County Borough and Urban District Council Elections January 1899. Members of previous body.' Colonial Office CO 904 papers, Microfilm 111, Box no. 184 pp 79, 82 & 83.   7 *Irish Times*, 20 Jan. 1899.   8 'Jacobin' was a pejorative term for radical left-wing revolutionaries.   9 McConnel, 'Fenians at Westminster', p. 46.   10 William Leo Feingold, 'The Irish Boards of Poor Law Guardians, 1872–86: a revolution in local government' (PhD, University of Chicago, 1974), p. 109.   11 LEA candidate John Clancy, elected with J.P. Nannetti in 1899,

fear of an accumulation of power but for the more practical reason that a new mayor required an inauguration parade and formal reception. The employment that this provided to the craftsmen of the city was lost in the case of a two-term mayor who spent nothing inaugurating a second year in office. Despite their campaign promises, labour decided to support the sitting lord mayor, Daniel Tallon, in his bid for a second term in 1899. As a prosperous vintner and influential newspaper director, Tallon was the quintessential Irish Parliamentary Party nationalist. To jeers and laughter from fellow councillors, the workers' representatives explained that as no labour candidate was likely to attract enough support to take the Mansion House, the incumbent nationalist was the 'least worst option'. It was an inauspicious beginning.

Initially, Nannetti upheld labour policies. He tried to introduce a motion favouring contractors who paid union wage rates.[12] His nationalist credentials were stronger however; he was among the minority of councillors opposed to presenting an official address of welcome to Queen Victoria on her visit in 1900.[13] He promoted the Irish language and supported the nomination of a controversial nationalist as an honorary freeman of the city.[14]

In January 1899, Nannetti retained his council seat when an electoral surge produced the team of ten labour councillors. A well-run campaign, and greater consciousness of working-class strength, contributed to this success. The LEA was quick to seize the opportunity afforded by the Parnellite split that had damaged the IPP's reputation and reduced its electoral appeal. The Irish Party was soon reunited, however, while labour struggled to maintain a distinctive identity. Nationalism swamped the movement inside and outside the council chamber.

At every election labour candidates had to recite the nationalist mantra calling for home rule, a Catholic University and freedom for political prisoners, while their IPP opponents claimed to represent the working man. This blurred the distinction between the two and labour was at a low ebb until 1905 when new and more radical members won seats.[15] From 1905 until 1913, labour councillors attacked the nationalist-dominated council's record on housing and social welfare. They criticized the IPP as a self-serving party of

---

was also a member of the IRB. Leon Ó'Broin, *Revolutionary underground. The story of the Irish Republican Brotherhood, 1858–1924* (Dublin, 1976), p. 46.   **12** Municipal council minutes [hereafter MC], 20 Nov. 1899, Item 535. His motion was ruled out of order.   **13** MC, 14 Mar. 1900, Item 248.   **14** MC, 30 Oct. 1901, Item 603. P.A. McHugh MP received the honour for his 'protest against the infamous system of jury packing'.   **15** Councillors Michael Lord and William Partridge brought fresh zeal to Labour's cause on the municipal council.

slum landlords and publicans. In particular they condemned the twin evils of
two-term mayors and double-jobbing, where the mayor would also serve as a
member of parliament. J.P. Nannetti was not a model workers' representative
in either regard. In 1900 he became the IPP MP for Dublin's College Green
Division, holding the seat until his death in 1915. This 'dual mandate' placed
Nannetti at the forefront of Dublin nationalism. His prominence in nationalist
circles also brought lucrative business opportunities; Nannetti the humble
tradesman became a trustee of the Royal Liver Assurance Company.

While his labour credentials may have weakened at home, Nannetti
remained a committed nationalist. His opposition to Queen Victoria's visit in
1900 placed him on the more radical end of the nationalist political spectrum.
In Westminster his questions and comments displayed a mixture of nationalist
and labour politics. He supported workers' causes when, for example, he
complained of soldiers being appointed as telegraph operators, resulting in the
loss of employment for civilians. He argued with the chief secretary for Ireland
over the exclusion of Gaelic games from the Phoenix Park, boldly claiming the
park's extensive territory for the citizens of Dublin. He raised workers'
concerns, promoted the cause of trade unionism and measures for relieving the
plight of the poor. By 1908 however, when forced to defend his city council
seat, a patronizing tone was evident in his printed address to voters. He
expressed satisfaction that 'the poor and lowly have benefited by my exertions'.
Referring to his work with the Distress Committee, a body set up in times of
high unemployment in the city, he spoke of helping 'the respectable poor'.[16]
The language may have been that of his generation and social class, but it was
not that of the younger radicals in the labour movement.

III

In January 1906 Nannetti was elected as lord mayor, with the support of
prominent IPP councillors and against the opposition of labour members.
With complete control of the municipal council the IPP could promote its
own men, and ensure their financial prosperity through the allocation of the
£3,000 annual salary that came with the Mansion House. During his two
mayoral terms, Joe Nannetti antagonized labour councillors on almost every

---

16 'To the burgesses of the Rotunda Ward. An address by J.P. Nannetti, lord mayor' in *Two cards and a letter
soliciting support for his re-election in the Rotunda ward, municipal election, Jan. 15th, 1908*, National Library
of Ireland (NLI), call number: LOP 116.

front. His dual mandate and double term in office flew in the face of labour
policy. His critics alleged that he profited from the high profile which his
position gave him, and that he only paid lip-service to the cause of labour.
Socialist James Connolly, a radical labour activist who had failed to win a seat
on the council in 1902 and 1903, described Nannetti as a 'nationalist-labour
poseur'. In a satirical response to his elevation to the mayoralty, the *Lepracaun
Cartoon Monthly* showed Nannetti as the infant of the IPP, being bottle-fed on
the mayor's large salary (fig. 19). In 1908 Nannetti defended his council seat
against the labour candidate Michael O'Flanagan. His opponents accused him
of using his influence at the *Freeman's Journal* to block coverage of
O'Flanagan's campaign and alleged that even Nannetti's own printers' union
did not support his candidacy. Gone were the days of 1899 when he was
counted among the labour team in City Hall.

Nannetti was criticized by commentators for milking the system. His
involvement with the Royal Liver Assurance Company, and his accumulation
of a lucrative two years-worth of salary as lord mayor added to his critics'

"THE TRIUMPH OF LABOUR."

19 Cartoon showing J.P. Nannetti as an infant being bottle-fed on the mayor's large salary, from *Lepracaun Cartoon Monthly*, February 1906: reproduced courtesy of the Board of Trinity College Dublin.

complaints. Although it could be argued in his favour that Nannetti won both parliamentary elections that he fought, it would appear that Irish political tribalism played an important role in his success. His opponent in each case was a unionist and simple electoral arithmetic meant that a nationalist was sure to take the seat.

In 1905 Sinn Féin entered City Hall on a platform of municipal reform. The party played a significant role on the municipal council up to 1912. Although a tiny minority, they enjoyed increasing electoral success, growing in confidence during Nannetti's tenure as lord mayor. Alongside their Irish-Ireland policies, the party promoted all the civic virtues familiar to municipal reformers in Britain and the US. City government had grown immeasurably over the preceding decades; patronage and jobbery were rife. Given that the IPP was heavily involved in the grocer-vintner and pub trades, it was significant that Sinn Féin promoted teetotalism, and attacked the publicans' bloc on the council whenever possible.[17] The greatest threat that Sinn Féin posed to the IPP, however, was their claim to be the true representatives of nationalism. This new 'upstart' party had far more radical policies on the Irish language, Irish industry and Gaelic games. Even at this early stage, Sinn Féin councillors claimed that representation at Westminster was worse than useless; this was a direct attack on a major plank in the IPP's political strategy.

The IPP still claimed to offer a big political tent sheltering the broad range of nationalists; workers and employers, women, rural and urban voters, slum-dwellers and landlords. From 1905 the party began to feel the sting of criticism coming from Sinn Féin and the reinvigorated labour representatives. In September 1907 the IPP leader John Redmond held an important meeting at the Round Room of the Mansion House, chaired by Lord Mayor Nannetti. This proved to be a significant occasion. Admission was by ticket only and the hall was crowded with party supporters. Nannetti, Redmond and others made speeches praising the party and its role in promoting the cause of home rule. Hecklers within the hall cried that the meeting was 'packed', that any dissenting voice had been kept out. Outside on Dawson Street, a crowd of around a thousand had failed to gain entry. They listened to highly critical speeches from Alderman Tom Kelly and other Sinn Féin representatives. Establishment nationalism was inside the hall while radical nationalism stood outside in the rain – the tent was clearly not big enough.

It is noteworthy that the IPP felt the need to defend its reputation in Dublin, the political heart of nationalism. The Round Room incident put the party's claim to be the true representatives of nationalism under great strain, as the radical element was visibly – and very audibly – excluded from the meeting. Slowly, sections of the public were coming to the realization that Ireland, and Irish nationalism, was more than merely the IPP. The heckler protesting inside the Round Room symbolized a shift in public understanding – the IPP was no longer the will of the Irish people in physical form, it was just another political party.

Nannetti presided over a second low moment for the IPP in 1907, when Richard 'Boss' Croker, the former leader of the disgraced Tammany regime in New York, arrived in Dublin and the IPP-controlled municipal council made him an honorary freeman of the city. Croker was a major donor to the IPP

---

17 Wallace, 'Local politics and government'. During the period 1899–1914 between 43% and 60% of nationalist councillors were involved in this sector. Occupational profile tables, pp 309–10 and 326.

Ciarán Wallace

and the parliamentary party acknowledged his aid through its control of the
municipal council, under the chairmanship of J.P. Nannetti.[18] It is startling to
think that anyone associated with Tammany, an international by-word for
municipal corruption, would be so honoured, but Croker was an exceptional
character. His colourful, and occasionally violent, career in politics had left
him a wealthy man with a prestigious address outside Dublin and a winning
racehorse that brought sporting glory to Ireland. Labour, Sinn Féin and
unionist councillors voted against the honour; the proposition merely confirmed
their low opinion of the complacent and corrupt establishment party, but the
permanent IPP majority voted it through. Only fifteen of the eighty councillors turned up when Lord Mayor Nannetti presided over the ceremonial
presentation to Croker.[19]

Despite this inglorious moment, Nannetti had not lost sight of his radical
roots. A major dispute arose between the city council and Dublin Castle; it
came to a head during his term as lord mayor. The Local Government Board
for Ireland (LGB) commissioned an annual audit of every council's finances.
In 1904 the municipal council objected strongly to criticism in the audit
report for the preceding year. The auditor, James W. Drury, had departed from
his brief to condemn what he saw as deplorable municipal administration.

The row escalated until, in March 1906, the council resolved that 'in view
of the continued violent and unjustifiable attacks on the City's credit and the
administration' they would refuse to submit any more accounts to Drury. The
LGB reassured the council that no offence was intended. Mr Drury, they
argued, was trying to guard the municipal council against any irregular or
illegal proceedings. Their letter implied that the council was merely being
oversensitive, 'it is scarcely conceivable in a City like Dublin, where municipal
administration is beset by so many difficulties, that the complicated financial
business of the council could be conducted in such a way as to be entirely
outside the pale of legitimate criticism'.[20]

The councillors were not convinced; the books were withheld and the affair
ended up in court. The LGB won the case of *King (Drury) v. the Corporation
of Dublin and the Town Clerk*, but the council lodged an appeal.[21] As lord

<hr>

18 MC, 1 July 1907, Item 404. The citation read that 'in view of [his] unique and distinguished position …
and of his intention to spend the remainder of his days in his native land and to support the Irish Parliamentary
Party in the struggle for Home Rule', he be made an honorary freeman of Dublin. Croker donated £3,000 to
the party in 1899 during Redmond's US tour. Expenses sheet, 20 Nov. 1899 (Redmond Papers, NLI, MS
15,238/10). It is likely that he made further donations.   **19** The municipal council had expanded from 60 to
80 members under the Dublin Boundaries Act, 1900.   **20** MC, 21 May 1906, Item 324.   **21** Feelings ran

mayor, Nannetti ensured that the account books were removed from the city when the auditor came to inspect them; neither the town clerk nor his staff could retrieve them. Eventually, the city found a flaw in Drury's appointment. This proved to be the undoing of the LGB's case, and in October 1907 Drury was replaced as auditor of the city's accounts.[22] Considering that it was his critique rather than his accountancy skills that caused offence, it is interesting to note that Drury was a Presbyterian from Tyrone. Perhaps underlying political or sectarian antipathies contributed to the intensity of the dispute. This small victory for the municipal council was to be a lesson well learned. Such non-cooperation with the Dublin Castle authorities later became a central part of the Revolutionary Dáil's campaign during the War of Independence.[23] Throughout the dispute, Lord Mayor Nannetti was resolute in his protest against Drury and Dublin Castle. Labour supported the cause, as did Sinn Féin. Perhaps the early radical resurfaced in Joe Nannetti, or maybe he felt the need to show the young political pups that the old party could still be militant. It was hard, however, to maintain the high moral ground when Boss Croker was awarded the Freedom of the city.

IV

Nannetti joined the Irish Republican Brotherhood in 1867, when he was 17 years of age. His claim to have been respected in the IRB's inner circles implies that he remained a member for some time. It is possible that the young Joe Nannetti was attracted to the secret and radical world of the Brotherhood, and that this prompted many of his later political decisions. However, it seems that as he grew older and more successful, Nannetti mellowed. In a 1910 article on Irish members of parliament the *Pall Mall Gazette* described him as 'quite a mild sort of rebel now'.[24]

Despite all the hopes and fears, in the years following Nannetti's mayoralty the IPP was not overtaken by labour or Sinn Féin. With the imminent prospect of home rule, the party regained much of its influence and reputation

very high, with one Sinn Féin councillor writing from his sick-bed to support continued resistance. MC, 6 July 1906, Item 421. It was significant that Henry Campbell, town clerk, was named in the court case. During the War of Independence he was forced from office by Sinn Féin councillors over his refusal to take part in similar acts of non-cooperation. **22** MC, 14 Oct. 1907, Item 581. Drury reappeared as auditor of the city's Distress Committee in 1909–10. MC, Reports 1911, Vol. 1. **23** Arthur Mitchell, *Revolutionary government in Ireland: Dáil Éireann, 1919–1922* (Dublin, 1993), passim. **24** McConnel, 'Fenians at Westminster', p. 46.

in municipal politics up to the time of the 1916 Rising. Joseph Nannetti, however, symbolizes the comfortable curse of the Irish Parliamentary Party. In its efforts to hold together a broad nationalist front, the party tried to absorb or placate competing movements such as labour, municipal reform and the campaign for women's votes. Everything else must wait for the advent of home rule. Nannetti was the voice of 'tame' labour. His DTC could claim to represent Dublin workers, but it spoke for an older established body of skilled tradesmen, not for the mass of semi-skilled or unskilled casual workers crowded into Dublin's slums and tenements. Nannetti's hard work brought him political, social and financial success. To the growing body of reformist opposition however, he represented the grasping hand of a party that controlled public life in Dublin, and across much of Ireland. The career of this prosperous parliamentary lord mayor illustrates the widening gap between the IPP and the range of emerging nationalist identities.

'Little' Lorcan Sherlock, 1912–15

LYDIA CARROLL

Lorcan Sherlock was lord mayor of Dublin for three successive terms of office, from 1912 to 1915. His small stature, on which contemporaries seemed to feel obliged to comment frequently, did not prevent him from looming large on the Dublin political scene. The description of him as 'Little Lorcan Sherlock' comes from no less a personage than James Joyce, who wrote in *Ulysses* of 'Hutchinson the lord mayor in Llandudno, and little Lorcan Sherlock doing *locum tenens* for him'.[1] Joseph Hutchinson was lord mayor from 1904–6 (see fig. 6), which suggests that Sherlock was seen as potential mayoral material far in advance of taking up residence in the Mansion House. When he did become lord mayor, some of the comments from his opponents – although we must allow for the exaggeration of political enmity – give some idea of his political style and personality. His Mountjoy electoral ward was described as Tammany Hall, with Sherlock as its Boss Croker or, again referring to his small stature, 'a miniature Boss Croker'.[2]

I

His father, Thomas Sherlock, had also been a councillor in Dublin Corporation, and had written a biography of Charles Stewart Parnell, of whom he was a close friend. Lorcan Sherlock shared his father's belief in home rule; elected for the Nationalist Party in Dublin Corporation, he was a supporter of John Redmond, and a member of the United Irish League. At the time of his election for the Mountjoy ward in 1905, he had a tobacconists and stationers shop in Summerhill.[3] The 1901 census shows that it was classed as a second class house, with four rooms, although the family, Sherlock, his first wife Lily, and two young sons, had a young female domestic servant. When he relinquished the lord mayoralty, he would say that he had entered politics as a working man and a poor man. He was, however, also Secretary of the Irish Cattle Traders' and Stockowners' Association, one of the most powerful lobby

---

1 James Joyce, *Ulysses*, Chapter 10, 'Wandering Rocks'. 2 *Irish Times*, 24 Jan. 1911. 3 *Irish Times*, 15 Aug. 1903.

THE MODERN DICK WHITTINGTON
(COUNCILLOR LORCAN G. SHERLOCK, LL.D.)
THRICE LORD MAYOR OF DUBLIN.

20 Cartoon of Lorcan Sherlock as Dick Whittington. Reproduced courtesy of
Dublin City Library and Archive.

groups in Dublin. He certainly was no shrinking political violet, which was no
bad thing in the political climate of the time. Discussions about home rule
were noisy and often violent affairs, and even the Council Chamber could be
dangerous. In 1910, Sherlock was awarded £50 damages against a fellow
councillor who assaulted him, and who had challenged him to come outside
and choose his own weapons.[4] He was an outstanding orator, one who could
be guaranteed to rouse an audience. For example, at a contentious meeting in
1906 at which a unionist and a nationalist candidate were speaking, it was
reported that 'the appearance of Mr Lorcan Sherlock on the scene added no
element making for peace. Throwing off his coat, he jumped on a chair, and
gesticulating vigorously, began an impassioned address.'[5]

Lorcan Sherlock became swiftly established as a member of Dublin
Corporation after his election in 1905, and during his time as councillor was
chairman of all of the important committees of the corporation, including the
Electricity Supply Committee, which brought the Pigeon House scheme to
fruition. From the time of his election, the three main foci of his interest, and
the causes for which he spoke out frequently, were improved housing for the
Dublin poor, workers' rights, and an increase in industry for Dublin.

4 *Irish Times*, 26 Feb. 1910.   5 *Irish Times*, 5 Jan. 1906.

In the early 1900s, the first two of these were closely interlinked; most of the employment in Dublin was casual and seasonal, in brewing, biscuit making, in transport or on the docks – industries that employed workers during busy seasons, and let them go during slack seasons. A large proportion of Dublin citizens lived an insecure, hand-to-mouth existence, barely able to afford one room in which to live, and that on a meagre diet, or on the verge of starvation. Charles Cameron, the city's medical officer of health, said that 'No inconsiderable number of poor get out of their beds, without knowing when they are to get their breakfast, for the simple reason that they have neither money nor credit. They must starve if they have got nothing which would be taken in pawn'.[6] More than 20,000 families in Dublin lived in one room in tenement houses, and the death rate was exceptionally high, exacerbated by undernourishment, insufficient clothing, and unsanitary living conditions (see fig. 22). This was the Dublin in which Lorcan Sherlock started his political career, and began to make an impact.

II

In 1906, the year after Lorcan Sherlock was first elected to Dublin Corporation, he publicly criticized his colleagues, revealing that a special meeting that had been called to deal with the housing problem had fallen through because not enough members of the corporation had shown up, and pointing out that another special meeting had been called for the following week, at which they would have an opportunity of showing whether there was any seriousness in their efforts to house the poor.[7]

On workers' rights, he had been outspoken as early as 1905, when he gave a vigorous speech in support of a resolution against a lockout in the building trade.[8] A few years later, in 1910, Sherlock was one of the main speakers at the event organized to welcome Jim Larkin on his release from prison. In his speech he described Larkin as 'an honest and honourable man', and said that he had emerged from his trial 'in a manner that very many of the merchant princes in Dublin would not have emerged from … in connection with their own trades and business'.[9] This comment about merchant princes seems

---

6 Charles Cameron, *How the poor live* (Dublin, 1904), p. 3 and *Report of the committee appointed by the Local Government Board for Ireland to inquire into the public health of the city of Dublin*, minutes of evidence, P.P.1900, vol. xxxix, col. 243.   7 *Irish Independent*, 12 Nov. 1906.   8 *Irish Independent*, 17 April 1905.   9 *Freeman's Journal*, 3 Oct. 1910.

somewhat at odds with a statement he had made two years previously in 1908, when he was presented with what was described as 'a substantial purse of sovereigns' by a committee of prominent citizens 'in recognition of his services as a member of the corporation'.[10] This seems a very strange gesture to modern eyes, but it was reported openly and with approval in the press, so it was obviously an acceptable and above-board gesture at the time. In his speech of thanks for the presentation, Sherlock called for industrial revival in Dublin, and said that there must be a radical change in the administration of the city if men of wealth who could push forward industrial enterprises were to be encouraged to enter civic life. It would seem, therefore, that in the years leading up to his election as lord mayor, he was tolerant of, and accepted by, both trade unionists and employers, and had managed to straddle the increasingly acrimonious divide between the two sides.

III

Lorcan G. Sherlock was elected lord mayor in 1912. He was recently married for the second time, his first wife having died in 1906 at the age of 28, while his young son Lorcan had died in 1911 at the age of 10. He was 38 years of age when he became lord mayor, and his second wife Marie was only 27 years of age; they would have been married for little over a year at the time, with a young baby, and probably had not bargained for their mayoralty containing events like those that occurred in 1913.

In 1913, Sherlock's cordial relationships with both labour and employer interests were put to the test. The militancy of trade unions in Dublin had been growing apace, in particular that of the union run by Jim Larkin, the Irish Transport and General Workers' Union (ITGWU). Larkin's weapon of choice was the sympathetic strike, whereby workers in firms not on strike would refuse to handle the goods of any firm where there was a strike. Larkin's main antagonist on the employers' side was William Martin Murphy, the chairman of the Dublin United Tramways Company, owner of the *Irish Independent*, and president of the Dublin Chamber of Commerce. The year 1913 saw an upsurge in industrial activity in Dublin; there were thirty major industrial disputes in the city between January and August of that year. In July, Lorcan Sherlock as lord mayor had taken action to mitigate the situation, and

---

10 *Irish Independent*, 24 July 1908.

21 Portrait of Lord Mayor Lorcan Sherlock by The MacEgan (Darius Joseph MacEgan, 1856–1939): reproduced courtesy of Dublin City Library and Archive.

after much difficult and protracted negotiation, managed to get both sides, the Trades Council for the workers, and the Dublin Chamber of Commerce for the employers, to agree to conciliation talks. William Martin Murphy, who had been unable to attend the meeting of the Chamber of Commerce that agreed to Sherlock's suggestion, was enraged at what he saw as conciliation towards Larkin, and when Larkin brought 200 of his tram workers out on strike on 26 August, the battle that would become known as the Lockout began. Murphy immediately sought and was given the support, not only of the Dublin Metropolitan Police, but also the armed Royal Irish Constabulary. Two meetings of workers, on Saturday 30 August at Beresford Place, and on Sunday 31 August in Sackville (now O'Connell) Street, were baton charged by police. Between 600 and 800 civilians were injured, and two men killed. Many of the injured were simply bystanders, and would later give evidence of indiscriminate violence and drunkenness among the police. As well as the baton charges, on Sunday night the police ransacked flats in the Corporation Street area, where some of the strikers had sought refuge the night before, breaking up furniture and terrorizing the residents.

It was at this point that Lorcan Sherlock, as lord mayor, spoke out.[11] This was a different Sherlock to the one who had flung off his coat and jumped on chairs. He now spoke in more restrained terms, but with palpable anger, and he spoke as the official leader of the city, aware that he was the linchpin between the two opposing forces of industry. He began by saying that he was aware of his position as one of enormous responsibility, in which he could be called on to act as peacemaker, and that it would be foolish to give any indication of his personal views.

> At the same time, when over 600 of my fellow citizens have had to be treated in hospital as the outcome of collisions between the police and themselves, I conceive it to be my duty to immediately demand from those in charge … a public enquiry at once, not only into the conduct of the police in the city during the past few days but also into the instructions given to them by the persons responsible – the Executive for the time being.

He went on to say that

11 *Dublin Evening Mail*, 1 Sept. 1913.

... in the event of the authorities refusing to hold the inquiry ... then, as lord mayor of this city, I will hold an inquiry myself in the most public manner, and I will invite by public communication those of my fellow-citizens who have evidence to give to come to such inquiry and tender their evidence.[12]

On 4 September, he again called for a truce between the unions and employers, saying 'Surely nothing should be left undone to save Dublin from the horrors of a terrible war!'[13]

In fact, the dispute worsened, as more employers supported Murphy and locked out any ITGWU supporters in their employ. Life for the poor of Dublin had been hard before the Lockout, now it became almost unbearable; they had always been hungry, now they were starving – in fact William Martin Murphy had helpfully pointed out even before the strike began that his shareholders would continue to eat three meals a day, unlike workers who went on strike.[14] Within weeks, 400 firms had joined the Lockout, with 15,000 union workers locked out, and many thousand more non-union workers laid off. The labouring poor of Dublin found themselves reliant on handouts of bread and food parcels simply to stay alive.

Throughout the Lockout, Lorcan Sherlock made continuous efforts to bring both sides together. The old frictions of class and religious warfare were re-ignited by the dispute. Faith, as well as workers' rights and employers' rights, fought for supremacy. It is almost certain that Sherlock acted in close co-operation with the Catholic archbishop of Dublin, William Walsh, who took a behind-the-scenes but active interest in the situation. Strategically placed clergy kept him informed of developments, including Fr Curran, who told the archbishop that public opinion was against the strikers, with the exception of the lord mayor and a few others.[15]

However, while Sherlock remained active in trying to settle the dispute, and his sympathy remained with the workers, it did not remain with Jim Larkin; their formerly cordial relationship deteriorated into acrimony. The feeling was mutual, with Larkin denouncing Sherlock and his supporters as, among other things, 'job-seekers and twisters'.[16] On Sherlock's part, his changed attitude to Larkin probably arose through a mixture of political expediency and

---

12 *Irish Times*, 2 Sept. 1913.   13 *Irish Times*, 4 Sept. 1913.   14 Padraig Yeates, *Lockout: Dublin 1913* (Dublin, 2000), p. 7.   15 Fr Curran to Dr Walsh, 18 Sept. 1913, Dublin Diocesan Archives.   16 *Irish Independent*, 8 Jan. 1914.

ideological differences. He had obviously become disillusioned with the dogma expounded by Larkin; in a letter to Archbishop Walsh, published in the *Freeman's Journal* on 17 January 1914, Sherlock congratulated the archbishop on having

> Struck a deadly blow against the insidious enemy of Socialism, and [for having] made it abundantly clear that there is no room for such views in Ireland's capital, once the people thoroughly understand what is the intention of its supporters.

Sherlock had begun to view Larkin and his supporters as a threat, not only to his political base in the Mountjoy Ward, but to the ultimate prize of home rule, which now seemed to be close to becoming a reality.

However, despite his differences with Larkin, Sherlock continued to mediate in the Lockout. His efforts still continued into December 1913, when he wrote once again to both sides, requesting them to come together on behalf of the citizens 'who are so deeply affected by the present deadlock'.[17]

On a more practical note, during the Lockout, Sherlock started a lord mayor's appeal for the families of the two men killed in the August riots, while his second wife Marie Sherlock had formed the Dublin Childrens' Distress fund in October, announcing that wherever nuns, teachers or ladies' school dinner committees were prepared to undertake the work, the Mansion House Ladies Committee was prepared to provide the money. She appealed for further subscriptions to extend the number of schools catered for, and for clothing for the children. A further small gesture, which was nonetheless important to those who received it, came from the Mansion House on 23 December 1913. A week previously, Lorcan Sherlock had heard that the *Daily Sketch* newspaper in Manchester had collected over 100,000 dolls. He applied for ten thousand of these for Dublin, and received five thousand. The schools had already closed, but Sherlock quickly organized volunteers to deliver tickets in the poorer areas of Dublin, and between 11.30 a.m. and 3.30 p.m., Marie Sherlock 'worked energetically' with her volunteers, handing out the dolls to a queue of little girls outside the Mansion House.[18]

Despite all efforts at mediation, the Lockout dispute was never solved. While food and money came from trade unionists in England, it was not enough to counteract the support given to the employers who imposed the

17 *Irish Times*, 13 Dec. 1913.   **18** *Weekly Irish Times*, 3 Jan. 1914.

Lockout, and by February 1914, the demoralized strikers had quite simply been starved back to work.

IV

Lorcan Sherlock's second term as lord mayor should not be seen solely in terms of the Lockout, because with another incident in 1913 he played perhaps his most important role as leader of the citizens of Dublin. On 3 September 1913, just a few days after the riots of 30 and 31 August, with the brutality against the poor of Dublin fresh in peoples' minds, a further disaster struck. Two tenement houses fell in Church Street, killing seven people. This was not the first time that tenement houses had fallen, but taken in conjunction with the heightened tension occasioned by the Lockout, the seven deaths in Church Street caused a public outcry. There was the added poignancy that one of those killed was a seventeen-year-old youth, Eugene Salmon, who had been locked out by Jacob's biscuit factory the week before, and had been killed while trying to rescue his young sister. The chief secretary, Augustine Birrell, announced that he would appoint a 'small Departmental Committee to enquire into the character and extent of the slum problem in Dublin'.[19] Lorcan Sherlock as lord mayor objected to this, demanding that the sittings for the taking of evidence ought to be public. He believed that the citizens of Dublin would not be satisfied with anything less than a Viceregal Commission, as a private enquiry would not throw the necessary amount of light on the ownership of the Dublin slums. He went on to say 'It is known that some members of the Dublin Corporation are tenement owners, and it is the corporation which must be the chief administrative authority in connection with any large scheme of housing reform'.[20] His demand, among others, resulted in the official 'Inquiry into the housing conditions of the working classes',[21] and its subsequent Report, the published record of which has been described as 'one of the most important social documents in the history of modern Dublin'.[22] Although it would be many years before the tenement problem in Dublin was finally resolved, the 1913 Inquiry was a turning point in a situation that had existed since at least the beginning of the nineteenth century.

19 *The Times*, 22 Oct. 1913.   **20** Ibid.   **21** *Report of the departmental committee appointed by the Local Government Board for Ireland to inquire into the housing conditions of the working classes in Dublin*, PP.1914, xix, cd.7273 (evidence of Inquiry) and cd.7317 (Report of Committee).   **22** Joseph V. O'Brien, *Dear dirty Dublin. A city in distress, 1899–1916* (London, 1982), p. 151.

V

There is no doubt that, from the beginning of his political career, Lorcan Sherlock was marked out as a leader, and quickly became one of the most influential councillors in the corporation. His three-term mayoralty was one of the most dramatic and important in the city's history. The first term of 1912–13 saw the great push towards home rule, with Sherlock as one of the campaign's most charismatic spokesmen. His second term of office in 1913–14 saw that ultimate goal of home rule come closer, only to be threatened by increasing instability and violence in the city as a result of the Lockout. The Lockout of 1913 remains a watershed in the history of the city, a word whose connotations have echoed down the generations. If ever the city needed a leader, it needed it then. Lorcan Sherlock, as the official leader of the city, took his role seriously. From being a firebrand councillor prior to his mayoralty, he developed into a more temperate and mature politician after he became lord mayor. He clearly saw his role as leader of all the citizens, and, although a committed nationalist, was tolerant of the opinions of unionists, who feared the introduction of home rule. He was even-handed in his mediation of the Lockout, steering a middle course between the opposing sides in mediation sessions, but at the same time leaving no doubt which side he was on when innocent citizens were brutalized by the forces of law and order. The year 1913 also saw the British government, at Sherlock's insistence, hold a public inquiry, one of many that had been held on the Dublin housing situation, but this time, one to the report of which they actually paid some attention. His third and final term of office in 1914–15 saw a bitter and deflated end to the Lockout, home rule put on hold, and Lorcan Sherlock once again speaking out when innocent citizens were gunned down in July 1914 by the King's Own Scottish Borderers on Bachelors' Walk.[23] He was offered a knighthood in 1915, but remained true to his nationalist principles, and declined it. Lorcan Sherlock later became sheriff of Dublin. He died in 1945, at the age of 71.

The record shows that Lorcan Sherlock as lord mayor rose to all the challenges that arose during his tenure, becoming the voice that tried to bring opposing factions in the city together, and asking that justice be done for those who could not speak for themselves. In other words, he tried to be the voice of the people, which is perhaps all that citizens can ask of their lord mayor.

---

23 *Irish Times*, 28 July 1914.

Lord Mayor Laurence O'Neill, Alderman Tom Kelly and Dublin's housing crisis

RUTH McMANUS

Laurence O'Neill, described on the occasion of his election to a fifth successive term of office as a 'popular, useful, independent and energetic lord mayor',[1] was the last person to hold the office under the British regime and the first to hold it under the Free State administration. His term, then, straddled a very turbulent period in Ireland's political and social history. It began in the midst of the First World War and continued through the 'troubles' of the early 1920s, coming to an end, perhaps, with the abolition of Dublin Corporation in 1924. The word 'perhaps' is apposite, because O'Neill did not vacate the Mansion House until 1925 and as late as 1926 a court case failed to conclude that he was no longer lord mayor, with the judge suggesting that 'probably' he remained lord mayor.[2] In any case, it was O'Neill who was the proposer, in 1930, of the next elected lord mayor of the city, that well-known and charismatic leader Alfie Byrne, discussed in the following chapter.

The focus of this essay is on O'Neill's attempts, during his term of office, to address Dublin's housing problems. In this task, he shared common cause with Alderman Tom Kelly, long-time chairman of the Dublin Corporation Housing Committee, and a man who was instrumental in shaping housing policy in the city.[3] Both expressed a burning desire to address the appalling housing conditions of the poor of the city. This second individual, Alderman Tom Kelly, also has the distinction of having been elected lord mayor in January 1920. He did not take office, as he was interned without charge in Wormwood Scrubs prison at the time of his election, as a result of which his health was broken.[4] In his absence, O'Neill remained on as lord mayor, while asserting that he would consult Kelly, pending the latter's recovery, and conduct the duties of lord mayor 'in accordance with Kelly's wishes'.[5] As Kelly was not inaugurated as mayor, he never officially held the office. Together, these two men were instrumental in shaping housing policy at a crucial period in the city's development.

---

1 *Irish Independent*, 1 Feb. 1921.   2 *Irish Independent*, 14 Dec. 1926.   3 For an in-depth consideration of the life and work of Tom Kelly, see Sheila Carden, *The Alderman: Alderman Tom Kelly (1868–1942) and Dublin Corporation* (Dublin, 2007).   4 *Irish Times*, 14 Feb. 1920.   5 *New York Times*, 24 Feb. 1920.

I

Born in 1874, Laurence O'Neill was educated in the Christian Brothers' Schools and at Belvedere College. First elected to Dublin Corporation in 1908, he was elected unanimously to the position of lord mayor in January 1917, an event without parallel for some years in the city. O'Neill served as lord mayor of Dublin through the tumultuous period in the aftermath of the 1916 Rising, while the First World War still raged, and through the War of Independence and Civil War. A moderate nationalist, he favoured a balanced, temperate approach to public office. For example, O'Neill expressed 'his ambition that the Mansion House would be the meeting place of the citizens of Dublin, no matter what their social qualifications, political leanings, or creed may be'.[6] While critical of the treatment of Irish prisoners in the wake of the 1916 Rising, O'Neill pleaded for a temperate approach, cautioning his fellow citizens that the eyes of the world were upon them.[7] He aimed to tread a middle ground, arguing the case for the people of his city while avoiding inflaming political sentiments. It must be recalled that this was a tremendously fraught period. The city was in grave distress, and early in his mayoralty, O'Neill spoke out on the 'food shortage peril',[8] and presided over a conference into the relief of distress.[9] In June 1917, O'Neill was present at an inquest into the death of a policeman that had occurred at a meeting concerning the fate of political prisoners. He led negotiations in a number of labour disputes, including that of the draymen at Boland's Mills,[10] and he made appeals on behalf of the unemployed of the city, arguing that unless they were provided with work in the rebuilding of Dublin, 'the present state of affairs would make them all turn into Sinn Féiners'.[11]

In his inaugural speech in January 1917, Laurence O'Neill identified the solution of the housing problem as one of his key aims.[12] When O'Neill made his first public appearance as lord mayor on 25 February 1917, he spoke on the topic of 'temperance and housing'. To his mind, 'the evils in their midst … might be traced to the wretched housing system … It seemed to him a miracle that their poor people were even so good or so temperate, regard being had to the disgusting surroundings in which they lived'.[13] This sentiment was shared by Alderman Tom Kelly, who had spoken in 1914 of life in the tenements,

6 *Irish Independent*, 30 Mar. 1917.   **7** *Irish Independent*, 22 May 1917.   **8** *Irish Independent*, 13 Mar. 1917.
9 *Irish Independent*, 15 Mar. 1917.   **10** *Irish Independent*, 26 June 1917.   **11** *Irish Independent*, 30 June
1917.   **12** *Irish Times*, 24 Jan. 1917.   **13** *Irish Independent*, 27 Feb. 1917.

22 Photograph of tenement houses at numbers 30 and 31 Grenville Street, off Mountjoy Square, taken by John Cooke in 1913: reproduced courtesy of Dublin City Library and Archive.

stating that 'those who, like myself, lived in them for years, know that life amongst the poor is only made tolerable by the help which one poor family renders another in times of stress, and until that state of affairs is permanently remedied, many of the social evils, in my judgement, will remain'.[14] However, although a worthy cause, housing reform was a vexed one. By the time that Laurence O'Neill took office in 1917, house construction in Dublin was almost at a stand-still. Wartime conditions and shortages were an issue, while the need to reconstruct the city centre following the destruction of Easter 1916 inevitably diverted money from the housing budget. In addition to these practical issues, however, there was a significant political issue, that of the strained relations between the Local Government Board for Ireland, which controlled government funding, and Dublin Corporation.

14 RPDCD, 1914, vol. 2, p. 179.

II

In order to gain an insight into the challenge facing O'Neill with regard to housing, it is necessary to review the experience of the corporation's Housing Committee over the years prior to his election. In particular, the difficulties surrounding the proposed housing scheme at Fairbrother's Fields, initiated in December 1912, illustrate the difficult circumstances under which housing reform was being attempted.[15] Problems emerged at the site acquisition stage, when a lengthy process of compulsory purchase became necessary, overseen by the Local Government Board (LGB) with the appointment of an arbitrator in March 1915. However, in May of that year a circular was issued by the LGB restricting borrowing by local authorities. The corporation's Housing Committee continued with the negotiations, on the basis that the work was of 'pressing necessity for reasons of public health' and therefore exempt from borrowing restrictions. Unfortunately, the LGB did not share that view, but by the time that the Housing Committee was informed that it was not exempt it was already 'irretrievably committed' to purchasing the site.[16] Eventually the chancellor of the exchequer stepped in, advising that the Treasury would advance the loans to acquire the site, but not to build on it. However, the Board of Works then refused to approve these loans, and it was not until December 1916, a full year later, that it finally advanced the money to acquire the lands.

Once the land was acquired, the corporation had to search for some means of paying for the building work at Fairbrother's Fields. The Housing Committee sought to gain a loan under the short-lived Housing (No. 2) Act, 1914 (which became law in August 1914, and operated for one year), and was supposed to provide £4 million for housing purposes in Great Britain and Ireland.[17] The necessary information was given to the LGB in March 1915, but when a reply was not received, and the Housing Committee pressed for a decision, it was discovered that the case of Dublin had never been submitted to the Treasury by the LGB. 'The foregoing circumstances will give some idea of the vexatious methods with which the Committee had to contend in their efforts to carry on their pressing work'.[18] At a special meeting of the corporation in October 1915, the council passed a resolution declaring its lack of confidence in the LGB.[19]

15 RPDCD 110/1920.   **16** Ibid.   **17** RPDCD 1920, no. 110, p. 364.   **18** Ibid.   **19** RPDCD 1915, vol. 3, p. 123.

Not for the first time, or the last, the plight of Dublin's poorest citizens apparently became subsumed into a battle of political wills. Given these circumstances, the very real efforts made by the Housing Committee, under the chairmanship of Tom Kelly, should not be underestimated. One of the most eloquent reports in the corporation records is the late 1915 'digest of the case for immediate housing loans for Dublin', which summarized the appalling conditions in the city: 'The poorer citizens in thousands pine away and die in surroundings which give them no fighting chance of life. Delay to them is death, and are they to be told that the State has no time and no money to bother about them?'[20] The report[21] continued by referring to the 'countless millions' of pounds being spent 'on the prosecution of a war to which Dublin alone has sent some 14,000 men to fight the Empire's battle ... Are they to find the Empire's gratitude on their return represented in the refusal of the government to allow the corporation to lift their wives and children from the horrors of life in dilapidated tenement houses or cellar dwellings into the atmosphere of light and life in a sanitary, self-contained, comfortable home?'[22]

Although in September 1916 the committee was informed that there was a possibility of obtaining money from American sources under the provisions of the Finance Act, 1916, negotiations fell through due to the prohibitive rates of interest demanded.[23] None of the Irish banks showed a disposition to give quotations for housing loans. Thus, 'every conceivable source was tapped with a view to obtaining funds for building, but without success, so that a hopeless deadlock was then created'.[24] This, then, was the circumstance which greeted Laurence O'Neill when he took office as lord mayor in February 1917.

III

Upon his election to the mayoralty, O'Neill found himself in the middle of an on-going campaign for the housing of Dublin's poor. His predecessor had promised a housing conference to consider the issue, but the new lord mayor was reluctant to proceed until funding, which appeared imminent, was secured.[25] On 5 April 1917, O'Neill led a deputation to Dublin Castle to seek

20 RPDCD 35/1916, p. 351. **21** Peter Cowan, the chief engineer of the Local Government Board, went so far as to suggest that 'the rebellion of 1916, with its terrible results in loss of life, vast material waste, the re-birth of dying antagonisms, the creation of new enmities, and the setting back of the clock in many most vital movements for the welfare of Ireland might possibly have been prevented if the people in Dublin had been better housed' (P.C. Cowan, *Report on Dublin housing* (Dublin, 1918), p. 31). **22** RPDCD 35/1916, p. 351. **23** RPDCD 103/1917. **24** RPDCD 110/1920, p. 364. **25** *Irish Independent*, 19 June 1917.

assistance and to highlight 'the gravity of the state of affairs in Dublin owing to the lack of employment, and to urge the Irish government to facilitate rebuilding operations by placing money at the disposal of the corporation for the erection of dwellings for the working classes'.[26] The chief secretary, Mr Duke, responded in a favourable way,[27] and subsequently inspected the housing areas for which schemes had been prepared; swayed by the distressing conditions he saw, he promised to make immediate arrangements with the chancellor of the exchequer to advance the necessary money. Within a fortnight, it seemed that approval had been received and that funding would be forthcoming to allow the schemes at Spitalfields, Fairbrother's Fields and McCaffrey estate to proceed.[28] The chief secretary was formally thanked by O'Neill at a meeting of Dublin Municipal Council 'for the great interest that he had taken, and was taking, in the work of housing'.[29]

Unfortunately, this was not to be a brave new dawn for Dublin's slum-dwellers. Despite this flurry of activity in April 1917, negotiations dragged on and the promised funding did not materialize. By late 1918, grave concern was expressed by the corporation regarding the differential treatment received by Irish local authorities compared to their counterparts in England with reference to financial aid for housing schemes. In November 1918, Tom Kelly, as chairman of the Housing Committee, spoke at a meeting of the Dublin Municipal Council at which O'Neill was presiding. Kelly outlined the failure of the LGB to uphold its promises, claiming that 'the whole correspondence showed that the British authorities were simply playing with the housing business'.[30] In a final attempt to put an end to this impasse, the lord mayor wrote directly to the prime minister, Lloyd George, 'in the hope that the corporation may obtain at an early date some definite decision as to the amount of state aid which will be available to enable the housing question here to be comprehensively dealt with'.[31] His letter was prompted, he said, by 'a deep sense of his responsibility as lord mayor'. In it, O'Neill reminded the prime minister of the assurances received that Ireland would participate in government housing grants after the war, pointing to the fact that a consensus

---

26 *Irish Times*, 6 Apr. 1917.   **27** *Irish Independent*, 6 Apr. 1917.   **28** *Irish Times*, 23 Apr. 1917. Laurence O'Neill was advised that £10,000 would be available immediately, followed by further amounts to total £100,000 by the end of the following March. This was to provide for Spitalfields (1st section), McCaffrey estate (10 acre site, Mount Brown), St James' Walk, Fairbrother's Fields (22 acres) and Crabbe Lane. While Spitalfields was completed in 1918, and McCaffrey and St James' Walk were in the hands of contractors, it was not until December 1918 that the Local Government Board sanctioned the loan to build on Fairbrother's Fields.   **29** *Irish Times*, 17 Apr. 1917.   **30** *Irish Times*, 16 Nov. 1918.   **31** *Weekly Irish Times*,

had been reached in 1914 that the housing problems in Dublin were beyond the resources of the municipality and that state aid was essential. He argued that the question was not a political one, but 'It is one which, on humanitarian grounds alone, demands immediate action on the part of the state, and the people of this city are entitled to know now what measure of assistance the government proposes to enable the very grave conditions in Dublin to be grappled with'.[32] Although the prime minister's reply, dated 26 November 1918, assured the lord mayor 'that I am taking steps to ascertain personally what is the actual position with regard to the progress of schemes for re-housing in Dublin', no further correspondence was recorded on the matter.[33]

Little wonder that by the time he was making his third inauguration speech, in February 1919, O'Neill was rather gloomy with regard to the possibilities of what could be achieved. 'He admitted with regret that his previous two years had been very barren of results, and he had no great hope of accomplishing much in the year to come, because with the world turned upside down it was very difficult to concentrate one's mind on anything practical'.[34] He singled out the LGB for criticism, stating that much more could and would have been done to improve housing conditions, had the LGB supplied the necessary information in relation to funding.

Throughout 1919 the efforts to obtain money to advance Dublin's housing programme continued. This was taking place against the background of an extremely grave political situation. There was huge frustration at the inaction of the LGB, contrasting with the clear-cut instructions for post-war housing schemes being sanctioned for local authorities in England. At the request of Tom Kelly, the lord mayor and town clerk wrote to the Irish banks to request a housing loan, but were turned down.[35] The difficulty of finding funding for housing remained an issue into 1920.

IV

Although they were not party colleagues, O'Neill and Kelly appear to have worked closely on the housing issue. Tom Kelly's strong voice, as chairman of the Dublin Corporation Housing Committee, was very influential throughout the decade and appears to have largely determined the direction of housing

23 Nov. 1918.   **32** RPDCD, 1918, vol. 1, pp 126–8.   **33** RPDCD, 1918, vol. 1, pp 126–8.   **34** *Irish Times*, 25 Feb. 1919.   **35** *Irish Times*, 25 Nov. 1919.

policy for the city.[36] However, the highly charged external political environment
was to intervene on 11 December 1919, when Kelly was taken from his bed
by the military, deported and imprisoned without charge until February of the
following year, effectively ruining his health. The outrage expressed by
members of Dublin Corporation at Kelly's arrest, reported in the newspapers
some days later, is palpable. The lord mayor stated that 'he had never heard so
much general indignation amongst all classes of the citizens as had arisen over
his [Kelly's] treatment and arrest'. He went on to refer to Alderman Kelly's
interest in the housing of the working classes, and asked them to 'think what
it was at this perilous juncture in their affairs to have such a man taken from
amongst them, treated worse than the meanest criminal, spirited away and
locked out of sight, God knew where, with no investigation, no charge, or no
trial whatever …'[37]

When the usual Local Inquiry concerning the proposed housing scheme at
Marino was opened in January 1920, Lord Mayor O'Neill, reluctant to
proceed with the inquiry in Kelly's absence, sent a telegram to the chief
secretary for Ireland asking for Kelly's release in view of his importance as both
witness and advisor. P.C. Cowan, the inspector for the LGB, stated that 'no
one could regret more sincerely Alderman Kelly's absence than he did, as very
many important issues needed to be worked out, in particular the great and
dominating difficulty of finance, and the nature of the houses'. He said that
Kelly was 'one of the pioneers who projected schemes like these in Dublin, and
that his heart and soul had been centred in this particular scheme. He added
that Kelly would have been a principal witness if he were free'. W.J. Larkin of
the Dublin Tenants' Association also regretted the absence of Kelly, whom he
described as 'an honourable and upright citizen, and as clear a gentleman as
there was in public life'.[38] In the event, the inquiry went ahead because it was
generally felt that Tom Kelly would have been the last to wish the work to be
postponed by even a day.[39] O'Neill paid warm tribute to Kelly when he stated
that his efforts to improve housing conditions in Dublin were 'worthy of the
highest admiration'.[40] A resolution moved by the lord mayor at the Housing
Committee meeting on 14 January 1920, and which was carried unanimously,
stated that

36 Murray Fraser, *John Bull's other homes* (Liverpool, 1996), passim.   37 *Irish Times*, 16 Dec. 1919.
38 *Evening Telegraph*, 2 Jan. 1920.   39 RPDCD, 1921, vol. 11, pp 386–7.   40 *Irish Times*, 15 Jan. 1920.

23 Design for Marino housing scheme; the design carried the heading 'For the Housing Committee, Ald Thomas Kelly Chairman': reproduced courtesy of Dublin City Library and Archive.

> We regret exceedingly that his confinement in a British gaol, without accusation or trial, has deprived us of his able counsel, and the citizens of the services of a man whose chief object has always been to improve the conditions of his native city.[41]

Kelly was released in February 1920, and never took office as lord mayor of Dublin, although when his health eventually recovered he returned to politics, and was elected as a city councillor in 1932 and Fianna Fáil TD for Dublin South in 1933, both of which positions he held till his death in 1942.[42] Instead, Laurence O'Neill continued in office as lord mayor. In 1924, when Dublin Corporation was controversially abolished, it was a mark of the esteem in which Laurence O'Neill was held that he was invited to accept the chairmanship of the commission established to run the city, and to continue in office as lord mayor for a further period of four years. It is a reflection of O'Neill's sense of integrity that he declined the offer.[43]

V

Dublin Corporation has frequently been criticized for its lack of action following the publication of the report of the Housing Inquiry in 1914.

41 RPDCD, 1921, vol. 1, p. 102. **42** Marie Coleman, 'Thomas Kelly', *Dictionary of Irish biography* [online]. **43** *Irish Independent*, 20 May 1924.

However, political circumstances made it extremely difficult for local government to function effectively. The inner city schemes that continued to be developed in the period from 1914 to 1920 were a considerable improvement on the horrors of the tenements. What is remarkable, is that whereas house-building almost ceased in British cities due to the Great War, in Ireland, despite the political situation, it did continue, albeit on a reduced scale. This was principally as a result of municipal activity in Dublin,[44] and due in no small part to the work of Alderman Tom Kelly and Laurence O'Neill.

O'Neill was undoubtedly popular and highly respected, as his – at the time – unrivalled record of re-election demonstrates. At the time, Mr Forrestal stated that

> it was the first time in the history of Dublin that a man was elected purely for his own personal worth, for his own intrinsic value, probity and utility, rather than for any other considerations ... despite the withdrawals of ... grants ..., the ejection of the administration from the city hall and municipal buildings, the constant harassment, raids and imprisonments of the members of the council ... they still survived, undeterred and undismayed, with an administration that strengthened under each rebuff, grew confident under each attack ...[45]

O'Neill continued to argue for relief, to support ecumenical undertakings, and to do his best for all of the citizens. In late 1920 he facilitated the establishment of the Irish White Cross, whose general council included two Catholic bishops, two bishops of the Church of Ireland, the chief rabbi, the ex-president of the Irish Methodist Conference, the lord mayor and mayors of nine Irish towns and cities, several Dáil deputies and some leading members of the Society of Friends. Its brief was to alleviate distress arising out of the Irish War of Independence. In an appeal for funds, O'Neill argued that

> in a time of political disturbance and violence it is still possible for men and women to forget their differences, religious and political alike, and to bend all their energies to a constructive effort for the preservation of their country ... no political distinctions exist in suffering, and none must exist in its relief.[46]

44 Fraser, *John Bull's other homes*, p. 168.   45 *Irish Times*, 1 Feb. 1921.   46 *Irish Independent*, 14 Mar. 1921.

O'Neill employed a similar tone when commenting on the completion of the first houses constructed by the St Barnabas public utility society in East Wall. His speech at the opening ceremony in June 1921 reveals both his concern for housing the poor and his strong belief in a moderate, ecumenical middle ground in political terms. He said that it was particularly pleasant 'to find ladies and gentlemen of different degrees and forms of thought and religion gathered together with the one common object of benefiting their fellow citizens', expressing the hope that this scheme would be 'a beacon of light, the influence of which would spread throughout their beloved land'. In laying the name-stone of the society, the lord mayor specifically thanked Reverend Hall, who had initiated the scheme, 'for the splendid patriotic services he had rendered to the locality, and indeed, by his example, for the whole city', as the housing of the working classes was a subject that must concern everyone.[47]

Laurence O'Neill's commitment to the poor of Dublin continued after he left office. In 1927, for example, as chairman of the Sick and Indigent Roomkeepers' Society, he referred to the great number of people who were in dire distress in the city, and called for an increase in public subscriptions.[48] O'Neill was elected to Dáil Éireann as an independent TD at the 1922 general election but did not contest the 1923 general election and was an unsuccessful candidate at the September 1927 general election. He was elected to the Irish Free State Seanad Éireann at a by-election on 20 June 1929 to fill the vacancy caused by the resignation of Henry Petty-Fitzmaurice. He was re-elected to the Seanad for a nine-year-term in 1931 and served until the Free State Seanad was abolished in 1936. He was nominated by the Taoiseach on the 2 January 1940 to the 3rd Seanad. He did not contest the 1943 Seanad election and died in July of that year.

---

47 *Church of Ireland Gazette*, 8 July 1921.   **48** *Irish Independent*, 29 Apr. 1927.

Legendary Lord Mayor Alfie Byrne

DAVID McELLIN

Since the role and function of the lord mayor of Dublin is largely symbolic, the personality and political experience of the holder have a large bearing on how he/she carries out the functions of the office. Probably the best-known lord mayor of modern times, Alfred (Alfie) Byrne, became lord mayor having served as a councillor and alderman of Dublin Corporation for thirteen years. He was a member of parliament at Westminster, a member of Dáil Éireann and of Seanad Éireann. He served continuously from 1930 to 1939 and again from 1954 to 1955, making him the longest-serving lord mayor in the history of the office. The affection in which he was held by the people of Dublin, particularly the poorer citizens, reflects his championing of their cause, as well as his role as a peacemaker in a variety of contexts, throughout his long and colourful career. Given his long and extensive career in a variety of roles, it is impossible to cover his full political career; accordingly, the focus in this essay will be on his first period in office from 1930 to 1939.

I

Alfred Byrne was born on 14 March 1882 at Seville Place, off Dublin's North Strand. The second of seven children of Thomas and Frances Byrne, he was educated at the local Christian Brothers School in the parish of St Laurence O'Toole. His father worked in shipping; his occupation in the 1901 census is given as 'engine fitter'. Alfie left school at the age of thirteen as his father had become unemployed, although it was not unusual for children to leave school at such an early age. He was apprenticed to the cycle trade in Dawson Street, and was to retain his interest in cycling throughout his life. At night, he worked as a theatre programme seller, thereby doubling his income. In the 1901 census Alfie's occupation is described as 'grocer's assistant'. He subsequently became a barman at a public house near the Dublin docks. With a combination of thrift and hard work, Alfie managed to save £500, which enabled him to buy his own public house, the *Verdon Bar*, at 37 Talbot Street in 1908.[1] Two years later, in 1910, he married Elizabeth Heagney of 1 North Wall.[2]

1 *Sunday Express*, 19 Feb. 1961. 2 *Freeman's Journal*, 20 Apr. 1910.

By the time of his marriage, Alfie Byrne had become an active member of the United Irish League (UIL) in the North Dock Ward. Since the reunification of the Irish Parliamentary Party (IPP) under the leadership of John Redmond in 1900, the UIL had been the main support organization of the Irish parliamentary nationalists. In December 1910 Alfie was selected by the UIL as a candidate for the Dublin Corporation elections, and was duly elected as a councillor for the North Dock Ward in January 1911. At the triennial elections in January 1914 he was elected an alderman. Alderman Byrne remained a member of Dublin Corporation, having been continuously elected, until its abolition in 1924. During the illness of the lord mayor, Laurence O'Neill (1917–1924), from September 1922 to September 1923, he acted as lord mayor *locum tenens*.[3]

As a member of the corporation, Alderman Byrne was diligent in fulfilling his duties and was a member of eleven committees. He was already demonstrating the concern for the poorest classes that was to be a feature of his mayoralty, showing a particular awareness of the concentration of poor housing available in the city centre tenements. The concentration of the poor living within the city boundaries had intensified with the late-nineteenth-century trend for more affluent classes to move to the growing suburbs.[4] Alfie Byrne was aware of the persistent problem and strove to address it (see Carroll, pp 131–40, McManus, pp 141–51).

While remaining active in city politics, Alfie Byrne was also involved in politics on the national stage. In October 1915 Alfie was elected member of parliament for the Harbour Division in a by-election held to fill a vacancy caused by the death of the sitting member, William Abraham of the Irish Parliamentary Party (IPP). Although not elected as an official candidate for the IPP, Byrne was subsequently admitted to that party. As an MP, he was critical of the government. His attendance at anti-conscription and anti-taxation meetings indicated how opinion in Dublin was turning against the war. Although not in support of the 1916 insurgents, he spent much of his subsequent career in the House of Commons lobbying on behalf of those interned after the Rising. Following appeals from those interned, including Michael Collins, he visited Republican prisoners in Frongoch, the Welsh internment camp, in July 1916.[5] He had become disillusioned with the Irish

3 Corporation minutes from 18 Sept. 1922 to 3 Sept. 1923. (At the meeting of 14 May 1923, Ald. J. Hubbard Clark took the chair as lord mayor, *locum tenens*.)   **4** See Ruth McManus, *Dublin, 1910–1940: shaping the city and suburbs* (Dublin, 2002), on the process of suburbanization.   **5** See Seán O'Mahony, *Frongoch: university of revolution* (Dublin, 1987).

Parliamentary Party and its failure to adapt to changing circumstances (see Wallace, pp 120–30). He was the only member of the IPP to attend the funeral of Thomas Ashe in September 1917. Meanwhile, electoral support for the Sinn Féin party was on the rise, with the party winning won four by-elections in 1917. Against this background, along with the great number of IPP MPs, Alfie lost his seat at the December 1918 general election, to the Sinn Féin candidate, Philip Shanahan.

He returned to national politics in 1922, by which time the Irish Free State had been established. At the general election in June 1922, Alfie Byrne was elected to the Third Dáil as an independent member for the Dublin Mid constituency. He was re-elected in 1923 and at the two elections held in 1927, but vacated his Dáil seat in December 1928, when he was elected to Seanad Éireann. Although re-elected to the Seanad at the triennial elections of December 1931, he resigned shortly thereafter to enable a defeated Cumann na nGaedheal candidate, George Crosbie, to be elected at the ensuing by-election.[6] This was characteristic of a politician who would later vote for his great rival for the mayoralty, Mrs Clarke (see the following chapter).

II

The year 1923 saw a major reorganization and restructuring of Dublin Corporation, including the appointment of a new city accountant. Allegations of misconduct by certain councillors in relation to the allocation of houses at the corporation's Fairbrother's Fields housing scheme led to an inquiry, under the chief engineering inspector for local government, on the instructions of the minister for local government. The outcome was the abolition of the corporation on 20 May 1924 and the transfer of its functions to three commissioners. For more than six years, the commissioners exercised the functions of the corporation, until its restoration on 14 October 1930. At the time of its restoration, under the terms of the Local Government (Dublin) Act, 1930, the area of the city was also extended. With the inclusion of the urban districts of Pembroke and Rathmines and Rathgar and certain rural areas, the new corporation had jurisdiction for a much larger area than heretofore.

Alfie had remained a member of Dublin Corporation from his first election in 1911 until its abolition in 1924. On its restoration in October 1930,

6 Donal O'Sullivan, *The Irish Free State and its senate* (London, 1940).

elections were held to fill the thirty-five seats on the new corporation. At the first meeting of the council, held on 14 October 1930, the first business was the election of a lord mayor. Following a two-and-a-half-hour long process, Senator Alderman Alfred Byrne defeated his opponent Seán T. O'Kelly TD (later president of Ireland) of Fianna Fáil by twenty votes to thirteen. Alderman Byrne had the support of the 'government party' or Cumann na nGaedheal (later Fine Gael) and he in turn invariably supported Fine Gael following his election to Dáil Éireann in 1932, although he retained his official status as an independent throughout his political life. He was also supported by a large number of independents at each mayoral election. Alfie Byrne's election in 1930 marked the start of a nine-year uninterrupted period in office, making him the longest serving lord mayor of Dublin.

In his years in the Mansion House his activities and civic charity made his name more widely known. He was very active in many aspects of Dublin's social, civic and religious life and it was not unusual for him to attend as many as four functions in one evening. His interest in the poor and destitute of Dublin was to the forefront at all times. At both national and local level he was a strong proponent of improved working-class housing. His humane disposition was instrumental in settling several industrial disputes. He was also an impartial peacemaker.

One example of Alfie Byrne's peace-making disposition can be found in November 1930, when on a visit to Belfast, the new lord mayor attempted to intervene in the case of three members of the Bohemian Football Club who had been suspended for playing at a recent amateur international between England and Ireland. Acting in an unofficial capacity, he suggested the setting up of a tribunal consisting of the lord mayor of Belfast, himself and an independent chairman to meet representatives of the Irish Football Association and the Football Association of the Irish Free State.[7] His intervention, however, did not result in a resolution of the dispute. He took a more formal role in efforts to resolve a building trade's dispute in January 1931, when he convened a meeting of the employers and the trade unions at the Mansion House.[8] Although not successful, the lord mayor resolved to continue to use his best efforts to bring about a settlement of the dispute and a resumption of work by the thousands that were idle.[9]

After a busy nine months he was re-elected lord mayor on 1 July 1931. It was not his intention to continue in national politics after his resignation from

7 *Irish Independent*, 28 Nov. 1930.   8 *Irish Independent*, 22 Jan. 1931.   9 *Irish Independent*, 22 Jan. 1931.

24 The Alfred Byrne ornamental spade, presented to the lord mayor in 1931: reproduced courtesy of Dublin City Library and Archive.

the Seanad at the end of 1931; however, before the 1932 general election the president of the Executive Council, William T. Cosgrave, requested that he be a candidate. In deference to the president's request he offered himself to the electorate and was duly elected to Dáil Éireann for the Dublin North constituency.[10]

Undoubtedly, the highlight of Alfie Byrne's mayoralty for the year 1932 was the Eucharistic Congress held in June of that year, when he welcomed the papal legate, Cardinal Lorenzo Lauri, and took an active part in the various ceremonies. In preparation for this event, on 16 October 1931 the lord mayor attended the cutting of the sod at the site of the altar in the Fifteen Acres, Phoenix Park. This was performed by Dublin's Archbishop Edward Byrne. At Alfie Byrne's request, the archbishop cut off a piece of the sod and blessed it. This was to be sent to the lord mayor's sister who was a nun in South Africa.[11]

10 *Irish Independent*, 9 Feb. 1932. 11 *Irish Independent*, 17 Oct. 1931.

This humble act contrasts with the pomp and circumstance of the events in June 1932. For example, the *Irish Independent* of 17 June 1932 has a photograph of the lord mayor showing his 'gold coach' to Captain Harrington, son of the late Mr T. Harrington MP, a former lord mayor of Dublin (1901–3). The caption observed that 'this coach was built for a lord mayor of Dublin nearly 200 years ago and will be drawn by six white horses, with postillions in old time uniforms, to the City Gates at Merrion on Monday next, to receive the papal legate. The coachman is to wear the same dress worn when Daniel O'Connell as lord mayor used the same coach' (see pp 91 and 111).[12] In his description of the ceremony of welcome for the papal legate, Dermot Keogh writes that 'The lord mayor of Dublin Alderman Alfred Byrne met the Papal Legate at the city boundary and fell on one knee to kiss the ring of his outstretched hand'.[13]

Alfie Byrne's activities during his mayoralty reflect the strong Roman Catholic ethos of the day. For example, in October 1933 he took part in the Irish National Pilgrimage to Rome to celebrate the extraordinary Holy Year called by Pope Pius XI. In the course of this visit, the lord mayor was granted an audience with the Pope. He would fly to Rome in February 1939 to attend the funeral of the pontiff. In March 1934 he was conferred with the Papal Knighthood of the Grand Cross of the Order of St Sylvester at a ceremony at the Apostolic Nunciature. The gold and diamond ornaments and the Cross, Star and Sash of the Knighthood of St Sylvester were to become one of Alfie Byrne's most treasured possessions. In June of that year, he participated in a pilgrimage to Lourdes.

III

During his time as lord mayor, Alderman Byrne strove to maintain good relations with the United Kingdom. In so doing he made numerous visits to various British cities. In September 1932 he visited Colwyn Bay, Wales, as guest of the Sanitary Inspectors' Association. At the dinner he spoke of the land annuities, saying that the time had come to bring the existing crisis to an end in the interest of both parties.[14] For St Patrick's Day 1934 Alfie Byrne visited London. In a speech at the annual dinner of the Holyhead and District

---

12 *Irish Independent*, 17 June 1932. **13** Dermot Keogh, *Ireland and the Vatican* (Cork, 1995), p. 96. **14** *Irish News*, 8 Sept. 1932.

Traders Association in December 1934 he said that 'an outsider would imagine that at least "bad feeling" existed between the two peoples but in reality this was not the case'.[15]

At national level, in December 1932 the lord mayor called a meeting aimed at forming a new political party, with the objective of ousting Fianna Fáil from government. This party was to stand resolutely behind the maintenance of the treaty which brought the Irish Free State into being.[16] However, this initiative was short lived as a general election was called for early 1933 that saw Fianna Fáil returned to office with an overall majority.

In 1935 Alfie Byrne made an extensive visit to the United States and Canada. He was the first lord mayor of Dublin to visit North America since Daniel Tallon had accompanied John Redmond some forty years earlier. He attended the St Patrick's Day parade in New York and also visited Boston, Washington and Baltimore. On the Canadian leg of the visit he went to Toronto, where he received the freedom of the city. Speaking at a luncheon in his honour the lord mayor said that 'the greatest crime against the peace and prosperity of Ireland was the boundary between North and South'.[17] He expressed similar sentiments in April 1936 when on a visit to Newry, where he received a warm welcome, to open the carnival. In his address on that occasion he expressed the hope that 'some day in the very early future by agreement and goodwill the people of Ireland would remove that Border which was put there by man and not by the Almighty'.[18]

An on-going theme of Alfie Byrne's mayoralty was his call for improved housing conditions. In an address at the annual congress of the Irish National Teachers Organization in April 1935, the lord mayor said that overcrowded tenements had long been a matter of grave concern for Dublin. He spoke of his visit to the United States saying that one thing that struck him forcibly was the great attention that the American people paid to the physical well-being of their voting people.[19] Later that year, on a visit to Leeds, he again addressed the subject, saying that from his own experience slum clearance ought to be carried out in the best interest of the tenants themselves. In giving evidence to a housing enquiry in the City Hall in October 1936, he called for 'sites somewhere in the centre of the city … the time has come for all the old tenements to come down no matter who owns them. They must come down and decent blocks of flats put in their places.'[20] In December 1938 the lord

15 *Manchester Guardian*, 12 Dec. 1934.   16 *Daily Mail*, 30 Dec. 1932.   17 *Irish Independent*, 3 Apr. 1935.   18 *Irish Times*, 18 Apr. 1936.   19 *Dublin Evening Mail*, 23 Apr. 1932.   20 *Irish Independent*, 21

mayor returned to one of his favourite themes, that of housing and slum clearance, in a speech to the annual dinner of the Insurance Institute, where he suggested that a share of the monies of the 'great insurance companies' be invested in the building of houses and industries in Ireland.[21]

In the year 1935 Alfie Byrne made a number of visits to Britain. For example, in July 1935 he visited Holyhead to open a 'fancie fayre' at the Bon Sauveur convent. In his address he said that he was glad to be in Holyhead, 'as it was one of the places where people lived in concord with one another, without regard to political or religious views'.[22] In October he visited London when at a luncheon in the Garrick Theatre he remarked that it was the first time in forty years that the lord mayors of Dublin and London had met.[23] In the same month he was a guest at the Nottingham lace ball.[24]

On 29 January 1936 the lord mayor represented the city of Dublin at the funeral of King George V, having attended pontifical high mass at Westminster Cathedral for the late king on the previous day.[25] Speaking on his return from the funeral Alderman Byrne said that the decision to attend the funeral was entirely his own. He added that he felt it was an act that the vast majority of Irish people would endorse.[26] In May 1937, at the invitation of Cardinal Hinsley of Westminster, he attended a thanksgiving mass at Westminster Cathedral to mark the coronation of King George VI. In a comment to the *Irish Independent* the lord mayor said that after the mass hundreds of Irish people shook his hand. During his visit to London Alderman Byrne was guest of honour at the Four Provinces Club. In the course of his address he stated that 'the great difficulty of partition could only be solved by goodwill and mutual understanding'.[27]

The triennial elections that were held in June 1936 were significant in that they were the first to be held on a universal franchise. The necessary legislation which was introduced by the minister for local government and public health, Seán T. O'Kelly TD, had the effect of increasing the number of voters in Dublin to about 363,000, an increase of more than 50 per cent on the old register. This was expected to benefit Fianna Fáil and the party campaigned strongly for a majority on the corporation. The then minister for industry and commerce, Seán Lemass TD, expressed the view that the capital city of a country with a Fianna Fáil government should have a Fianna Fáil corporation.[28]

Oct. 1936. **21** *Sunday Independent*, 4 Dec. 1938. **22** *Irish Independent*, 10 July 1935. **23** *Irish Independent*, 3 Oct. 1935. **24** *Nottingham Guardian*, 4 Oct. 1935. **25** *Irish Times*, 28 Jan. 1936. **26** *Irish Times*, 31 Jan. 1936. **27** *Irish Independent*, 21 May 1937. **28** *Irish Times*, 6 June 1936.

This approach was strongly critiqued by the *Irish Times*, which wrote in glowing terms of Alfie Byrne's term as lord mayor.

> To some extent the contests in Greater Dublin will centre around the personality of the lord mayor, Alderman Byrne. Mr Byrne has been lord mayor now for six years – since the rehabilitation of the city council; and, although his period in office has been unusually long, we venture to say that Dublin never has had a chief magistrate of greater efficiency or more valuable qualities. Throughout his term in the Mansion House Alderman Byrne has preserved a sturdy independence which has won him golden opinions in all quarters. He never has forgotten the fact that, as lord mayor, he is the representative, not of a class, a creed or a party but of all the citizens of Ireland's ancient capital. His capacity for hard work is almost incredible, and his popularity is without parallel in the annals of our city. We are convinced that no other man in Ireland to-day can replace Alderman Byrne as lord mayor. For that reason we regret very much that Mr Lemass should declare publicly that a member of the Fianna Fáil party ought to be chosen.[29]

The election results were a huge personal triumph for Alfie Byrne. Out of a poll of 137,749, a total of 72,658 votes (over 52 per cent) were cast for the lord mayor's panel. He polled 14,297 first preferences, being twice as great as the votes of any other candidate with one exception.[30] Commenting on the results under the headline 'The Lord Mayor's Triumph', the *Dublin Evening Mail* described the results of the elections as 'a remarkable personal triumph for the lord mayor. His personality has dominated the campaign and there can be little doubt that his action in publicly giving his blessing to the Fine Gael and Independent candidates has been the chief factor in the defeat of the Fianna Fáil and Labour combine'.[31] On 10 July 1936, Alderman Byrne was re-elected lord mayor, his opponent again being Mrs Clarke.

Throughout 1937 the lord mayor continued with his usual busy round of activities. On 30 January he opened the Robert Emmet Bridge over the Grand Canal at Harold's Cross. In February he paid a visit to Manchester.[32] The purpose of this visit was to attend a Liver Workers' Mutual Society's dinner. Alderman Byrne was a trustee of the Royal Liver Friendly Society. In his

29 Ibid.   **30** *Irish Times*, 2 July 1936. Mr E. Benson (UIP) had 9,469 votes.   **31** *Dublin Evening Mail*, 3 July 1936.   **32** *Irish Independent*, 5 Feb. 1937.

25 Portrait of Alderman Senator Alfred Byrne, first lord mayor of Greater Dublin, by The MacEgan: reproduced courtesy of Dublin City Library and Archive.

address the lord mayor again referred to the land annuities question and the question of the 'boundary' in the context of President de Valera's statement that 'The unity of Ireland is essential before we will ever get a complete and final settlement with England.' Byrne said 'The significance of the last statement has, apparently, not been fully realized. It means that the man-made boundary by your politicians dividing Northern and Southern Ireland must go. Is it not worth a big, determined effort to find a solution that will bring the three peoples together – Free State, Great Britain and Northern Ireland?'[33]

In August 1937 in a speech to the North Dublin Horticultural Society Alfie Byrne raised the issue of what he called 'savage sentences' of three to five years imposed on 7- to 11-year-olds for robbing orchards. Senior Justice Little of the District Court took issue with the lord mayor's comments, both denying that there had been such sentences and offering a strong defence of industrial schools. In response to the senior justice the lord mayor said 'I have no further comment to make. All I wanted to do is express my opinion that for the punishment of trifling offences the home of the children is better than any institution. I do not like to see children being taken from their parents' homes'.[34]

The new constitution, Bunreacht na hÉireann, approved in a referendum on 1 July 1937 provided for the office of president to be directly elected by the people. For much of the latter part of 1937 and early 1938 the name of Alderman Byrne was being mentioned as a possible candidate to oppose the most likely Fianna Fáil candidate, Seán T. O'Kelly TD, vice president of the Executive Council / Tánaiste. However the election never took place, as Fianna Fáil and Fine Gael eventually agreed on the Irish scholar Dr Douglas Hyde, who became the first president of Ireland on 25 June 1938.

As with 1937, the year 1938 was equally busy for Alfie Byrne. In January there was a visit to Leeds. In February he received the freedom of Kilkenny. In March he visited Swansea to attend an Ireland/Wales rugby match. In April Byrne visited Belfast to address the Rotary Club.[35] There followed a visit to Manchester in May for the city's centenary celebrations. Throughout the remainder of 1938 the lord mayor made a number of visits to Britain. In July there were visits to Holyhead and London. In September he visited Rhyl in Wales to open a garden fete where he spoke of his hope that peace would be maintained in the world.[36] Later that month he was in Glasgow to visit the Empire Exhibition and toured the exhibits with the lord mayor of Belfast.[37]

33 Ibid.   **34** *Cork Examiner*, 26 Aug. 1937.   **35** *Irish Times*, 27 Apr. 1938.   **36** *Irish Press*, 9 Sept. 1938. **37** *Irish Times*, 14 Sept. 1938.

IV

Throughout his period as lord mayor in the 1930s, Alderman Byrne's principal opponent at each election was the Fianna Fáil candidate, Mrs Kathleen Clarke, widow of 1916 leader Tom Clarke. He successfully defeated her on seven successive occasions. (She was not his opponent in 1930 and 1931.)

During his time in office, lord mayor Alfie Byrne was assiduous in his acceptance of invitations to various functions and events. In an interview with the *Daily Express* he revealed that the greatest number of functions he had attended in one day was thirty-one 'including meetings, dinners and dances'. Unsurprisingly, this busy schedule took its toll and as 1938 drew to a close Alfie Byrne referred to the fact that he might not contest the mayoralty for a tenth successive year, largely on health grounds. Speaking at the annual Christmas treat for over 3,000 inmates of the Dublin Union he said that the enormous amount of correspondence together with the vast number of callers to the Mansion House and the many disappointments he met in trying to remedy grievances had affected his health so that, on the direction of his medical advisor, he would not be a candidate again for the mayoral office.[38]

As he had indicated Alfie decided to withdraw from the 1939 mayoral election. At the meeting of the corporation on 26 June 1939 to elect a lord mayor, Alderman Byrne allowed himself to be nominated after two other candidates, Alderman Peadar S. Doyle TD, and Patrick Belton, both of Fine Gael, had been defeated. On the division to elect a lord mayor, Alderman Byrne defeated the Fianna Fáil candidate Mrs Clarke by 17 votes to 14.[39] Subsequently Byrne withdrew and on 27 June 1939 at the resumed election to elect a lord mayor, Mrs Clarke defeated the only other candidate Alderman Peadar Doyle TD. On the substantive vote there was a tie and Alderman Byrne gave his casting vote in favour of Mrs Clarke, having already voted for her.[40] Thus Mrs Kathleen Clarke became the first woman lord mayor in the city's history.

Alderman Alfred Byrne TD continued to represent his northside constituency at local and national level. He had successfully retained his seat in Dáil Éireann at each general election from 1932. Nevertheless, continued electoral success was not guaranteed. In 1953, for example, he received just four votes when he contested the mayoral election. However, in the following year, in June 1954, he was elected lord mayor for a final, record tenth time with the support of Fine Gael and numerous independents.

38 *Irish Weekly Independent*, 2 Jan. 1939. **39** *Irish Times*, 27 June 1939. **40** *Irish Times*, 28 June 1939.

This time Alfie Byrne did not live in the Mansion House, instead travelling daily by bus from his home in Rathmines to his official residence. One of the benefits of this arrangement was that it provided him with another way of meeting the people of the city. When in December 1954, disastrous floods swept his old native district at Fairview and the North Strand, the 71-year-old rose from his sick bed to offer what assistance he could. Some 20,000 homes were under water, so the need was urgent. In the Mansion House he organized a distress fund and insisted on payments being made before Christmas. He was again a candidate for the mayoralty in 1955 but was defeated by the Labour Party candidate Denis Larkin who received the support of Fianna Fáil. On the following day, 5 July 1955, Alderman Byrne was conferred with the honorary degree of Doctor of Laws by the University of Dublin (Trinity College). The citation recalled that from the earliest days there had been friendly relations with the corporation of Dublin. 'Today', it continued, 'we welcome Ald. Byrne who has held the office of lord mayor more frequently than any other man, whose name is linked all over the world with that of Dublin; a champion of the poor and needy, a friend of all men. We have not forgotten how in the floods of last year he rose from his bed in the cold and darkness of the winter night to organize relief and assistance'.[41] A few months later, on 13 March 1956, Alfie Byrne died. At the time he was still a serving member of both Dáil Éireann and Dublin Corporation.

V

On becoming the first lord mayor of the enlarged Dublin Corporation in 1930, Alfie Byrne brought to this office almost twenty years of political experience. Not only had he served as a member of the corporation for thirteen years and acted as lord mayor, but he had also served in the national parliaments of the United Kingdom and the Irish Free State.

An astute politician, he was a constitutional nationalist. Although an independent, he supported Cumann na nGeadheal/Fine Gael and that party in turn supported him on the corporation. His championship of the poor and the underprivileged saw him continuously elected at local and national level. His kindness to children was legendary. He was famous for the lollipops and sweets that he purchased from Urney's of Tallaght and which he dispensed to

41 *Irish Press*, 6 July 1955.

thousands of children. On a more serious note, he showed a socially advanced outlook towards children in the stance he took on child sentencing.

Alfie Byrne was a reconciler and peacemaker. He took every opportunity to promote reconciliation between Britain and Ireland and on the island between North and South. With his old world courtesy, kindly nature and friendly disposition (he was often referred to as 'the shaking hand of Dublin'), he was Dublin's most popular and best-known lord mayor and deserving of the description legendary lord mayor of Dublin.

Kathleen Clarke, first woman lord mayor of Dublin

HELEN LITTON

Just over seventy years ago, on Tuesday 27 June 1939, Mrs Kathleen Clarke was elected as the first woman lord mayor of Dublin. No woman had yet been elected mayor or lord mayor anywhere in Ireland, and it was seen as a momentous step; indeed, the excitement could be compared with that caused by the election of Mary Robinson as first female president of Ireland in 1990.

Mrs Clarke's election was the product of the usual feuds and voting pacts, and her main competitors were from within her own party, Fianna Fáil. She had stood for the position seven times in previous years, and in the end was elected on the casting vote of the outgoing lord mayor, the highly popular Alfie Byrne, who was retiring after nine years (see p. 163).[1] Thanking him, she said that during his term of office 'he never seemed to forget … that he had in my person the representative of a man whom all Ireland honours. It is because I represent that man, not anything that I believe within myself, that he has put me in this chair here tonight'.[2]

Mrs Clarke, a widow with three adult sons, was referring to her husband, Thomas Clarke, one of the leaders of the Easter Rising and a signatory of the Proclamation of the Republic. Following his execution, Kathleen Clarke entered political life herself, vowing to carry on the fight for Ireland's independence on his behalf. A prime mover of the Irish Volunteer Dependants' Fund, which helped the families of dead or imprisoned Volunteers, she had given Michael Collins a new standing in republican circles by appointing him secretary to the Fund, and she remained active in Cumann na mBan for many years, taking the anti-Treaty side in the Civil War. A founder member of Fianna Fáil, she had entered Dáil Éireann with Éamon de Valera in 1927, and was a Senator from 1928 to 1936. With such a strong republican background, it is not surprising that her mayoralty was characterized by a robust stance on nationalist issues, but it was also an interesting period in terms of her changing relationship with Fianna Fáil and de Valera, as well as the way in which the presence of a woman in a traditionally male role was portrayed by the media.

---

1 Minutes of Municipal Council of City of Dublin, 27 June 1939, Gilbert Library, Dublin. **2** *Irish Times*, 28 June 1939.

26 Photograph of Lord Mayor Kathleen Clarke wearing the chain of the president of the court of conscience, which she wore in place of the lord mayor's chain of office, presented by William III: reproduced courtesy of Dublin City Library and Archive.

I

Kathleen Clarke represented the old republican Ireland. The Daly family of Limerick, into which she had been born in 1878, maintained a proud Fenian tradition, and her only brother, Commandant Edward (Ned) Daly, like her husband, had been executed in 1916 at the age of 25. She began her mayoralty as she meant to go on, refusing to accept the lord mayor's chain because it had been presented to Dublin Corporation by King William III (apparently Labour councillor James Larkin cried 'Don't put on King Billy's chain!').[3] A smaller chain, known as the City Chain, was hastily produced, and she was ceremonially invested with it. She also refused the robes of office, calling them 'red rags from the British period'.[4] However, she stated that she would not be partisan, or 'only to the extent that the man or woman who put Ireland first would always get a better show from her than the person who did not give Ireland his allegiance'.[5]

Her election was enthusiastically greeted by crowds outside City Hall, and immediately the women's pages of the newspapers swung into action. The *Irish Times* asserted that she would have 'the good wishes of all women in the country and their support in her new exalted position'.[6] She was quoted in the *Irish Press* as saying: 'I am terribly keen on the fact that women, if given the opportunity, could do as well in positions in public life as the men. I have great faith in my own sex.' In the *Irish Independent*, Gertrude Gaffney proclaimed that 'the women of the country look to her to maintain the average housewife's reputation for canny and discriminating administration of affairs, and I am sure that every one of them wishes her well'.[7]

She would have described herself as a nationalist first and a feminist second, and had not, for example, involved herself in the fight for women's suffrage, but she laid her cards firmly on the table in the *Evening Mail*: 'On the surface, women have equal rights in this country. But, under the surface, there is a great feeling against women, especially in public life … Nobody would dispute the fact that it is very nice for a woman to be supported in comfort by a husband or father. But there are many women who have neither; and there are many women who would be a great loss to public life if they allowed domestic cares to occupy their time to the exclusion of all else'.[8] So much for the vice-

3 *New York Times*, 28 June 1939. **4** Unidentified press cutting (possibly *Herald Tribune*), no date. **5** *Irish Times*, 28 June 1939. **6** Kitty Clive, 'Echoes of the Town', *Irish Times*, 30 June 1939. **7** *Irish Press*, *Irish Independent*, 29 June 1939. **8** *Dublin Evening Mail*, 4 July 1939.

27 Lord Mayor Kathleen Clarke mixing the christmas pudding at St Patrick's Home (Little Sisters of the Poor), Kilmainham, December 1939. Alderman P.S. Doyle TD, her successor as lord mayor, observes: reproduced courtesy of Independent Newspapers.

chairman of Athy Urban Council, who had referred to ladies on public bodies as 'the curse of the country'. She accused him of 'blather', and stated that 'Sex is not a test of ability for a job. In actual fact, women have an individual and clearer point of view than men'.[9]

Interviewed by the *Evening Herald*, Mrs Clarke paid tribute to the talents and energies of her predecessor, adding, 'I could not possibly attend the number of functions that he managed to fit into one day. I want to conserve my strength so that on really big occasions I will be fit, mentally and physically, for the task they will impose on me'. Aged 61, she had not been in good health for many years; she had suffered a miscarriage after the Easter Rising, followed by a serious illness, and her imprisonment in Holloway Jail with Maud Gonne and Countess Markievicz, following the 'German Plot' in 1918, had ended early on health grounds because of a heart condition. However, despite an operation in March 1940, followed by a long illness, she was re-elected as lord mayor on 2 July 1940, and served out her second term.

II

The election of Dublin's first woman lord mayor naturally caused great interest all over the country, as her press-cutting album shows. Patriotic commentators

9 *Daily Sketch*, 25 Aug. 1939.

dwelt on her republican background, and hoped that her election would work
against the perceived tendency of independent Ireland to be ruled by the
moneyed classes and the civil service. Congratulations poured in from health
boards, county councils, and the National Council of Women of Ireland, and
the *Standard* published a poem in her honour, to the tune of 'The Croppy Boy':

> ... So here's a health to our dear First Lady
> Daughter of Daly, a Fenian too;
> Ned Daly of Limerick, a rebel ever,
> To God and to Ireland staunch and true.
>
> Long may you lord it in Dublin city
> Honouring us while we honour you
> For great is this day in Ireland's story
> And we'll cherish forever this daughter true![10]

As R.M. Fox said in the *Irish Press*, 'Her career spans a momentous period of
Ireland's history and shows the strength of the resurgent spirit in Ireland'.[11]
However, the Dublin ratepayers, who were largely unionist in sympathy, were
suspicious of her republican tendencies, and their worst fears were soon to be
realized.

The election of a woman lord mayor threw up several anomalies in Irish
public life. For example, the Dublin Port and Docks Board found itself
welcoming its first ever woman member, because Dublin's lord mayor was a
representative of the Admiralty. She had to be called 'lord mayor', because
'lady mayoress' is the official title of a lord mayor's wife, and Quidnunc in the
Irish Times suggested that it was time a new title was devised, on the lines of
'taoiseach' or 'uachtarain', which did not alter with the sex of the holder.[12]

A family crest then had to be researched for the plaque which was to be
placed in the collection of mayoral arms in City Hall. The Ó Cléirigh plaque,
with its motif of a robin bearing an olive branch, was apparently the first coat
of arms with its motto in the Irish language: 'Siothchain de bheirim
chughaibh' (I bring peace to you). When she announced this motto, she
added, 'If I have brought a new era in the fact that I occupy the mayoral chair,
it is significant that my crest is peace, and I hope my crest will be true ...'[13]

10 *Standard*, 12 Jan. 1940. **11** *Irish Press*, 30 June 1939. **12** *Irish Times*, 5 July 1939. **13** *Dublin Evening Mail*, 24 July 1939, address to Annual Association of Gas Managers.

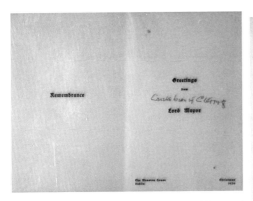

28 Christmas card circulated by Lord Mayor Kathleen Clarke in 1939 commemorating the Easter Rising, front and inside views. Note her signature in the Irish language: reproduced courtesy of Dublin City Library and Archive.

Peace was not, however, to be the dominant note of her mayoralty. Moving into the Mansion House on 19 July, Kathleen Clarke immediately ordered the removal of a portrait of the young Queen Victoria, which had hung in the entrance hall for many years. In her memoirs, published long after her death, she stated, 'I felt I could not sleep in the house until she was out of it, she had been so bitterly hostile to Ireland and everything Irish'.[14] Along with portraits of other British monarchs, Victoria was moved out early one morning, and passengers in the early trams were greeted by a row of paintings ranged along the railings in Dawson Street. This action hit the front pages of both Irish and English newspapers, and the reactions of Dublin ratepayers filled correspondence columns for weeks; they paid her salary of £2,500 p.a., and they insisted that she should listen to them.

14 Kathleen Clarke, *Revolutionary woman: Kathleen Clarke, 1878–1972*, ed. Helen Litton (Dublin, 1991), p. 222.

Correspondents were allowed to use pseudonyms in those days, and the signatures reflect the opinions expressed: 'Patriotic Anti-Fanatic', 'A Supporter of Royalty', 'A Southern Loyalist', 'Plain Citizen', 'One Who Is Pained'. She was accused of having a 'pettish school-girl mentality', but fought back with the example of her uncle John Daly, a Fenian ex-prisoner, who as first nationalist mayor of Limerick in 1898–9 had had the royal coat of arms removed from Limerick Town Hall. She had some support: the *Evening Mail* pointed out that Alfie Byrne had carried out many structural improvements in the Mansion House without anyone suggesting that he had no right to do so.[15] Others scornfully accused her opponents of pretending to be interested in art simply as a weapon of attack. The paintings were put in storage, and have since been restored and rehung.

III

The life of a lord mayor is one of constant public occasions and distinguished visitors, and Mrs Clarke was a focus of interest and curiosity, although her state of health curtailed her activities for a period during her first term. The first signature in her Visitor's Book was that of Éamon de Valera, and she made formal visits to President Douglas Hyde, the Apostolic Nuncio, and the two archbishops of Dublin; she appointed Father Dermot, OFM Cap, as her chaplain. She entertained film stars such as Gene Autry, the Singing Cowboy, and Valerie Hobson,[16] as well as the United States postmaster-general, James A. Farley. Her press-cutting album is full of meetings here and speeches there, presentations, prize-givings and theatre trips.[17] She had no male escort for social events, but sometimes her youngest son, Emmet, would accompany her. Her stylish costumes were often a matter of comment, since she had trained and worked as a tailor, and made most of her own garments. Whenever she bought clothes, she made it clear that she was a strong supporter of Irish manufacturers,[18] and one of her evening dresses was a full-length gown of Limerick lace.

Kathleen Clarke was already active in the National Graves Association, and president of the Dublin branch of the Irish Red Cross. As mayor, she attended

---

15 *Dublin Evening Mail*, 1 Aug. 1939. **16** 'Together they discussed flying, and their homes', *Irish Press*, 30 July 1939. **17** 'Mrs Clarke was in a pretty dress of black tissue lace, the hem appliqued with white flowers', Report of annual reception of Friends of National College, no source, 26 Jan. 1940. **18** Speech to Women's Industrial Development Association, 4 Dec. 1939.

such events as the 50th anniversary of the founding of the National Society for the Prevention of Cruelty to Children, where she urged people to subscribe to Dublin Corporation's housing loan to alleviate the 'slum evil': 'No matter which way the war goes, corporation loans will be a good investment'. She addressed Craobh na hAiseirige, the Irish language revival movement, with an appeal for a greater use of Irish in daily life (she did not speak Irish herself). As senior vice-chair of the Royal Irish Academy of Music, she attended their prize-givings, and called for greater development of 'our own music' to encourage national and patriotic feelings. She always had a great interest in child welfare, and was on the board of St Ultan's Children's Hospital; she opened several child health clinics, and hosted a St John's Ambulance party for 250 mothers at the Mansion House, as well as Christmas treats for under-privileged children.

In November 1940 she laid the foundation stone for a scheme of flats in Charlemont Street, funded by public subscription, and the plaque with her name on it is still there. She donated two copies of her husband's prison memoir, *Glimpses of an Irish felon's prison life*, signed by her, to be raffled in aid of the Dublin Brigade of the National Association of the Old IRA. She drafted an address to be given by Dublin Corporation to the archbishop of Dublin-elect, Dr John Charles McQuaid, placing on record their sincere pleasure at his elevation, and was also involved in discussions on the siting of a new cathedral for Dublin – the proposed site of Merrion Square was being displaced by plans for a new emphasis on the riverside of Dublin, making the proposed Cathedral the centrepiece.

IV

The mayoralty of Kathleen Clarke was, of course, immediately overtaken by the Second World War, and the Declaration of Emergency in the Irish Free State, with consequent rationing and fuel shortages. She was president of the Irish Red Cross, headed appeals for charities and hospitals, and appealed to the striking Municipal Employees' Union to provide essential services, as well as mediating in a milk strike. A Mansion House coal fund, to which she contributed £25, provided fuel, and the Red Cross fund helped victims of the German bombs which fell in Dublin in May 1941, killing thirty-five people.

As war clouds gathered, Mrs Clarke said in an interview, 'It is all very well for England to denounce Herr Hitler, and to talk of the atrocities and brutalities, but it is up to us to point out to Irish children that atrocities and brutalities began in Ireland by England and by the people England sent across to Ireland'.[19] She supported Ireland's policy of neutrality, but she seems to have been suspicious that Éamon de Valera was 'neutral towards the British', giving clandestine support to British aims.[20] Worried about the consequences of offending Germany, at a time when it was expected that Germany would win the war, she expressed disapproval when de Valera sent the Dublin Fire Brigade to a bombed Belfast in April 1941, an act of generosity for which he has always been commended. She was notorious in Dublin for friendly acts towards the legations of the Axis powers, hosting an official dinner for Eduard Hempel, the German ambassador. The Japanese ambassador, Setsuya Beppu, would apparently present her with a flower on each 3 May, the anniversary of her husband's execution.[21]

Kathleen Clarke tended to regard herself as a semi-detached member of Fianna Fáil, and was often out of sympathy with its decisions. She had clashed with the party over de Valera's 1937 Constitution, and its 'anti-women' aspects, and this led to the Thomas Clarke Cumann, which she had established, seeking her resignation from the party. This was not forthcoming, however; de Valera informed them that party members were permitted to express disagreement. Her strongly republican attitudes led, during her mayoralty, to more disagreements over de Valera's policies, particularly in regard to the IRA. She believed that the IRA should have called off its British bombing campaign when the war started, but she opposed the setting up of military courts to try IRA offences.

As lord mayor, she was part of a deputation that pleaded for the release of Patrick McGrath, an IRA prisoner on hunger strike, and she visited him in Jervis Street Hospital after he was freed. He was later rearrested, however, after a raid that resulted in the death of a policeman, and was sentenced to death. Kathleen Clarke's representations for mercy were refused, and on the day of the execution she drew the blinds of the Mansion House, lowered the flag to half-mast, and ordered the city manager to fly the City Hall flag at half-mast as well. This was a very public repudiation of government policies by a party member; as she said in her memoirs, 'I never could see why as a member of a party or organization I was bound to approve of everything the leaders did'.[22]

19 *Standard*, 7 July 1939. 20 The Free State did in fact give a lot of covert support to the Allies, unknown at the time. See Michael Kennedy, Catriona Crowe et al. (eds), *Documents on Irish foreign policy, vol. VII, 1941–45* (Dublin, 2010). 21 Family sources. 22 Clarke, *Revolutionary woman*, p. 224.

Clarke supported appeals for Tomás Óg MacCurtain, son of the lord mayor of Cork who had been murdered by the Black and Tans in 1920. The boy had been sentenced to death for shooting a policeman, but pressure of public opinion forced a reprieve. She also headed a public appeal for Barnes and McCormick, sentenced to death in Britain for an IRA bomb which had killed five people in Coventry, but no reprieve was granted.

V

In June 1941, Kathleen Clarke announced that she would not seek re-election as lord mayor, on health grounds. Shortly after this, she resigned from Fianna Fáil, feeling that its views and hers had moved too far apart. She lived an active life, serving on numerous boards and committees, for another thirty years, and stood unsuccessfully as a Dáil candidate for Clann na Poblachta in 1948. In 1966, with other relatives of Proclamation signatories, she was conferred with an honorary doctorate by the National University of Ireland. She died on 19 September 1972 in Liverpool, where she was living with her last surviving son, Dr Emmet Clarke, and his family. She was given a State funeral in Dublin, and the cortege, pausing for one minute outside the GPO, was accompanied to Dean's Grange cemetery by President Éamon de Valera and Taoiseach Jack Lynch.

Her mayoralty was a fitting culmination to a life spent fighting for Ireland's right to absolute freedom, a cause for which she suffered great loss. She picked up her husband's baton, at a time when women were strongly discouraged from public careers, and drove his republicanism forward. She lived to see her attitudes decried as anachronistic and backward-looking, but Kathleen Clarke never doubted her right to express her opinions, and used the role of lord mayor to support republican causes.

Dublin's mayors from 1500 to 2012

DUBLIN CITY LIBRARY AND ARCHIVE

The most comprehensive list published to date was compiled by Jacqueline Hill. This covered the period 1229 to 1983 and was published in T.W. Moody, F.X. Martin & F.J. Byrne (eds), *A new history of Ireland*, ix (Oxford, 1984), pp 548–64. This was based on lists published annually in the *Dublin Corporation Yearbook*, which in turn were drawn from Sir John T. and Lady Gilbert (eds), *Calendar of ancient records of Dublin* (19 vols, 1889–1944) and, from 1841 onwards, from the minutes of Dublin City Council. This present list draws on all of the above sources, supplemented with names of mayors published in Colm Lennon and James Murray (eds), *The Dublin city franchise roll, 1468–1512* (Dublin, 1998), and with names of certain lord mayors uniquely recorded in contemporary leases which are preserved in the Dublin City Archive. Since 2004, these lists have been published on the website www.dublincity.ie, where they are updated annually.

Incumbent	Date of office	Commencement
Robert Forster	1500–1	Michaelmas 1500
Hugh Talbot	1501–2	Michaelmas 1501
Richard Tyrell	1502–3	Michaelmas 1502
John Blake	1503–4	Michaelmas 1503
Thomas Newman	1504–5	Michaelmas 1504
Nicholas Hertbard	1505–6	Michaelmas 1505
William English	1506–7	Michaelmas 1507
William Canterell (Cauterell)	1507–8	Michaelmas 1507
Thomas Philip	1508–9	Michaelmas 1508
William [blank]	1509–10	Michaelmas 1509
Nicholas Roch	1510–11	Michaelmas 1510
Thomas Bermyngham (Brymingham)	1511–12	Michaelmas 1511
Not recorded	1512–23	

Incumbent	Date of office	Commencement
Nicholas Queytrot	1523–4	Michaelmas 1523
Not recorded	1524–5	
Richard Talbot	1525–6	Michaelmas 1525
Walter Ewstas (Eustace)	1526–7	Michaelmas 1526
Not recorded	1527–30	
Thomas Barbe	1530–1	Michaelmas 1530
John Sarsewell	1531–2	Michaelmas 1532
Nicholas Gaydon	1532–3	Michaelmas 1532
Walter FitzSymon	1533–4	Michaelmas 1533
Robert Shilyngford	1534–5	Michaelmas 1534
Thomas Stephens	1535–6	Michaelmas 1535
John Shilton	1536 –7	Michaelmas 1536
John Scuyr	1537–8	Michaelmas 1537
James FitzSymond	1538–9	Michaelmas 1538
Nicholas Bennet	1539–40	Michaelmas 1539
Walter Tirrell	1540–1	Michaelmas 1540
Nicholas Umfre	1541–2	Michaelmas 1541
Nicholas Stanyhurst	1542–3	Michaelmas 1542
Not recorded	1543–6	
Henry Plunket	1546–7	Michaelmas 1546
Thady Duff	1547–8	Michaelmas 1547
James Hancoke	1548–9	Michaelmas 1548
Richard Fyane (Fian)	1549–50	Michaelmas 1549
John Money	1550–1	Michaelmas 1550
Michael Penteny	1551–2	Michaelmas 1551
Robert Cusake	1552–3	Michaelmas 1552
Bartholomew Ball	1555–4	Michaelmas 1553
Patrick Sarsfield	1554–5	Michaelmas 1554
Thomas Rogers	1555–6	Michaelmas 1555
John Challyner	1556–7	Michaelmas 1556
John Spensfelde	1557–8	Michaelmas 1557
Robert Golding	1558–9	Michaelmas 1558
Christopher Sedgrave	1559–60	Michaelmas 1559
Thomas FitzSymon	1560–1	Michaelmas 1560
Robert Ussher	1561–2	Michaelmas 1561

Incumbent	Date of office	Commencement
Thomas Fininge	1562–3	Michaelmas 1562
Robert Cusake	1563–4	Michaelmas 1563
Richard Fiand (Fian)	1564–5	Michaelmas 1564
Nicholas FitzSimon	1565–6	Michaelmas 1565
Sir William Sarsfield	1566–7	Michaelmas 1566
John FitzSymon	1567–8	Michaelmas 1567
Michael Bea	1568–9	Michaelmas 1568
Walter Cusake	1569–70	Michaelmas 1569
Henry Browne	1570–1	Michaelmas 1570
Patrick Dowdall	1571–2	Michaelmas 1571
James Bellewe (Bedlow)	1572–3	Michaelmas 1572
Christopher Fagan	1573–4	Michaelmas 1573
John Ussher	1574–5	Michaelmas 1574
Patrick Goghe (Googhe)	1575–6	Michaelmas 1575
John Goughe	1576–7	Michaelmas 1576
Giles Allen	1577–8	Michaelmas 1577
Richard Rownsell	1578–9	Michaelmas 1578
Nicholas Duffe	1579–80	Michaelmas 1579
Walter Ball	1580–1	Michaelmas 1580
John Gaydon	1581–2	Michaelmas 1581
Nicholas Ball	1582–3	Michaelmas 1582
John Lennan	1583–4	Michaelmas 1583
Thomas Cosgrave	1584–5	Michaelmas 1584
William Piccott	1585–6	Michaelmas 1585
Richard Rounsell	1586–7	Michaelmas 1586
Richard Fagan	1587–8	Michaelmas 1587
Walter Sedgrave	1588–9	Michaelmas 1588
John Forster	1589–90	Michaelmas 1589
Edmond Devenish	1590–1	Michaelmas 1590
Thomas Smith	1591–2	Michaelmas 1591
Philip Conran	1592–3	Michaelmas 1592
James Janes	1593–4	Michaelmas 1593
Thomas Gerrald	1594–5	Michaelmas 1594
Francis Taylor	1595–6	Michaelmas 1595
Michael Chamberlen	1596–7	Michaelmas 1596

Incumbent	Date of office	Commencement
Nicholas Weston	1597–8	Michaelmas 1597
James Bellewe (Bedlow)	1598–9	Michaelmas 1598
Gerald Yonge	1599–1600	Michaelmas 1599
Nicholas Barran	1600–1	Michaelmas 1600
Matthew Handcocke	1601–2	Michaelmas 1601
John Terrell	1602–3	Michaelmas 1602
William Gough	1603–4[1]	Michaelmas 1603
John Elliott	1604[2]	1604
Robert Ball	1604–5	Michaelmas 1604
John Brice	1605–6	Michaelmas 1605
John Arthur	1606–7	Michaelmas 1606
Nicholas Barran	1607–8	Michaelmas 1607
John Cusake	1608–9	Michaelmas 1608
Robert Ball	1609–10	Michaelmas 1609
Richard Barrye	1610–11	Michaelmas 1610
Thomas Buyshoppe	1611–12	Michaelmas 1611
Sir James Carroll	1612–13	Michaelmas 1612
Richard Forster	1613–14	Michaelmas 1613
Richard Brown (Browne)	1614–16[3]	Michaelmas 1614
John Bennes	1616–17	Michaelmas 1616
Sir James Carroll	1617–18	Michaelmas 1617
John Lany	1618–19	Michaelmas 1618
Richard Forster	1619–20	Michaelmas 1619
Richard Browne	1620–1	Michaelmas 1620
Edward Ball	1621–2	Michaelmas 1621
Richard Wiggett	1622–3	Michaelmas 1622
Thady Duff	1623–4	Michaelmas 1623
William Bushopp	1624–5	Michaelmas 1624
Sir James Carroll	1625–6	Michaelmas 1625
Thomas Evans	1626–7	Michaelmas 1626
Edward Jans	1627–8	Michaelmas 1627
Robert Bennett	1628–9	Michaelmas 1628

1 Died in office, 1604.   **2** Elected for remainder of Gough's term of office.   **3** Elected for two consecutive terms of office.

Incumbent	Date of office	Commencement
Christopher Forster	1629–30	Michaelmas 1629
Thomas Evans	1630–1	Michaelmas 1630
George Jones	1631–2	Michaelmas 1631
Robert Bennett	1632–3	Michaelmas 1632
Robert Dixon	1633–4	Michaelmas 1633
Sir James Carroll	1634–5	Michaelmas 1634
Sir Christopher Forster	1635–7[4]	Michaelmas 1635
James Watson	1637–8	Michaelmas 1637
Sir Christopher Forster	1638–9	Michaelmas 1638
Charles Forster	1639–40	Michaelmas 1639
Thomas Wakefield	1640–2[5]	Michaelmas 1640
William Smith	1642–7[6]	Michaelmas 1642
William Bladen	1647–8	Michaelmas 1647
John Pue	1648–9	Michaelmas 1648
Thomas Pemberton	1649–50[7]	Michaelmas 1649
Sankey Sullyard	1650[8]	Michaelmas 1650
Raphael Hunt	1650–1	Michaelmas 1650
Richard Tighe	1651–2	Michaelmas 1651
Daniel Hutchinson	1652–3	Michaelmas 1652
John Preston	1653–4	Michaelmas 1653
Thomas Hooke	1654–5	Michaelmas 1654
Richard Tighe	1655–6	Michaelmas 1655
Ridgley Hatfield	1656–7	Michaelmas 1656
Thomas Waterhouse	1657–8	Michaelmas 1658
Peter Wybrants	1658–9	Michaelmas 1658
Robert Deey	1659–60	Michaelmas 1659
Hubart Adryan Verneer	1660–1	Michaelmas 1660
George Gilbert	1661–2	Michaelmas 1661
John Cranwell	1662–3	Michaelmas 1662
William Smith	1663–5[9]	Michaelmas 1663
Sir Daniel Bellingham	1665–6[10]	Michaelmas 1665
John Desmynieres	1666–7	Michaelmas 1666

4 Elected for two consecutive terms of office.   **5** Ibid.   **6** Elected for five consecutive terms of office.
7 Believed to have died in office.   **8** Elected for remainder of Pemberton's term of office.   **9** Elected for two consecutive terms of office, serving as the last mayor of Dublin, 1664–5.   **10** Inaugural lord mayor of Dublin.

Incumbent	Date of office	Commencement
Mark Quinn	1667–8	Michaelmas 1667
John Forrest	1668–9	Michaelmas 1668
Lewis Desmynieres	1669–70	Michaelmas 1669
Enoch Reader	1670–1	Michaelmas 1670
Sir John Totty	1671–2	Michaelmas 1671
Robert Deey	1672–3	Michaelmas 1672
Sir Joshua Allen	1673–4	Michaelmas 1673
Sir Francis Brewster	1674–5	Michaelmas 1674
William Smith	1675–6	Michaelmas 1675
Christopher Lovett	1676–7	Michaelmas 1676
John Smith	1677–8	Michaelmas 1677
Peter Ward	1678–9	Michaelmas 1678
John Eastwood	1679–80	Michaelmas 1679
Luke Lowther	1680–1	Michaelmas 1680
Sir Humphrey Jervis	1681–3[11]	Michaelmas 1681
Sir Elias Best	1683–4	Michaelmas 1683
Sir Abel Ram	1684–5	Michaelmas 1684
Sir John Knox	1685–6	Michaelmas 1685
Sir John Castleton	1686–7	Michaelmas 1686
Sir Thomas Hackett	1687–8	Michaelmas 1687
Sir Michael Creagh	1688–9	Michaelmas 1688
Terence McDermott	1689–90	Michaelmas 1689
John Otrington	1690–1	Michaelmas 1690
Sir Michael Mitchell	1691–3[12]	Michaelmas 1691
Sir John Rogerson	1693–4	Michaelmas 1693
George Blackhall	1694–5	Michaelmas 1694
William Watts	1695–6	Michaelmas 1695
Sir William Billington	1696–7	Michaelmas 1696
Bartholomew Vanhomrigh	1697–8	Michaelmas 1697
Thomas Quinn	1698–9	Michaelmas 1698
Sir Anthony Percy	1699–1700	Michaelmas 1699
Sir Mark Rainsford	1700–1	Michaelmas 1700
Samuel Walton	1701–2	Michaelmas 1701

11 Elected for two consecutive terms of office.   **12** Ibid.

Incumbent	Date of office	Commencement
Thomas Bell	1702–3	Michaelmas 1702
John Page	1703–4	Michaelmas 1703
Sir Francis Stoyte	1704–5	Michaelmas 1704
William Gibbons	1705–6	Michaelmas 1705
Benjamin Burton	1706–7	Michaelmas 1706
John Pearson	1707–8	Michaelmas 1707
Sir William Fownes	1708–9	Michaelmas 1708
Charles Forrest	1709–10	Michaelmas 1709
Sir John Eccles	1710–11	Michaelmas 1710
Ralph Gore	1711–12	Michaelmas 1711
Sir Samuel Cooke	1712–13[13]	Michaelmas 1712
Sir James Barlow	1714–15	Michaelmas 1714
John Stoyte	1715–16	Michaelmas 1715
Thomas Bolton	1716–17	Michaelmas 1716
Anthony Barkey	1717–18	Michaelmas 1717
William Quaill	1718–19	Michaelmas 1718
Thomas Wilkinson	1719–20	Michaelmas 1719
George Forbes	1720–1	Michaelmas 1720
Thomas Curtis	1721–2	Michaelmas 1721
William Dickson	1722–3	Michaelmas 1722
John Porter	1723–4	Michaelmas 1723
John Reyson	1724–5	Michaelmas 1724
Joseph Kane	1725–6	Michaelmas 1725
William Empson	1726–7	Michaelmas 1726
Sir Nathaniel Whitwell	1727–8	Michaelmas 1727
Henry Burrowes	1728–9[14]	Michaelmas 1728
John Page	1729[15]	17 June 1729
Sir Peter Verdoen	1729–30	Michaelmas 1729
Nathaniel Pearson	1730–1	Michaelmas 1730
Joseph Nuttall	1731–2	Michaelmas 1731
Humphrey French	1732–3	Michaelmas 1732
Thomas How	1733–4	Michaelmas 1733

13 Retained office illegally, 1713–4.   **14** Resigned in disgrace, 17 June 1729.   **15** Elected for rest of Burrowes' term.

Incumbent	Date of office	Commencement
Nathaniel Kane	1734–5	Michaelmas 1734
Sir Richard Grattan	1735–6[16]	Michaelmas 1735
George Forbes	1736[17]	22 June 1736
James Somerville	1736–7	Michaelmas 1736
William Walker	1737–8	Michaelmas 1737
John Macarroll	1738–9	Michaelmas 1738
Daniel Falkiner	1739–40	Michaelmas 1739
Sir Samuel Cooke	1740–1	Michaelmas 1740
William Aldrich	1741–2	Michaelmas 1741
Gilbert King	1742–3	Michaelmas 1742
David Tew	1743–4[18]	Michaelmas 1743
William Aldrich	1744[19]	21 Aug. 1744
John Walker	1744–5	Michaelmas 1744
Daniel Cooke	1745–6	Michaelmas 1745
Richard White	1746–7[20]	Michaelmas 1746
William Walker	1747[21]	19 March 1747
Sir George Ribton	1747–8	Michaelmas 1747
Robert Ross	1748–9	Michaelmas 1748
John Adamson	1749–50	Michaelmas 1749
Thomas Taylor	1750–1	Michaelmas 1750
John Cooke	1751–2	Michaelmas 1751
Sir Charles Barton	1752–3	Michaelmas 1752
Andrew Murray	1753–4	Michaelmas 1753
Hans Bailie	1754–5	Michaelmas 1754
Percival Hunt	1755–6	Michaelmas 1755
John Forbes	1756–7	Michaelmas 1756
Thomas Meade	1757–8	Michaelmas 1757
Philip Crampton	1758–9	Michaelmas 1758
John Tew	1759–60	Michaelmas 1759
Sir Patrick Hamilton	1760–1	Michaelmas 1760
Sir Timothy Allen	1761–2	Michaelmas 1761
Charles Russell	1762–3	Michaelmas 1762

16 Died in office, 1736. **17** Elected for rest of Grattan's term. **18** Died in office, 1744. **19** Elected for rest of Tew's term. **20** Died in office, 1747. **21** Elected for rest of White's term.

Incumbent	Date of office	Commencement
William Forbes	1763–4	Michaelmas 1763
Benjamin Geale	1764–5	Michaelmas 1764
Sir James Taylor	1765–6	Michaelmas 1765
Edward Sankey	1766–7	Michaelmas 1766
Francis Fetherston	1767–8	Michaelmas 1767
Benjamin Barton	1768–9	Michaelmas 1768
Sir Thomas Blackhall	1769–70	Michaelmas 1769
George Reynolds	1770–1	Michaelmas 1770
Francis Booker	1771–2[22]	Michaelmas 1771
William Forbes	1772[23]	11 Feb. 1772
Richard French	1772–3	Michaelmas 1772
William Lightburne	1773–4	Michaelmas 1773
Henry Hart	1774–5	Michaelmas 1774
Thomas Emerson	1775–6	Michaelmas 1775
Henry Bevan	1776–7	Michaelmas 1776
William Dunne	1777–8	Michaelmas 1777
Sir Anthony King	1778–9	Michaelmas 1778
James Hamilton	1779–80	Michaelmas 1779
Kilner Swettenham	1780–1	Michaelmas 1780
John Darragh	1781–2	Michaelmas 1781
Nathaniel Warren	1782–3	Michaelmas 1782
Thomas Green	1783–4	Michaelmas 1783
James Horan	1784–5	Michaelmas 1784
James Sheil	1785–6	Michaelmas 1785
George Alcock	1786–7	Michaelmas 1786
William Alexander	1787–8	Michaelmas 1787
John Ross	1788–9	Michaelmas 1788
John Exshaw	1789–90	Michaelmas 1789
Henry Hewison	1790–1	Michaelmas 1790
Henry Gore Sankey	1791–2	Michaelmas 1791
John Carleton	1792–3	Michaelmas 1792
William James	1793–4	Michaelmas 1793
Richard Moncrieff	1794–5	Michaelmas 1794

22 Died in office, 1772.   **23** Elected for rest of Booker's term.

Incumbent	Date of office	Commencement
Sir William Worthington	1795–6	Michaelmas 1795
Samuel Reed	1796–7	Michaelmas 1796
Thomas Fleming	1797–8	Michaelmas 1797
Thomas Andrews	1798–9	Michaelmas 1798
John Sutton	1799–1800[24]	Michaelmas 1799
John Exshaw	1800[25]	Feb. 1800
Charles Thorp	1800–1	Michaelmas 1800
Richard Manders	1801–2	Michaelmas 1801
Jacob Poole	1802–3	Michaelmas 1802
Henry Hutton	1803–4	Michaelmas 1803
Meredith Jenkins	1804–5	Michaelmas 1804
James Vance	1805–6	Michaelmas 1805
Joseph Pemberton	1806–7	Michaelmas 1806
Hugh Trevor	1807–8	Michaelmas 1807
Frederick Darley	1808–9	Michaelmas 1808
Sir William Stamer, bt	1809–10	Michaelmas 1809
Nathaniel Hone	1810–11	Michaelmas 1810
William Henry Archer	1811–12	Michaelmas 1811
Abraham Bradley King	1812–13	Michaelmas 1812
John Cash	1813–14	Michaelmas 1813
John Claudius Beresford	1814–15	Michaelmas 1814
Robert Shaw	1815–16	Michaelmas 1815
Mark Bloxham	1816–17	Michaelmas 1816
John Alley	1817–18	Michaelmas 1817
Sir Thomas McKenny	1818–19	Michaelmas 1818
Sir William Stamer, bt	1819–20	Michaelmas 1819
Sir Abraham Bradley King, bt	1820–1	Michaelmas 1820
Sir John Kingston James, bt	1822–2	Michaelmas 1821
John Smith Fleming	1822–3	Michaelmas 1822
Richard Smyth	1823–4	Michaelmas 1823
Drury Jones	1824–5	Michaelmas 1824
Thomas Abbott	1825–6	Michaelmas 1825
Samuel Wilkinson Tyndall	1826–7	Michaelmas 1826

24 Died in office, 9 Feb. 1800.   **25** Elected for rest of Sutton's term.

Incumbent	Date of office	Commencement
Sir Edmond Nugent	1827–8	Michaelmas 1827
Alexander Montgomery	1828–9	Michaelmas 1828
Jacob West	1829–30	Michaelmas 1829
Sir Robert Way Harty, bt	1830–1	Michaelmas 1830
Sir Thomas Whelan	1831–2	Michaelmas 1831
Charles Palmer Archer	1832–3	Michaelmas 1832
Sir George Whiteford	1833–4	Michaelmas 1833
Arthur Perrin	1834–5	Michaelmas 1834
Arthur Morrison	1835–6	Michaelmas 1835
William Hodges	1836–7	Michaelmas 1836
Samuel Warren	1837–8	Michaelmas 1837
George Hoyte	1838–9	Michaelmas 1838
Sir Nicholas William Brady	1839–40	Michaelmas 1839
Sir John Kingston James, bt	1840–1[26]	Michaelmas 1840
Daniel O'Connell	1841–2[27]	1 November 1841
George Roe	1842–3	1 November 1842
Sir Timothy O'Brien, bt	1844	1 January 1844
John L. Arabin	1845	1 January 1845
John Keshan	1846	1 January 1846
Michael Staunton	1847	1 January 1847
Jeremiah Dunne	1848	1 January 1848
Sir Timothy O'Brien, bt	1849	1 January 1849
John Reynolds	1850	1 January 1850
Benjamin Lee Guinness	1851	1 January 1851
John D'Arcy	1852	1 January 1852
Robert Henry Kinahan	1853	1 January 1853
Sir Edward McDonnell	1854	1 January 1854
Joseph Boyce	1855	1 January 1855
Fergus Farrell	1856	1 January 1856
Richard Atkinson	1857	1 January 1857
John Campbell	1858	1 January 1858
James Lambert	1859	1 January 1859
Redmond Carroll	1860	1 January 1860

26 Last lord mayor elected by Dublin City Assembly.　**27** First lord mayor elected by Dublin City Council.

Incumbent	Date of office	Commencement
Richard Atkinson	1861	1 January 1861
Denis Moylan	1862	1 January 1862
John Prendergast Vereker	1863	1 January 1863
Peter Paul McSwiney	1864	1 January 1864
Sir John Barrington	1865	1 January 1865
James William Mackey	1866	1 January 1866
William Lane Joynt	1867	1 January 1867
Sir William Carroll	1868–9[28]	1 January 1868
Edward Purdon	1870	1 January 1870
Patrick Bulfin	1871[29]	1 January 1871
John Campbell	1871[30]	21 June 1871
Robert Garde Durdin	1872	1 January 1872
Sir James William Mackey	1873	1 January 1873
Maurice Brooks	1874	1 January 1874
Peter Paul McSwiney	1875	1 January 1875
Sir George Bolster Owens, bt	1876	1 January 1876
Hugh Tarpey	1877–8[31]	1 January 1877
Sir John Barrington	1879	1 January 1879
Edmund Dwyer Gray	1880	1 January 1880
George Moyers	1881	1 January 1881
Charles Dawson	1882–3[32]	1 January 1882
William Meagher	1884	1 January 1884
John O'Connor	1885	1 January 1885
Timothy Daniel Sullivan	1886–7[33]	1 January 1886
Thomas Sexton	1888–90[34]	1 January 1888
Edward Joseph Kennedy	1890	1 January 1890
Joseph Michael Meade	1891–2[35]	1 January 1891
James Shanks	1893	1 January 1893
Valentine Blake Dillon	1894	1 January 1894
Valentine Blake Dillon	1895	1 January 1895
Richard F. McCoy	1896–7[36]	1 January 1896
Daniel Tallon	1898–1900[37]	1 January 1898

28 Elected for two consecutive terms of office.   **29** Died in office, 12/13 June 1871.   **30** Elected for rest of Bulfin's term.   **31** Elected for two consecutive terms of office.   **32** Elected for two consecutive terms of office.   **33** Ibid.   **34** Ibid.   **35** Ibid.   **36** Ibid.   **37** Ibid.

Incumbent	Date of office	Commencement
Sir Thomas Devereux Pile, bt	1900–1	23 February 1900
Timothy Charles Harrington	1901–4[38]	23 February 1901
Joseph Hutchinson	1904–6	23 February 1904
Joseph Patrick Nannetti	1906–8[39]	23 February 1906
Gerald O'Reilly	1908–9	23 February 1908
William Coffey	1909–10	23 February 1909
Michael Doyle	1910–11	23 February 1910
John J. Farrell	1911–12	23 February 1911
Lorcan George Sherlock	1912–15[40]	23 February 1912
James Michael Gallagher	1915–18[41]	23 February 1915
Laurence O'Neill	1918–24[42]	23 February 1918
Alfred Byrne	1930–39[43]	14 October 1930
Caitlin Bean Ui Chleirigh	1939–41[44]	27 June 1939
Peadar Sean Ua Dubhghaill	1941–3[45]	30 June 1941
Martin O'Sullivan	1943–5[46]	28 June 1943
Peadar Sean Ua Dubhghaill	1945–6	26 June 1945
John McCann	1946–7	1 July 1946
Patrick Joseph Cahill	1947–8	30 June 1947
John Breen	1948–9	28 June 1948
Cormac Breathnach	1949–50	27 June 1949
John Belton	1950–1	30 Sept 1950
Andrew S. Clarkin	1951–3[47]	25 June 1951
Bernard Butler	1953–4	30 June 1953
Alfred Byrne	1954–5	28 June 1954
Denis Larkin	1955–6	4 July 1955
Robert Briscoe	1956–7	25 June 1956
James Carroll	1957–8	1 July 1957

38 Elected for three consecutive terms of office.   39 Elected for two consecutive terms of office.
40 Elected for three consecutive terms of office.   41 Ibid.   42 Elected for six consecutive terms of office
and served until Dublin City Council was dissolved by the minister for local government at 6.00 p.m. on
20 May 1924. The city council was replaced by three commissioners, Seamus O Murchadha, Patrick J.
Hernon and Dr William C. Dwyer, who were appointed by the minister. The commissioners remained in
office until a new Dublin City Council was elected on 30 September 1930, taking office on 14 October
1930. Dublin was therefore without a lord mayor from 20 May 1924 until 14 October 1930.   43 Elected
for nine consecutive terms of office.   44 Elected for two consecutive terms of office. First woman lord
mayor of Dublin.   45 Elected for two consecutive terms of office.   46 Ibid.   47 Ibid.

Incumbent	Date of office	Commencement
Catherine Byrne	1958–9	30 June 1958
Philip Brady	1959–60	29 June 1959
Maurice Edward Dockrell	1960–1	4 July 1960
Robert Briscoe	1961–2	26 June 1961
James O'Keefe	1962–3	25 June 1962
Sean Moore	1963–4	24 June 1963
John McCann	1964–5	1 July 1964
Eugene Timmons	1965–7[48]	1 July 1965
Thomas Stafford	1967–8	8 July 1967
Frank Cluskey	1968–9[49]	8 July 1968
James O'Keefe	1974–5	28 June 1974
Patrick Dunne	1975–6	30 June 1975
Jim Mitchell	1976–7	5 July 1976
Michael Collins	1977–8	4 July 1977
Patrick Belton	1978–9	3 July 1978
William Cumiskey	1979–80	18 June 1979
Fergus O'Brien	1980–1	30 June 1980
Alexis Fitzgerald	1981–2	29 June 1981
Daniel Browne	1982–3	28 June 1982
Michael Keating	1983–4	27 June 1983
Michael O'Halloran	1984–5	2 July 1984
James Tunney	1985–6	1 July 1985
Bertie Ahern	1986–7	7 July 1986
Carmencita Hederman	1987–8	22 June 1987
Ben Briscoe	1988–9	4 July 1988
Sean Haughey	1989–90	3 July 1989
Michael Donnelly	1990–1	2 July 1990
Sean Kenny	1991–2	8 July 1991
Gay Mitchell	1992–3	6 July 1992

48 Ibid.   **49** Held office until 25 April 1969, when Dublin City Council was dissolved by the minister for Local Government on 25 April 1969, because of its refusal to strike a rate. The city council was replaced by a Commissioner, Dr John Garvin, who was appointed by the minister. Dr Garvin held office until 30 April 1973, when he was replaced by 45 commissioners appointed by the minister, and they remained in office until a new Dublin City Council was elected in 1974. The city council held its first meeting after the local elections on 28 June 1974, when James O'Keefe was elected as lord mayor of Dublin. Dublin was therefore without a lord mayor from 25 April 1969 until 28 June 1974.

Incumbent	Date of office	Commencement
Tomás Mac Giolla	1993–4	5 July 1993
John Gormley	1994–5	4 July 1994
Sean D. Dublin Bay-Rockall Loftus	1995–6	3 July 1995
Brendan Lynch	1996–7	1 July 1996
John Stafford	1997–8	7 July 1997
Joe Doyle	1998–9	13 July 1998
Mary Freehill	1999–2000	5 July 1999
Maurice Ahern	2000–1	3 July 2000
Michael Mulcahy	2001–2[50]	2 July 2001
Anthony Creevey	June 2002[51]	10 June 2002
Dermot Lacey	2002–3	1 July 2002
Royston Brady	2003–4	7 July 2003
Michael Conaghan	2004–5	21 June 2004
Catherine Byrne	2005–6	27 June 2005
Vincent Jackson	2006–7	26 June 2006
Patrick Bourke	2007–8	25 June 2007
Eibhlin Byrne	2008–9	30 June 2008
Emer Costello	2009–10	15 June 2009
Gerry Breen	2010–11	28 June 2010
Andrew Montague	2011–12	27 June 2011
Naoise Ó Muirí	2012–	25 June 2012

50 Resigned as lord mayor on election to Dáil Eireann, 24 May 2007.   **51** Elected for rest of Mulcahy's term.

A brief history of the Mansion House, Dublin

MARY E. CLARK

Dublin's Mansion House has been the official residence of the city's lord mayor since 1715. It is the sole mayoral residence in Ireland, where the only other Mansion House, in Cork, became a seminary in 1842 and has been part of the Mercy Hospital since 1857. Dublin's Mansion House is also older than any surviving in Britain, where the earliest, built at Newcastle-upon-Tyne in 1691, was sold in 1837 and destroyed by fire in 1895. Of England's surviving mayoral residences, York built its Mansion House in 1735, followed by Doncaster and then by London, where the Mansion House was completed in 1752.

The provision of hospitality has long been a primary function of the Dublin mayoralty. Writing in the sixteenth century, the historian Richard Stanihurst noted that £500 was the minimum amount that each mayor was expected to spend on entertainment from his own personal fortune. In 1665, the office was raised to the status of lord mayor and the first incumbent, Sir Daniel Bellingham, built a large personal residence at the corner of Fishamble Street and Castle Street so that he could entertain on a lavish scale. However, Bellingham was a wealthy goldsmith and not every lord mayor owned a house of the requisite size and splendour. Most were obliged to rent a dwelling large enough to entertain 'the government and persons of quality' because their own accommodation was too confined for this purpose. A rent allowance of £100 was supplied to each lord mayor but it was not always spent wisely: when the 2nd duke of Ormond arrived in Dublin as lord lieutenant on 12 August 1703, the lord mayor, Thomas Bell, received him not in a house but in a tent on St Stephen's Green.

In 1713, the Dublin City Assembly set up a committee to obtain a suitable house as a residence for the lord mayor and the following Easter the property developer Joshua Dawson offered a choice of two buildings: 'a good house' near St Andrew's Church, off Dame Street, or his own residence near St Stephen's Green. After careful consideration, the city assembly purchased Dawson's residence on 25 April 1715 at a cost of £3,500 and agreed to pay a yearly rent of 40s., with two fat capons and a loaf of double-refined sugar weighing six pounds each Christmas – if demanded. In return, Dawson agreed to construct an adjoining wainscoted room which could be used for civic receptions – the famous Oak Room.

Dublin's new mayoral residence underwent many changes of name before settling on the Mansion House. At first, it was known as 'the Lord Mayor's House', appearing under this title in an engraving published as part of Charles Brooking's map of Dublin, dated 1728 (fig. 29). Here it is shown as a plain but dignified Queen Anne house set in its own wooded grounds, with two storeys surmounted by a frieze inset with life-size male statues, possibly representing mythological figures. These statues have long since vanished, and the original façade is hidden under a Victorian exterior, while the woodlands have been largely built over, leaving only a small garden beside the residence. The architect is unknown, but it is likely that Joshua Dawson was in part responsible for the design.

The Mansion House has been the centre of Dublin's civic life for almost three centuries. During the eighteenth century, the lord mayor had an entertainment allowance of £500 sterling along with ten thousand oysters from the civic oyster beds. His domestic comforts were also provided for, with a housekeeper in residence and fresh milk available from a dairy in the then extensive gardens. The annual City Ball was held at the mayoral residence on St Stephen's night but was discontinued in 1728 because of riotous behaviour. It was replaced by a more sedate dinner for the aldermen and their wives, hosted by the lord mayor and lady mayoress, after which two silver loving cups, the Williamson Cup and the Fownes Cup were circulated for a communal toast.

The state visit to Dublin by George IV in 1821 provided fresh impetus for improving the Mansion House. Over £600 was spent in repairing the building and the large sum of £8,000 sterling was raised from the city's aldermen for an extension to allow space for a reception of the king. Designed by the noted architect John Semple, this took the form of a large circular room, known officially as the King's Room and popularly as the Round Room. The royal visit was announced on 18 January 1821 and was to begin on 23 August, leaving just seven months to raise the money, commission the design and construct the Round Room, which was built by the Dublin firm of Mountiford John Hay. The *Freeman's Journal* of 24 August noted that the Round Room 'was intended to resemble the circular court-yard of an Arabian Palace. It is surrounded by a battlemented rampart about 22 feet high ... [and]

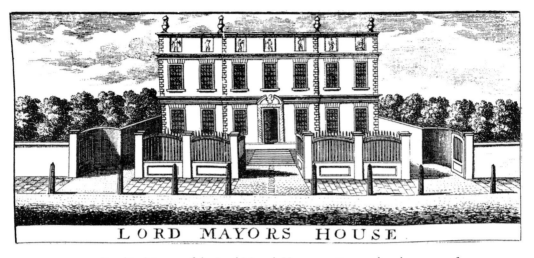

29 Brooking's image of the Lord Mayor's House, 1728: reproduced courtesy of Dublin City Library and Archive.

the ceiling was painted to represent a sky'. Many have marvelled at the speed with which the Round Room was constructed but the secret was simple: it was built with a temporary roof. A permanent roof was not supplied until 1824, again to the design of John Semple, and this remained in place until it was replaced by Dublin City Council in 1999. In 1864, the original Supper Room was built to afford additional space for civic events; the current building, dating from the 1890s, is the third on this site.

Hospitality at the Mansion House continued throughout the nineteenth century. A good example is the civic reception for Queen Victoria's son, the duke of Edinburgh, who visited Dublin in June 1872. The Round Room was decorated and the Supper Room was wallpapered; curtains were taken down, cleaned and put back; the mayoral portraits were restored; pot-plants were hired to give a festive air; a brand-new City Flag was designed and commissioned; and a pavilion was erected in the garden.

The Mansion House, and especially the Round Room, played its part in the movement towards independence that was triggered by the 1916 Rising. Following the General Election of 1918, the First Dáil was convened in the Round Room on Tuesday 21 January 1919 when the Declaration of Independence was passed. The First Dáil continued to meet there, while the Second Dáil, elected on 19 May 1921, also met in the Round Room. In 1920, Dublin City Council moved to the Mansion House, where it was forced to

30 Contemporary view of the Mansion House: © Dublin City Council, photograph by
Joanna Travers.

remain for nearly four years while City Hall was under military occupation,
first by the British army and later by the Irish Free State army. The Round
Room was fitted out as a temporary council chamber, furnished with benches
from the original chamber in City Hall, supplemented by sofas borrowed from
the drawing room in the Mansion House. The lord mayor's chair, another
import from City Hall, lent a certain dignity to the proceedings, which were
overlooked by a motley gathering of civic portraits assembled on the Round
Room balcony, seeming to peer down on deliberations.

Today, the Mansion House is still the home of the lord mayor of Dublin
during his or her term of office, which at the time of writing, lasts one year.
Here, the lord mayor welcomes groups from the city, from Ireland and from
all over the world. Important civic events are held in the Mansion House, such
as the conferring of the honorary freedom of Dublin and the IMPAC Dublin
Literary Award, the world's most valuable literary prize. As the 300th
anniversary of its existence as a mayoral residence approaches in 2015, Dublin's
Mansion House continues to dispense hospitality in the heart of the city.

The Dublin city regalia and Dublin city silverware

Summary list of the historic collections.
Catalogue entries drawn from descriptions commissioned by Dublin City
Council from Douglas Bennett and Associates, Fine Art and Antique Valuers.
Edited by Mary E. Clark, Dublin City Archivist

SECTION A: SEALS

The Dublin city seal

31 Dublin city seal: reproduced courtesy of Dublin City Library and Archive.

Early thirteenth century, bronze The medieval Dublin city seal is considered to be among the finest of its kind extant from western Europe. It is first mentioned in the year 1229/30, when it was used by the Dublin City Assembly to issue a deed to the town clerk, William FitzRobert. The seal consists of two matrices in bronze. It is likely that it was made for Dublin by a travelling craftsman who specialized in the manufacture of seals. When issuing documents, wax was melted and poured into the matrices, which were placed over each other with a seal cord in between, attached to the document at the other end. When the wax cooled, the matrices were removed, leaving the imprint on the seal as follows:

Obverse/Dublin at war:	Three watchtowers above one of the city gates, defended by archers holding cross-bows with watchmen sounding an alarm
Reverse/Dublin at peace:	A merchant ship at sea under sail, with sailors and passengers clearly visible
Motto/obverse:	+SIGILLUM:COMMUNE:CIUIUM:DUBLNIE:
Motto/reverse:	+SIGILLUM:COMMUNE:CIUIUM:DUBLINIE:
Size:	Seal and counterseal Each 95 mm in diameter
Note:	On display in City Hall Exhibition

The hanaper for the Dublin city seal

Sixteenth century: oak The hanaper was an oak casket which was used to hold the Dublin city seal for security. It is first mentioned in the year 1573, but may be much older. The hanaper was fitted with six separate and individual locks and one key to each lock was held by six different officials: the mayor, the mayor of the staple, the city treasurer, the sheriffs (who held one key between them) and two guild masters, who held one key each. The hanaper could only be opened when all six key-holders were present, thus preventing fraudulent use of the city seal.

Note:	On display in City Hall Exhibition

The lord mayor's official seal

1863, steel, Dublin The lord mayor's official seal was obtained in 1863 to replace an earlier provost's seal which no longer exists. It is kept in the Mansion House and bears the lions of England (as in the original provost's seal) with the motto:

SIGILUM MAYORI CIVITATIS DUBLINII

It is used to seal documents which are issued directly from the lord mayor's office, such as scrolls for the Lord Mayor's Awards.

The lord mayor's fob seal

*c.*1821, **Dublin** This seal seems to have been made for Sir Abraham Bradley King, who was lord mayor at the time of George IV's visit to Dublin in 1821.

It shows the lord mayor's official arms, with the inscription: THE LOYAL CORPORATION OF DUBLIN.

32 Lord mayor's official seal: reproduced courtesy of Dublin City Library and Archive.

SECTION B: SWORDS AND MACES

The great Dublin civic sword[1]

1390s London cruciform sword, 1,385mm in length, with a pommel and cross of iron encased in thick silver-gilt sheet decorated with engraved designs and inscriptions, including forget-me-not floral device and motto 'Souereyne' used by Henry of Bolingbroke and ostrich feather used by him as earl of Derby. Made originally for Bolingbroke's use during the 1390s, before he became Henry IV of England in 1399. Delivered to Dublin in 1409 or 1410.

1 Claude Blair and Ida Delamer, 'The Dublin Civic Swords', *Proceedings of the Royal Irish Academy*, 88 (1988), Section C, 87–142.

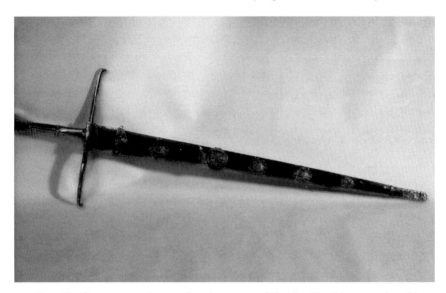

33 Great Dublin civic sword: reproduced courtesy of Dublin City Library and Archive.

Maker: Attributed to Herman van Cleve of London
Exhibited: The Age of Chivalry, Royal Academy, London, 1987–8
                Dublin City Treasures, 1991
Note: On display in City Hall Exhibition

1690s Dublin scabbard, 1,106 mm in length, is of wood covered in red velvet mounted in silver-gilt. It bears eight silver-gilt bands, some of which come from the original medieval scabbard, the remainder from the seventeenth century.

Maker: Attributed to William Drayton of Dublin, 1690s
Exhibited: The Age of Chivalry, Royal Academy, London, 1987–8
                Dublin City Treasures, 1991
Note: On display in City Hall Exhibition

The lesser Dublin civic sword[2]

16th-century cruciform sword, 1,132 mm in length, with a hilt of engraved silver-gilt including the grip. The steel blade is in good condition. The scabbard is not extant.

2 Blair and Delamer, 'The Dublin Civic Swords'.

Maker:	Not known
	Silver-gilt grip is attributed to James Bee of Dublin, *c.*1609
Exhibited:	Dublin City Treasures, 1991
Note:	On display in City Hall Exhibition

The great mace of Dublin

1717–18 Dublin silver-gilt mace, 1,545 mm in length and 610 mm around the head, incorporating parts of an earlier mace made *c.*1665 for the first lord mayor of Dublin, Sir Daniel Bellingham. The gilded shaft, which is made in three separate pieces screwed together, encloses a wooden shaft and is ornamented with a flat chased foliate design, and has two knops elaborately ornamented with repoussé chasing in a similar manner. The head of the mace, which is 483 mm in height, is supported on the shaft by four ornamental brackets. The arches are topped with an orb and cross under which is a flat plate with the arms of George I.

Maker:	Thomas Bolton
Exhibited:	Dublin City Treasures, 1991
Note:	On display in City Hall Exhibition

The minor mace

1762 Dublin silver mace, 305 mm in length. The head has applied harp, rose and thistle and fleur-de-lys all aurmounted by crowns. The top plate bears the royal arms with an empty shield and the shaft is capped with the Three Castles of Dublin.

Maker:	Thomas Johnston
Exhibited:	Dublin City Treasures, 1991

Two officer's maces

1717 Dublin silver mace, with mahogany shank and silver ferrule

Maker:	Not given

1760 Dublin silver mace, with mahogany shank and silver ferrule

Maker:	William Townsend

Two identical maces, carried by officers in attendance on the lord mayor. The heads each have a plate bearing the royal arms of England impaling Scotland,

France, Ireland and Hanover and applied harps, roses, thistles and fleur-de-lys. The silver ferrules bear the Three Castles of Dublin.

Exhibited: Dublin City Treasures, 1991

SECTION C: CHAINS OF OFFICE

The lord mayor's great chain of office [also known as The collar of SS]

34 The lord mayor's great chain of office, or collar of SS: reproduced courtesy of Dublin City Library and Archive.

1698 22 ct. gold chain of office composed of links representing the Tudor rose (12) by a trefoil-shaped knot (12) and links in the shape of the letter S (26) – [hence the alternative title for this chain, *the collar of SS*]. The design is repeated throughout the length of the collar. On each side is a harp and at the lowest point is a link in the shape of a portcullis which is repeated in the centre. Made on receipt of a grant to the city of Dublin from William III.

Maker:	Not known

From the front is suspended a circular **gold medal** 83 mm in diameter with bust of William III in relief, showing extensive wear.

Maker:	James Roettier of London
Note:	Original on display in City Hall Exhibition. Replica worn by lord mayor on a daily basis

The Clancy chain

1913 Dublin 18 ct. gold chain with a medallion in centre 57 mm x 83 mm inscribed on front 1014–1914. The total length of the chain is 660 mm and it is composed of two types of links, cushion-shaped with cruciform motifs from Book of Kells and elongated ribbon matter. The pattern is broken with two Brian Borumha harps. At the base is a circular centre-piece in the form of a gorgette 38 mm in diameter from which is suspended a pierced interlaced design pendant 76 mm x 51 mm bearing the Dublin arms and motto in blue and red enamel. Presented to John Clancy 1914.

Maker:	William Stokes

The high sheriff's chain

1792 Dublin 22 ct gold chain comprising 141 links many of which are of recent origin. Each high sheriff was supposed to add a link with his name, for his term of office. The earliest name on the chain is that of James Moore for the year 1826: the office of high sheriff was abolished in 1926.

Maker:	Not known

1882 Dublin gold medal 51 mm in diameter, is attached to the swivel ends and bears an inscription 'August 16, 1882. E. Dwyer Gray, Esquire, MP High Sheriff of Dublin City, committed to Richmond Prison by Mr Justice Lawson for three months, fined £500 and ordered to find bail in £10,000 or be imprisoned for a further three months for "contempt of Court". 30 September, Mr Gray without solicitation liberated by the same Judge on payment of the fine which had been provided by Public Subscription'. On the other side: 'October 24th, 1882. Right Hon. W.E. Gladstone, prime minister, declared in the House of Commons, in reference to Mr Gray's case, the intention of Housing Committee to introduce a bill in the coming session to amend the law regarding "contempt of court". Presented to the High Sheriff in commemoration of these events by the Gray Indemnity Committee, Decr., 1882'.

Maker: John Waterhouse

The D'Olier chain

1796 Dublin 22 ct gold chain, approximately 3,500 mm in length, consisting of 167 folded links, connected by an ornament 45 mm x 20 mm now much worn, probably a castle with crossed swords behind it. The chain is now worn by the deputy lord mayor.

Maker: Jeremiah D'Olier

The court of conscience chain

22 ct gold chain of office, approximately 2,745 mm in length, consisting of 179 fold over links. Originally worn by president of the court of conscience, for settlement of small debts (see fig. 26).

Maker: Not known
Note: On display in City Hall Exhibition

The modern deputy lord mayor's chain

1990 Dublin silver chain of office consisting of 26 hinged plates with applied motifs tracing the history of Dublin. A 115 mm circular medallion with extended angles is looped on, in the centre of which is a parcel-gilt casting of a ship of the Dublin city seal. Presented by Arthur Guinness & Company to mark Dublin's term as European City of Culture 1991.

Maker: Michael D. Hilliar
Note: On display in City Hall Exhibition

The lady mayoress' suite

This suite consists of two separate chains, which may be worn together, along with a Tara brooch, which may be worn with the chains or on its own.

1961 18 ct Dublin gold chain made of triple close links with double bolt rings. To this is attached a medallion having three castles imposed on a background of blue enamel and a pierced intertwined border with the motto of the city engraved. On reverse is engraved: 'Presented to Isobel Dockrell by J.J. McDowell … etc.' At lowest point is blue enamel shield with Three Castles of Dublin in gold.

Maker: Jack McDowell

1961 18 ct Dublin gold chain with interlinking links joined to above chain by two bolt rings. This chain has a small shield in blue enamel bearing the three castles of Dublin.

Maker: Jack McDowell

1961 18 ct. Dublin gold Tara brooch

Maker: Jack McDowell

SECTION D: CEREMONIAL LOVING CUPS

The Williamson cup and cover

1695 Dublin silver goblet-shaped cup with cover 724 mm high with ornamental knop stem and large spreading base. The cup is engraved with the arms of Sir Joseph Williamson impaling those of his wife, together with supporters, ribbon and motto. The Three Castles of Dublin are also engraved with scroll mantling and an inscription: 'The gift of the Right Honourable Sir Joseph Williamson, Knight, to the Right Honourable the lord mayor, Sheriffs, Commons and Citizens of the City of Dublin, Anno Dom. 1696'. The cover is surmounted by Sir Joseph's falcon crest issuing from a coronet.

Maker: Thomas Bolton
Exhibited: Dublin City Treasures, 1991
Note: On display in City Hall Exhibition

The Fownes cup and cover

1700 Dublin silver goblet-shaped cup with cover 648 mm high with ornamental knop stem on a large spreading base. The cup is engraved with the Three Castles of Dublin with scroll mantling. The cover is surmounted by a falcon crest issuing from a coronet and is engraved with a demi-falcon issuing from a coronet beneath which are a crest and motto.

Maker:	Thomas Bolton
Exhibited:	Dublin City Treasures, 1991
Note:	On display in City Hall Exhibition

Queen Victoria cup and cover

1899 London silver-gilt cup with cover 445 mm high. The cup is supported on a squat spreading base and has harp-shaped handles. On one side is engraved the royal arms while on the other is the arms and motto of the city of Dublin with supporters and an inscription: 'Presented by Queen Victoria to the citizens of Dublin as a memento of Her Majesty's visit to the Viceregal Lodge, April 1900'. The domed cover is surmounted by an acanthus-covered finial.

Maker:	R.S. Garrard & Co. Haymarket, London

SECTION E: OCCASIONAL SILVERWARE

Card tray

1760 Dublin silver card tray, circular with gadroon and shell border on three feet. Presented to Dublin Corporation to mark the Dublin Millennium, 1988.

Maker:	Robert Calderwood

Set of salt dishes

1786 Dublin silver gilt. Set of four boat-shaped salt dishes, together with four Georgian Irish silver salt spoons of earlier dates. Presented to Dublin Corporation to mark the Dublin Millennium, 1988.

Maker:	Christopher Haines

The water bailiff's oar

1842 Dublin silver. Symbolic of the lord mayor's role as admiral of the port of Dublin.

Exhibited: Dublin City Treasures, 1991

The Alfred Byrne ornamental spade

1931 Dublin silver spade, 845 mm in length. The shield shape, 140 mm x 170 mm has an interlaced engraved border in the Celtic tradition and an inscription recording that it was presented to the Right Honourable the Lord Mayor Alderman Senator Alfred Byrne, on the occasion of cutting the first sod at the Roundwood waterworks, 15 September 1931. Above the blade there is a silver collar 87 mm with three interlaced bands and gothic tracing; below a curved handle with silver-mounted ends is another collar 4.5 cm with two interlaced bands and engraved intertwining loops. The wooden handle measures 675 mm (see fig. 24).

Maker: Thomas Weir & Sons

Abbreviations

CARD	*Calendar of ancient records of Dublin*, ed. J.T. Gilbert (19 vols, Dublin, 1889–1944)
CSPI	*Calendar of the state papers relating to Ireland, 1509–73* [etc.] (24 vols, London, 1860–1911)
CO	Colonial Office
DCA	Dublin City Archives
DCLA	Dublin City Library and Archives
DIB	*Dictionary of Irish biography from the earliest times to the year 2002*, ed. James McGuire and James Quinn (9 vols, Cambridge, 2009)
DTC	Dublin Trades Council
ESTC	English Short Title Catalogue
GPO	General Post Office
IPP	Irish Parliamentary Party
IRA	Irish Republican Army
IRB	Irish Republican Brotherhood
ITGWU	Irish Transport and General Workers' Union
JRSAI	*Journal of the Royal Society of Antiquaries of Ireland* (Dublin, 1892–)
LEA	Labour Electoral Association
LGB	Local Government Board for Ireland
MC	Municipal council minutes
NAI	National Archives of Ireland
NGI	National Gallery of Ireland
NLI	National Library of Ireland
NUI	National University of Ireland
RHA	Royal Hibernia Academy
RIA	Royal Irish Academy
RIA Proc	*Proceedings of the Royal Irish Academy* (Dublin, 1836–)
RPDCD	Reports and Printed Documents of the Corporation of Dublin
TCD	Trinity College Dublin
TNA	The National Archives, Kew
UIL	United Irish League
UIP	Ulster Independent Party

Select bibliography

Bartlett, Thomas (ed.), *Revolutionary Dublin, 1795–1801: the letters of Francis Higgins to Dublin Castle* (Dublin, 2004).

Bellingham, Thomas, *Diary of Thomas Bellingham, an officer under William III* http://www.archive.org/details/diaryofthomasbeloobelluoft.

Bennett, Douglas, *The Company of Goldsmiths of Dublin, 1637–1987* (Dublin, 1987).

Berry, Henry F., 'Catalogue of the mayors, provosts and bailiffs of Dublin City, AD 1229–1447' in Howard Clarke (ed.), *Medieval Dublin: the living city* (Dublin, 1990), pp 151–62.

— 'The Goldsmiths' Company of Dublin (Gild of All Saints)', *Journal of the Royal Society of Antiquaries of Ireland*, 5th ser., 31 (1901), 119–33.

Boyd, Gary A., *Dublin, 1745–1920: hospitals, spectacle and vice* (Dublin, 2005).

Brady, Joseph, and Anngret Simms (eds), *Dublin through space and time* (Dublin, 2002).

Butel, Paul, and Louis Cullen (eds), *Cities and merchants: French and Irish perspectives on urban development, 1500–1800* (Dublin, 1986).

Cameron, Charles, *How the poor live* (Dublin, 1904).

Carden Sheila, *The Alderman: Alderman Tom Kelly (1868–1942) and Dublin Corporation* (Dublin, 2007).

Clarke, Howard, *Dublin, Part I: to 1610, Irish Historic Towns Atlas, no. 11*, Royal Irish Academy (Dublin, 2003).

Clark, Mary, and Raymond Refaussé (eds), *Directory of historic Dublin guilds* (Dublin, 1993).

Clark, Mary, *Dublin city pipe water accounts* (Dublin City Public Libraries).

— 'The Mansion House, Dublin', *Dublin Historical Record*, 60:2 (Autumn 2007), 218–27.

— and Grainne Doran, *Serving the city: the Dublin city managers and town clerks, 1230–1996* (Dublin, 1996).

Cullen, Louis, 'The Dublin merchant community in the eighteenth century' in Paul Butel and Louis M. Cullen (eds), *Cities and merchants: French and Irish perspectives on urban development, 1500–1900* (Dublin, 1986), pp 195–209.

— *Princes and pirates: the Dublin Chamber of Commerce, 1783–1983* (Dublin, 1983).

— 'Landlords, bankers and merchants: the early Irish banking world, 1700–1820', *Hermathena*, 135 (1983), 25–44.

Daly, Mary, *Dublin, the deposed capital* (Cork, 1985).

Dickson, David, 'The demographic implications of Dublin's growth' in R. Lawton and R. Lee (eds), *Urban population development in western Europe from the late eighteenth century to the early twentieth century* (Liverpool, 1989), pp 178–89.

— 'Capital and country: 1600–1800' in Art Cosgrove (ed.), *Dublin through the ages* (Dublin, 1988), pp 63–76.

— (ed.), *The gorgeous mask: Dublin 1700–1850* (Dublin, 1987).

— 'Large-scale developers and the growth of eighteenth-century Irish cities' in Paul Butel and Louis M. Cullen (eds), *Cities and merchants: French and Irish perspectives on urban development, 1500–1900* (Dublin, 1986), pp 109–23.

— 'The place of Dublin in the eighteenth-century Irish economy' in T.M. Devine and David Dickson (eds), *Ireland and Scotland, 1600–1850: parallels and contrasts in economic and social development* (Edinburgh, 1983), pp 177–92.

Dudley, Edward, 'The beginnings of municipal government in Dublin', *Dublin Historical Record,* 1:1 (1938), 2–10.

Elias, A.C., Jr, 'Dublin at mid-century: the tricks of the "tricks of the town" laid open', *Eighteenth-Century Ireland,* 10 (1995), 108–20.

Garnham, Neal, 'Police and public order in eighteenth-century Dublin' in P. Clark and Raymond Gillespie (eds), *Two capitals: London and Dublin, 1500–1840: Proceedings of the British Academy,* 107 (Oxford, 2001), pp 81–91.

Gilbert, John T., *A history of the city of Dublin*, 3 vols (Dublin, 1973).

— and Rosa Mulholland Gilbert (eds), *Calendar of ancient records of Dublin, in the possession of the Municipal Corporation of that city*, 9 vols (Dublin, 1889–1944).

Gillespie, Raymond, 'Religion and urban society: the case of early modern Dublin' in Peter Clark and Raymond Gillespie (eds), *Two capitals: London and Dublin, 1500–1840: Proceedings of the British Academy,* 107 (Oxford, 2001), pp 223–38.

— 'Robert Ware's telling tale: a medieval Dublin story and its significance' in Seán Duffy (ed.), *Medieval Dublin V* (Dublin, 2004), pp 291–301.

Gilligan, H.A., *A history of the port of Dublin* (Dublin, 1988).

Herlihy, Jim, *The Dublin Metropolitan Police: a short history and genealogical guide* (Dublin, 2001).

Hill, J.R., 'The 1847 general election in Dublin City' in Allan Blackstock and Eoin Magennis (eds), *Politics and political culture in Britain and Ireland, 1750–1850: essays in tribute to Peter Jupp* (Belfast, 2007).

— 'Dublin after the Union: the age of the ultra Protestants, 1801–22' in Michael Brown, Patrick Geoghegan & James Kelly (eds), *The Irish Act of Union, 1800: bicentennial essays* (Dublin, 2003), pp 144–56.

— 'The shaping of Dublin government in the long eighteenth century' in Peter Clark and Raymond Gillespie (eds), *Two capitals: London and Dublin, 1500–1840, Proceedings of the British Academy,* 7 (Oxford, 2001).

— *From patriots to unionists: Dublin civic politics and Irish Protestant patriotism, 1660–1840* (Oxford, 1997).

— 'Mayors and lord mayors of Dublin from 1229' in T.W. Moody, F.X. Martin & F.J. Byrne (eds), *A new history of Ireland,* ix: *maps, genealogies, lists* (Oxford, 1984), pp 547–64.

— 'National festivals, the state, and "Protestant ascendancy" in Ireland, 1790–1829', *Irish Historical Studies,* 24 (1984), 30–51.

— 'Artisans, sectarianism and politics in Dublin, 1829–1848', *Saothar,* 7 (1981), 12–27.

Holden, F.J., 'Property taxes in old Dublin', *Dublin Historical Record,* 13:3&4 (1953), 133–7.

Jackson, Charles, *English goldsmiths and their marks: a history of the goldsmiths and plate workers of England, Scotland, and Ireland* (Dover, 1964).

Jones, Randolph, 'Dublin's Great Civic Sword', *Dublin Historical Record,* 60:1 (Spring 2007), 44–53.

Kennedy, Máire, 'Printer to the city: John Exshaw (1751–1827), printer, bookseller and lord mayor of Dublin', *Long Room,* 52–3 (2007–8), 15–25.

Keogh, Dermot, *Ireland and the Vatican* (Cork, 1995).

Lennon, Colm, *Dublin, Part II: 1610–1756, Irish Historic Towns Atlas, no. 19,* Royal Irish Academy (Dublin, 2008).

— 'Fraternity and community in early modern Dublin' in Robert Armstrong and Tadhg Ó hAnnracháin (eds), *Community in early modern Ireland* (Dublin, 2006), pp 167–78.

— 'The changing face of Dublin 1550–1750' in Peter Clark and Raymond Gillespie (eds), *Two capitals: London and Dublin 1500–1800* (Oxford, 2001).

— *Lords of Dublin in the age of reformation* (Dublin, 1989).

Litton, Falkiner C., *Illustrations of Irish history and topography, mainly of the seventeenth century* (London, 1904).

Luanaigh, Donall, 'Alderman Edward Purdon, lord mayor of Dublin, 1870', *Dublin Historical Record*, 61:2 (Autumn 2008), 155–7.

Mahaffy Pentland, Robert (ed.), *Calendar of State Papers, Charles II, 1660–62, 1663–65, 1666–69* (Nendeln Kraus, 1979).

Mansfield, Brocard Fr, 'Father Paul Browne O.D.C., 1598–1671', *Dublin Historical Record*, 37 (1984), 54–80.

Maume, Patrick, *The long gestation: Irish national life, 1891–1918* (Dublin, 1999).

Maxwell, Constantia, *Dublin under the Georges, 1714–1830* (London, 1939).

McConnel, James, 'Fenians at Westminster: the Edwardian Irish Parliamentary Party and the legacy of the New Departure', *Irish Historical Studies*, 34:133 (May 2004), 42–64.

McEvansoneya, Philip, 'A colourful spectacle restored: the state coach of the lord mayor of Dublin', *Irish Arts Review Yearbook* (2001) 81–7.

McGrath, Bríd, 'The Irish elections of 1640–1641' in Ciarán Brady and Jane Ohlmeyer (eds), *British interventions in early modern Ireland* (Cambridge, 2005), pp 186–206.

McManus Ruth, *Dublin, 1910–1940: shaping the city and suburbs* (Dublin, 2002).

Meehan, Patrick, *The civic regalia, insignia, charters and manuscripts of Dublin*, delivered in Muniment Room, City Hall, Dublin, July 1931.

Meredith, Jane, *Around and about the Custom House* (Dublin, 1997).

Monks, Patrick J., 'The Aldermen of Skinners' Alley', *Dublin Historical Record*, 19:2 (1964), 45–63.

Moore, Niamh, *Dublin docklands reinvented: the post-industrial regeneration of a European city quarter* (Dublin, 2008).

Morrissey, Thomas, 'The 1913 Lock-Out: letters for the archbishop', *Studies*, 75:297 (Spring, 1986), 86–101.

—, *Edward J. Byrne, 1872–194: the forgotten archbishop of Dublin* (Dublin, 2011).

Mullan, John, *Idea togatae constantiae, sive Francisci Tailleri praetoris in persecutione congressus at religionis Catholicae defensione interitus* (Paris, 1629).

Murphy, Sean, 'Municipal politics and popular disturbances 1660–1800' in Art Cosgrove (ed.), *Dublin through the ages* (Dublin, 1988), pp 77–92.

— 'Monumental inscriptions from Rathfarnham Graveyard, Dublin', *Irish Genealogist*, 7 (1986), 293–306.

Murphy, Sean, 'The Corporation of Dublin 1660–1760', *Dublin Historical Record*, 38 (1984), 22–35.

Ní Mhurchadha, Maighréad, *Fingal, 1603–60: contending neighbours in north Dublin* (Dublin, 2005).

O'Brien, Gillian, and Finola O'Kane (eds), *Georgian Dublin* (Dublin, 2008).

O'Brien, Joseph V., *Dear dirty Dublin: a city in distress, 1899–1916* (London, 1982).

O'Connor, Emmet, *A labour history of Ireland, 1824–1960* (Dublin, 1992).

Ó Maitiú, Séamus, *Dublin's suburban towns, 1834–1930* (Dublin, 2003).

O'Neill, Marie, 'Dublin Corporation in the troubled times, 1914–1924', *Dublin Historical Record*, 47:1 (1994), 56–70.

O'Sullivan, Donal, *The Irish Free State and its senate* (London, 1940).

Parkinson, Danny, 'Arthur Morrisson, 1765–1837, lord mayor of Dublin 1835', *Dublin Historical Record*, 47:2 (1994) 183–6.

Phillips, James W., *Printing and bookselling in Dublin, 1670–1800* (Dublin, 1998).

Pollard, M., *A dictionary of members of the Dublin book trade 1550–1800: based on the records of the Guild of St Luke the Evangelist Dublin* (London, 2000).

Ronan, Myles V., 'Archbishop Bulkeley's visitation of Dublin, 1630', ed. in *Archivium Hibernicum*, 8 (1941), 56–98.

Shaw, Henry, *The Dublin pictorial guide and directory of 1850* (reprinted Belfast, 1988).

Strickland, W.G., 'The state coach of the lord mayor of the city of Dublin and the state coach of the earl of Clare, lord chancellor of Ireland', *Journal of the Royal Society of Antiquaries of Ireland*, 51 (1921), 49–67.

— 'The civic insignia of Dublin', *Journal of the Royal Society of Antiquaries of Ireland*, 2 (1922), 117–32.

— 'The ancient official seals of the city of Dublin' in H.B. Clarke (ed.), *Medieval Dublin: the living city* (Dublin, 1990), pp 163–71.

Tait, Clodagh, '"As legacie upon my soule": the wills of the Irish Catholic community, c.1550–1660' in Robert Armstrong and Tadhg Ó hAnnracháin (eds), *Communities in early modern Ireland* (Dublin, 2006), pp 179–98.

Townend, Peter (ed.), *Burke's peerage, baronetage and knightage* (London, 1963).

Twomey, Brendan, *Dublin in 1707: a year in the life of the city* (Dublin, 2009).

Webb, John, 'The guilds of Dublin', *Irish Monthly*, 45 (August 1917), 507–14.

Walker, John W. Boyle, *The Irish labour movement in the nineteenth century* (Washington, 1988).

Yeates, Pádraig, *Lockout: Dublin 1913* (Dublin, 2000).

Index

Page references in italics refer to illustrations

King, Sir Abraham Bradley, 196
*King (Drury) v. the Corporation of Dublin
    and the Town Clerk*, 128–9
Kinge, John, 64
King's Hospital, 71–2
King's Own Scottish Borderers, 140
Kirk, Joseph, 116
knights of the shire, 47

La Touche, James, 89
Labour Electoral Association, 122, 123
Labour Gazette, 121
labour movement, 120–2, 127, 129, 142
    lockouts, 133
    and Nannetti, 124–5
    and nationalism, 122–4
    workers' rights, 132, 133–4
Labour Party, 160, 164
lady mayoress' suite, 203
land annuities, 161
land re-zoning, 19
land surveys, 37
Larkin, Denis, 164
Larkin, James (junior), 168
Larkin, Jim, 133, 134, 136, 137–8
Larkin, W.J., 148
Latouche, David, 82
Laudian reform, 56–7
Lauri, Cardinal Lorenzo, 156
Lawson, Justice, 201–2
Leeds, 158, 162
legal publications, 78
Leigh, Sir Arthur, 56
Leinster, duke of, 103, 104, 106
Lemass, Seán, 159, 160
Lennon, Colm, 20, 25, 44
Lepracaun Cartoon Monthly, 125, 126
lighting, 27
Limerick, 46, 168, 172
Linen Hall ward, 109
literacy, 74, 76
Little, Justice, 162
Liverpool, 121, 175
Lloyd George, David, 146, 147
local government
    central government intrusion, 43, 44,
        47–52

nationalism in, 122–4, 126–32
    reform acts, 27–32, 30, 32, 120, 154
Local Government, department of, 154,
    159
Local Government Act, 2001, 32
Local Government Board for Ireland, 128,
    143, 144, 146, 147, 148
Local Government (Dublin) Act, 1930,
    154
Local Government (Dublin Mayor and
    Regional Authority) Bill, 2010, 33, 34
Local Government (Ireland) Act, 1898,
    30, 120
Local Government (Ireland) Act, 1919, 30
Loftus, Dudley, 58
London, 83, 106, 118, 198, 201, 204
    booksellers, 77, 83
    Byrne in, 157–8, 159, 162
    Dublin equal with, 68
    Gordon riots, 89
    Mansion House, 191
London Magazine, 75
Longford, County, 64
Lord, Michael, 123n
lord lieutenant, 26, 27–8
lottery commissioners, 79
Louth, Co., 64
Lovett, Christopher, 62, 69
loving cups, 203–4
Lowther, Gerard, 64
Lucas, Charles, 89
Lynch, Jack, 175
Lynch, John, 42

MacBride, Maud Gonne, 169
McCaffrey estate, 146
McCormick, James, 175
MacCurtain, Tomás Óg, 175
McDowell, J.J., 203
maces, 199–200
    Great Mace, 65, *65*, 69, 71
McGrath, Bríd, 48
McGrath, Patrick, 174
McHugh, P.A., 123n
McKenny, Dennis, 100
McKenny, James, 99
McKenny, Jane, 99